Finally it came closer to D-Day. We were not too well informed about what it was and what type of obstacles we would be called upon to blow—and found out that our services were seriously in demand. We each had a gap to blow on the beach in a time slot, with Omaha Beach as our objective. We could see that the beach was filled with rows of mines and obstacles of different shapes, sizes, and density. The beach was three hundred yards wide at low tide. There was a twenty-six foot tide that came in a foot every eight minutes. Water temperature was cold. Our job was to blow an obstacle-free gap fifty yards wide and three hundred and fifty feet long through the mines and obstacles. We didn't have enough land mines and explosives in our squad to do it, so we grouped with the Army Engineer Demolition men. We had trained with them for six weeks, and had five engineers and three untrained seamen assigned to our unit.

So we had units of thirteen to fourteen men for each gap. The Army demolition men had gap teams of twenty-six men. We all went in on the same gap assignment and riding the same landing craft at the same time to blow one gap. That was the plan.

ALSO BY CHET CUNNINGHAM

SEAL Team Seven Series
Firestorm
Battleground
Deathrace
Pacific Siege
Warcry
Frontal Assault
Flashpoint
Tropical Terror
Bloodstorm
Deathblow
Ambush
Counterfire
Payback
Deadly Force
Field of Fire
Attack Mode
Hostile Fire
Under Siege

The Specialists Series
Plunder
Nuke Down
Deadly Strike

Crazy Horse
Cripple Creek Bonanza
Hell Wouldn't Stop

THE FROGMEN
OF
WORLD WAR II

AN ORAL HISTORY OF THE U.S. NAVY'S UNDERWATER DEMOLITION TEAMS

★ ★ ★

CHET CUNNINGHAM

POCKET **STAR** BOOKS
New York London Toronto Sydney

440.545973
CUN

T 26789

ANCHOR P... ...BRARY
ANCHOR 556

The sale of this book without its cover is unauthorized. If you purchased this book without a cover, you should be aware that it was reported to the publisher as "unsold and destroyed." Neither the author nor the publisher has received payment for the sale of this "stripped book."

An *Original* Publication of POCKET BOOKS

A Pocket Star Book published by
POCKET BOOKS, a division of Simon & Schuster, Inc.
1230 Avenue of the Americas, New York, NY 10020

Copyright © 2005 by Chet Cunningham

All rights reserved, including the right to reproduce
this book or portions thereof in any form whatsoever.
For information address Pocket Books, 1230 Avenue
of the Americas, New York, NY 10020

ISBN: 0-7434-8216-6

First Pocket Books printing January 2005

10 9 8 7 6 5 4 3 2

POCKET STAR BOOKS and colophon are registered
trademarks of Simon & Schuster, Inc.

Cover design by Jesse Sanchez
Front cover image © Corbis

Manufactured in the United States of America

For information regarding special discounts for bulk purchases,
please contact Simon & Schuster Special Sales at 1-800-456-6798
or business@simonandschuster.com.

CONTENTS

Introduction	1
Naval Special Services Unit No. 1: The First Frogmen	4
The Army's Alamo Scouts	26
The First World War II Use of a Demolition Unit	29
The Navy Combat Demolition Units	33
The U.S. Navy's Scouts & Raiders	120
Underwater Demolition Teams	232
Selected Bibliography	323
Appendix 1	324
Appendix 2	328
Appendix 3	332
Appendix 4	336
Appendix 5	343
Appendix 6	354
Appendix 7	362

INTRODUCTION

Mention the word *SEALs* in a Navy town and there is a feeling of instant respect, of awe, of genuine amazement at what these men do in the service of their country. The U.S. Navy SEALs are without question the best-trained and the world's premier quick-strike Special Operations Unit. They can hit an enemy from the air, from the ground, or from over the water—*SE*a, *A*ir, *L*and.

Today's SEALs are the result of many years of development and evolved from the early days of World War II, when the Navy discovered, at the bloody near-disaster at Tarawa, that something more than air reconnaissance was needed before an invasion. There was a desperate need for today what we call "humint," or human intelligence. This means a fragile, expendable human being must be on the site, at the spot where the action must take place, to relay in absolute accuracy all of the intelligence needed in any attack, invasion, or offensive operation.

The Navy had been experimenting with amphibious landings from the early days of the mid-1930s. They knew that with Japan as a potential enemy, there would be the need for many amphibious landings in a war with them. Landing exercises continued into 1940, and with the start of the war on December 7, 1941, the need became more and more important.

In August of 1941 in New River, Virginia, more amphibious landing trials and tests were made, and progress was noted. After one hazardous operation, the multiservice officers decided that there was a need for a reconnaissance capability. Infantry Second Lieutenant Lloyd E. Peddicord was given the assignment to develop this capability.

Through the spring of 1942 many more amphibious exercises and landings were made. Lieutenant Peddicord worked on his recon assignment. In the middle of August 1942, an amphibious training base was being constructed at Little Creek, Virginia. Peddicord checked it out and decided it was where he would set up his recon school and he would call his men Scouts & Raiders.

The hammer blow that pushed the Navy into critical development of the humint capacity was the Tarawa invasion. Aerial recon photos led to several misconceptions, and they led to planning mistakes that wound up putting thousands of Marines off their landing craft into chest-deep or deeper water a thousand yards from the beaches they were attacking.

Japanese gunners did their work and thousands of Marines died in the water before they ever touched the dry beach. Reefs that were supposed to be under enough water so the landing craft could float over them were only deep enough to be out of sight and rip the landing craft to shreds and stop them in the water, making them perfect targets for Japanese gunners onshore.

Today's SEAL teams have a long heritage behind them. The very first men who did this type of work were in the Navy and called Special Service Units. After them were the Navy Underwater Demolition Units. Then came the Scouts & Raiders, and then the Underwater Demolition Teams. After the war the UDT teams served for many years until President Kennedy created the military Special Forces, including the modern-day SEALs.

This book is not a history of the units described. It has a touch of history to keep the stories in perspective. Over 95 percent of the book is an oral history, told by the men who were there and bled in the service of their country during World War II. It covers only the actions of the men up to the time of the Japanese surrender, on August 15, 1945.

Some of these stories are tragic, some humorous, a few angry, but most are told with understanding and candor after the buffeting of nearly sixty years of remembering those days.

Memories of the same landing and the same incident may vary from one Navy Frogman to the next, but the intent of telling what happened to each fighting swimmer is there.

Naval Special Services Unit No. 1:
THE FIRST FROGMEN

Before the Navy SEALs, there were the Underwater Demolition Teams. Before them came the Scouts & Raiders, and before them were the Navy Combat Demolition Units. But there was another group even before the NCDUs. It was called the Naval Special Services Unit No. 1, also known as the Amphibious Scouts.

A lot of military historians know little about Special Services Unit No. 1 because it was a top-secret group in the U.S. Navy created for a special purpose. Pat and Hank Staudt have done a heroic job of researching the beginnings of the group and much of that work is included here.

Pat and Hank Staudt

COAST WATCHERS IN the Pacific Theater had provided much information since their formation on September 8, 1939, but the need in 1942 exceeded their personnel. Most of the first watchers were planters, teachers, missionaries, and prospectors who lived in the affected areas. Soon the need for more extensive reliable intelligence prompted a plan for the formation of a new group. In March 1942 the Allied Intelligence Bureau took over the duties of the coast watchers and renamed them Ferdinand.

The Ferdinands worked in the Solomons and New Britain and were given service ranks for compensation and to protect them from charges of spying if captured. The Ferdinands continued to transmit information by radio through 1942.

Amphibious landing schools and training had begun in the Pacific. In February 1943 the amphibious training command was started in Newcastle, Australia. In April 1943 the First Marine Division began amphibious reconnaissance training in Australia. In May of 1943 Standard Landing Craft Units Nos. 4 and 5 were trained at the amphibious base in San Diego.

But there was still a need for precise and accurate intelligence about landing sites. This meant there was a need for forming a unique, highly skilled, and cohesive force unlike any the military had ever seen before.

The duties these men would be required to perform would be hazardous in the extreme. They required the abilities of men of very differing background, training, and experience to subordinate individual identities and work successfully in unison and covertly to achieve crucial goals.

This group was needed because of the failure of aerial photos and no onsite recon to produce precise intelligence about landing sites.

The Navy brass at last decided: "It follows that amphibious intelligence as complete and accurate knowledge of all sea, land and air factors whether natural or artificial affecting an amphibious landing is required."

Mid-June of 1943 saw whirlwind activity initiated in gathering volunteers from the 7th Amphibious Area. Volunteers were sought with many and varied skills. Included were knowledge of the geography, native customs, and language of the theater; recon experience; small-craft handling; hydrographic knowledge; and the ability to evaluate beach suitability for amphibious craft.

Volunteers came from the landing-craft units at Nelson Bay, Australia. They included Ensigns Alva E. Gipe, Rudolph A. Horak, and Donald E. Root. Also volunteering were BM 2/C Richard Bardy, Jack Brandau, Cox'n Calvin W. Byrd, MB 2/C Paul L. Dougherty, PMH 1/C Milton J. Kolb, MM/lC Bill Luger, Wayne Pettis, RM 2/C Taylor, BM 2/C Robert Thomas, RM 2/C R. Toman, M 2/C Rosaire Trudeau, and MB 1/C Joshua Weintraub.

From ATB Toorbul came Ensigns Henry Staudt, Franklin Meredith, and John C. Goodridge; also, Navy Combat Demolition Unit officers Lt. (jg) Lloyd Anders, Lt. (jg) Hamilton, and "Beach Jumper" Mathews.

There were also contingents from the Marines, from the Army, and from Australia's 9th Army Division.

On July 7, 1943, the commanding officer of the Amphibious 7th Fleet ordered that "there be established a school for Amphibious Scouts in the vicinity of Cairns and that they were to be called SPECIAL SERVICE UNIT 1."

By July 18, 1943, the majority of the group were at Cairns Base and began training in physical education, martial arts, panoramic sketching to identify precise locations, as well as rubber-raft work. There also was jungle survival training, pidgin English, and recognition of underwater coral formations and sea creatures.

About August 28, Special Services Unit No. 1 moved to a new base at Fergusson Island off in the D'Entrecasteaux Islands, New Guinea. More men joined the teams there, including Lt. Bernard C. Wildgen, USNRMC Ensign David De Windt, and Ensign Morris B. Tichener.

Coxswain Calvin Byrd (deceased)
Corinth, Mississippi

IN NOVEMBER 1942, I was assigned to Unit No. 5 of the Amphibious Landing Forces at the destroyer base in San Diego, where we practiced landing daily in the surf at the Silver Strand near Coronado. We used personnel craft.

This training continued there and at Camp Pendleton near Oceanside until April 30, 1943. On May 1, Unit No. 5 was sent to Treasure Island Naval Base, San Francisco, for transport to the Southeast Pacific Command.

Before leaving San Diego, we were ordered to go to the U.S. Marine base there and pick up the following supplies: a 1903 rifle, high-top Marine shoes, khaki pants and shirts, socks, and a camouflage poncho. We had to carry all that plus our regular seabag. By the time the two hundred of us were ready to board the ship, Bosn's Mate First Class Griggs walked around calling out: "Do not forget to bring your poncho." That was funny, because many of us guys had already forgotten our ponchos somewhere. I never saw anyone wearing one.

The USS *Mizar* took us directly to Sydney, Australia. From there we moved to the Newcastle area. The main purpose there was to train troops in beach landings.

While I was there, Commander Coultas came to ask

for volunteers for a new unit named Special Service Unit No. 1. I was interviewed for this service and volunteered sometime around June 30, 1943.

Unfortunate events occurred in the Solomon Islands and other areas during amphibious landings, due to lack of intelligence regarding excessive coral off the beaches and the existence of swampy land behind the beaches. Lives were lost and equipment lost due to these unknown hazards. It would be our job to gather this type of intelligence.

About forty men were selected for Unit No. 1: eight or ten Australians, two or three Marine Corps officers, two or three U.S. Army officers, and the balance being Navy officers and enlisted men. We all were transferred to Cairns, Australia.

At Cairns the base for Unit No. 1 was set up across the inlet from the town of Cairns and a little east toward the ocean. Training consisted of martial arts taught by one of the Aussie officers, methods of drawing or sketching landscapes in order to identify locations, and survival on food provided by jungle plants and animals. We also learned basic words of pidgin English taught by Aborigines in case we needed to talk with New Guinea natives. We made trips to the Great Barrier Reef to observe coral formations and the tropical sea creatures. We did a lot of physical exercises and swimming.

From there we went to Fergusson Island. It had been a PT boat base abandoned only a few days before we moved in. The U.S. Army had a base on Goodenough Island, six or eight miles to the west. There was a wharf we used to dock our two LCP (landing craft, personnel) boats.

Our base was on a beautiful lagoon, and there were

some palm frond buildings that had been a religious mission before our LCP boats landed.

Commander Coultas and staff arranged for the natives to build a mess hall/meeting room, medical house, storage room, radio shack, and sleeping rooms. We were amazed how quickly the natives did this using logs, palm fronds, and vines.

Lessons were given in the use of rubber boats for landing from PT boats and submarines. We practiced landing on beaches in the surf, pulling boats ashore, deflating them so they could be hidden in the jungle and later inflating them with a small cylinder of compressed air for the return after the mission was completed.

We made many trips into the jungle for stays of two or three days or more. We landed at night along the coast. We had classes on what intelligence was likely to be gathered.

We played physical fitness exercises such as five-mile fast marches. We learned to communicate with the natives. We had target practice with our carbines and .45 pistols.

Some nights we could see flashes of antiaircraft fire to the east, probably from Woodlark Island. One night coming back to base, we shut down our LCP's engine when a Japanese plane flew over so he would not see the wake of our moving boat.

In October of 1943 one of our teams made a mission to the Finschhafen, New Guinea, area. The team had three Australians and our Lt. (jg) Hank Staudt. One of the Aussies was "Blue" Harris, who had been one of the first coast watchers.

In late November 1943 we moved from Fergusson Island to Milne Bay. Some of us were given recreation—R & R—leave to Australia. When we returned, most of the Special Service Unit No. 1 trainees had been reassigned to other duties. John Grady and I remained in the unit along with Lt. Root and Lt. Gipe. We were then assigned to the staff on the USS *Blue Ridge*, Admiral Barbey's flagship. Lt. Root and I became a team, as did Lt. Gibe and John Grady.

Around February 1944 the Army First Cavalry Division invaded the Admiralty Islands. Lt. Root and I were given the assignment to move from our base and take the USS *Oyster Bay*, a PT boat tender, and then to board one of the PT boats for transport to Bat Island, in the Purdy Group. There we were to perform surveillance and to gather tidal information to be used in the proposed invasion of Aitape, New Guinea. Near the Admiralty Islands we transferred to a PT boat for the final leg of the journey.

On arrival at Bat Island it was just after dark. We were challenged by someone onshore and found that it was a U.S. Army unit that had landed the day before. They said they almost opened fire on us. They said an Aussie team was located on the south shore of the island.

We spent the rest of the night with the soldiers. The next morning we moved to the north shore to set up tidal recordings. Our location had been a copra shed owned by some Australian and abandoned after the war started. We also found on the island huge hogs that fed off coconuts and birds.

We set a stake marked for tidal readings in a location partially sheltered from big waves. Readings were taken once an hour, but that was later changed to once every two hours. Tidal changes were small at Bat Island.

We learned by radio that several Aussies had become seriously ill and a seaplane from Manus Island had picked them up. Doctors found the illness to be typhus fever caused by ticks.

Later it was decided to evacuate the island because of the sickness. Before we left, we all met at the original landing site. The Aussies had volunteered to kill and dress out and barbecue one of the hogs. It worked, but the meat was almost too fat and greasy to eat.

We had been there sixteen days when an Australian corvette picked us up and took us back to Manus Island.

Word came to us that an Aussie team led by "Blue" Harris was detected and eliminated by Japanese in the Hollandia area.

At times John Grady and I were assigned to the staff on the USS *Henry T. Allen*. It and other ships were moored to buoys anchored in Humboldt Bay. The buoys were equipped with telephone lines the ships could tap into.

Lt. Root and I were assigned to scout Biak Island. An Army Alamo Scout team was also assigned. We would use two PT boats. We would have to refuel at Wakde because of the distance from the PT base near Hollandia. A problem was that Wakde was not yet secure and fighting was still going on. Shortly after we tied up there at a small pier, a rifle shot came our way, causing us to seek cover, which delayed our departure.

Lt. Dove and his Alamo team were in one PT and Lt. Root and I and two Alamo Scouts were in the other. After refueling, we left for Biak. The seas became rough, and about midnight our PT hit a log, which disabled one of our propellers. Due to rough seas, we couldn't transfer to the other PT. Our mission was canceled and we returned to Hollandia. Later, Lt. Gipe and John Grady went into Biak with the invasion forces. They told us we were fortunate not to have landed on the Biak beaches, which were heavily occupied. The stop at Wakde was my first time to observe a mop-up operation and to see the corpses of the enemy.

In late May we learned that the USS *Blueridge*, where we were assigned, was taking a trip to Sydney, Australia. As we sailed through the Coral Sea we heard about the invasion of France. Shortly after that we learned that Lt. Root and I were ordered to return to the Army G-2 base near Finschhafen, New Guinea. We were all packed, and when the ship hit Sydney, a Navy auto picked us up and took us directly to the airport. We went on a commercial flight to Brisbane. Then we caught a military mail plane and flew to Port Moresby. From there we flew on to Finschhafen and met with the Alamo Scout team at the Army G-2 headquarters.

There we learned about the Sansapor mission, where we would be inserted by a submarine, the USS *S-47* based at Manus harbor in the Admiralty Islands. Two Javanese scouts would accompany us for translation if needed.

After several meetings we left for Manus harbor and met with the submarine people. For several days we practiced and became familiar with the men and the facilities. All extra torpedoes had been removed forward to provide space for the enlisted scouts to sleep on cots.

Compressed air was available for inflating our rubber boats. The distance the main deck was above sea level could be regulated to ease boarding and unloading our rubber boats. The crew of the *S-47* was great and treated us like celebrities.

The trip from Manus to Sansapor was about 1,100 miles. We ran submerged during the day and on the surface at night. We arrived off Sansapor during daylight on June 27, 1944. The captain raised the periscope so we could view the coast and locate the river mouth we were to enter that night. Photos were taken via the periscope for us to study. The coast and silhouette of the background also helped.

That night we prepared to go ashore. The sub's sonar man reported heavy Japanese barge traffic moving along the coast. The *S-47* crew members were to inform us by radio when to proceed or to stop in order to prevent detection. This worked well, so we avoided the barges and landed on the beach about 0100.

But we had missed the river mouth by five hundred yards. We had to drag our rubber boats through the surf to the river. The waves kept driving the boats back onshore and we had to drag them off again. We were tired when we got to the river mouth and could board the boats again.

Both teams proceeded up the river to a suitable place to unload and deflate and hide the boats. Then we waited for daylight to go to our objective. I went to sleep and an Alamo Scout woke me, saying I was snoring too loud and that a Japanese barge had landed near us. We saw the Japanese camouflage their barge with limbs and palm fronds. It was evident that our planes raided them during the day. This forced them to operate at night for resupply.

We decided to lay low until the Japs left, then continue our mission. It was important that we not be detected. Our planes appeared about 1000 and fired on several locations, but they didn't see the Jap barge. The planes left an hour later and the Jap barges left an hour after that.

The Alamo Scouts went inland for their survey, and we went to the beach to do our work. We recorded information concerning the condition of the beach, the terrain leading inland away from the beach, the water depth, coral, surf, and slope. We saw a small island about three miles offshore. It appeared to have a building. Apparently it was subjected to air attacks. That night we rested and napped at a secluded spot just off a jungle trail. The chiggers were worse there than anyplace I had been. They could partly be removed using a knife blade to scrape them off.

The next day we worked gaining similar information on the beach to the east. On June 30 we were scheduled to meet the other team at the place we had left the rubber boats. As we moved along a trail I was in the lead position. I saw a small group of Japanese apparently finishing a meal. We sought cover and were able to alert the Alamo Scouts when they arrived to take cover. After a short break we checked again and the Japs were gone, probably to their barge for the night's travel.

We found our boats and inflated them. After dark we contacted the *S-47*, and with the help of their sonar man via our radio we made a safe return to the boat. We had showers to get rid of the chiggers, and then a brandy and big steak dinner.

For my work at Sansapor, I was awarded the Bronze Star. The citation:

> For meritorious achievement as an Amphibious Scout, during operations against enemy Japanese forces in the Sansapor area of Dutch New Guinea, from June 27 to 30, 1944. When an enemy barge containing six men landed within twenty yards of the party, Coxswain Calvin Worth Byrd coolly and methodically recorded intelligence data. Later when the party retracted

for the return to the submarine, he sighted an enemy campfire and by his timely warning, enabled his party to escape detection. His courage and devotion to duty were in keeping with the highest traditions of the United States Naval Service.

It was signed by James Forrestal, secretary of the Navy, for the President.

On September 15, 1944, we were set to go into Morotai without prior scouting information. Amphibious Scouts were assigned to participate with the initial landing forces in the event our services would be needed for scouting or beach party work.

Lt. Don Root and I were assigned to a LCI (landing craft, infantry), and one practice run was made in the Aitape area. The Army troops had not been in combat and were not familiar with LCIs.

Later, when we reached Morotai, the landing was made without opposition. It was evident that scouting would have been beneficial because of equipment lost and damaged due to coral and mudflats along the chosen beach.

As I went along the beach I was hailed by some old friends from Gulfport, Mississippi. This was a pleasant surprise. We were about ten thousand miles from home and had not seen each other in three or four years.

Morotai was rapidly secured. Our services were not needed, so we were ordered to board an empty LST for transportation back to the USS *Blue Ridge*.

Dinagat and Homonhon in the Leyte Gulf were our next targets. In late September 1944 meetings were held on the *Blue Ridge* to plan and organize a mission to set up navigation lights on Dinagat and Homonhon Islands to mark a channel that was clear of mines. The mine swept channel with lights would be ready for use on October 19, 1944 by invasion forces attacking Leyte on the morning of October 20, 1944.

Lt. Don Root and Paul Dougherty and I were assigned to install a light on Dinagat while Lt. Earl Gipe, John Grady, and another enlisted man would install a light on Homonhon. The lights were made by a machine shop on one of the ships in Humboldt Bay. The poles consisted of three-inch pipe joints that could be coupled together. The lights could be screwed to the top of the pole. Lights could be adjusted up or down and from side to side. Power would come from truck batteries. There would be three hundred U.S. 6th Army Rangers involved. One hundred would land on Dinagat with Lt. Root, Dougherty, and me. One hundred would land with Lt. Gipe. The other one hundred Rangers would be in reserve. Three APDs would be used to transport the Rangers and us.

In addition to the three APDs, the convoy would consist of twelve minesweepers, three destroyers, and one seagoing tug. It would be necessary to fuel at sea before arriving at the destination.

Except for some bad weather at sea, everything worked well and we landed on Dinagat about 1100 on 17 October. It was raining. We loaded the light on a medical stretcher for transporting it to Desolation Point. The Rangers arranged to move inland, except for one platoon assigned for our protection.

There were a few Japs in the area, so we moved slowly and did not make it to Desolation Point before dark. It continued to rain. We spent the night in a small building that had been damaged by a destroyer shelling before we landed. The Ranger platoon set up a perimeter for protection. During the night a weird noise got our attention. It turned out to be a little dog crying for food.

The next morning, October 18, 1944, we continued on to Desolation Point. The platoon of Rangers were soaking wet after spending the night in the rain. The minesweepers were actively engaged in floating mines and exploding them with gunfire. They had done this since the morning of October 17, 1944. The channel was to be close to Dinagat.

Soon after arriving at Desolation Point, we put the light together and had it ready for testing and adjusting that night. There was a small shack on the point. On the walls were charts of American planes, which indicated the Japs had a plane spotter in the area. The view of the ocean from this location was exceptionally good.

Early that night we contacted by radio the Navy captain on a destroyer. He instructed us to turn on the light and then gave us directions to adjust the position to conform with the navigation channel for the ships in the invasion fleet. The light was then turned out and secured for the night.

The Ranger platoon set up a semiperimeter around the land side of the point. Orders for the night were no smoking, no talking, and no walking or other upright movement. Sometime around 2100 or 2200 we heard two shots. According to orders, we remained still.

The next morning we found that one of the Rangers had detected a moving figure and fired the two shots. Both struck and killed the figure, who was a Jap. We assumed he was the plane spotter going to the shack.

On October 19 the minesweepers continued to destroy mines but were close to finishing. During the day a Ranger colonel came by. He was enthusiastic about our mission. He took our names, ranks, and serial numbers, and indicated he would recommend awards for our accomplishments.

Around 2100 on the night of October 19–20, 1944, we turned on Dinagat's Desolation Point light. Sometime around midnight we could hear some of the ships in the invasion fleet as they passed by.

The invasion was a complete success, partly due to the navigation lights that we installed.

The *Blue Ridge* had moved into Leyte Gulf with the invasion forces. They sent a boat for us on October 24 after the naval battle of Leyte Gulf. Several days later we went back to Hollandia. Leyte was our last mission for the Special Services Unit No. 1 and the Amphibious Scouts.

First Lieutenant R.B. Firm, USMCR

LIFE ON FERGUSSON Island was almost idyllic after Guadalcanal. The routine was as follows: eight days in the bivouac area, followed by eight days in the bush. The time in the hinterland was spent in team groups. Two teams would be taken up the coast to set up camps in different spots. In the morning they would try to ambush each other. The afternoons were spent hunting and fishing. The natives who had been assigned to us were at our elbows constantly during this time in the jungle. We were becoming proficient to a much greater degree in pidgin.

The Sixth Army had moved up to Goodenough Island, six miles across the straight from us. We would go over every few days to get a supply of rations from their quartermaster. The PTs would ferry us over, and we did our shopping in a weapons carrier that we kept chained to a tree. We had painted prominently *Special Service Unit No. 2* on the sides. This aroused curiosity of some of the Army brass. We told them where we were from. But when they asked us who we were and what we did, we clammed up. An Army colonel came over one day to pay us a visit. He never got past our jetty where Commander Coultas stopped him in his tracks.

The first mission of the group was to Finschhafen in September and rapidly followed by operations to Gasmata, Arawe, and Cape Gloucester.

Lieutenant (jg) Rudy Horak
Dallas, Texas

I GRADUATED FROM the University of Texas in June 1942 in Austin, Texas. Just before graduation, I joined the Navy V-7 program. In August, I was sent to Notre Dame for a few weeks' indoctrination and then to Columbia University Midshipman School in New York. I graduated there as an ensign, USNR, on December 2, 1942.

Three of us, A. E. Gipe, Donald E. Root, and I, requested and were granted orders to attend the Navy Amphibious School, Destroyer Base, San Diego. In April, after training, we shipped out on the USS *Mizar* and arrived in Sydney, Australia three weeks later. We practiced landing with the U.S. Marines and the Army's 32nd Division on the beaches northward along the east coast of Australia.

In July 1943, Lt. Commander William F. Coultas came to Port Stephens to interview Navy personnel for the Amphibious Scouts, also called Special Services Unit No. 1. Earl Gipe, Donald G. Root and I volunteered and were selected after the interviews. We were sent to training camp at Cairns, Australia, and trained in all aspects of jungle warfare.

Later we went to a vacated PT boat base on Fergusson Island. Nearby was Goodenough Island, which was a staging area for the 6th Army.

Our scout team went to Cape Gloucester from September 24 to October 6, 1943. Our team included Australian Kirkwall Smith, a radioman, Marine John Bradbeer, 32nd Division Army Lt. Daily Gambill, and two natives, Sabra and Tablo. We paddled our rubber boats shoreward after launching from a PT boat. Japanese armed barges were in the area and we finally got past them and landed. Our two natives panicked and ran into the brush, leaving our boats unattended. They turned over in the surf and dumped all of our food and provisions into the salty water. So we spent the next eleven days without any substantial food. All I had was a banana and a yam. The villages had no food due to our aerial blockade, which kept the Japanese from bringing in supplies.

One day I was cleaning my carbine, had it all taken apart, when I heard a gunshot. Within a minute a native came running up to me saying "Japon he come," in pidgin English. I never had assembled my carbine so fast in my life, and we both were out of there hiding in the brush. Turned out a Japanese patrol came into the native's village demanding food. The chief told them he had no food for his villagers.

Another time I remember during that recon we were given specific orders to stay at our posts during the night. About midnight I saw a figure walking along the beach coming right toward my position. My brain told me it had to be a Jap, so I aimed my carbine and started to pull the trigger. Just then the figure called out my name. It was Lt. Gambill of the 6th Army who had been my tent mate on Fergusson Island. I almost killed my buddy. He didn't say why he left his post. I don't know if I could have lived with myself if I had pulled the trigger that night.

During our scouting, Sabra and I located two entrenched coastal guns guarding Dampier Strait between New Guinea and Cape Gloucester. We took coordinates and pinpointed these guns and relayed the information. Later we found out the Allied bombers neutralized these guns, so our landing forces sailed through the straits uninterrupted during the landing at Borgen Bay.

Our scouting report showed that the southern coast was rocky, the immediate inland terrain densely vegetated, and that a large scale landing there was not feasible. So the powers decided on the northern part of the cape, Borgen Bay, which our team recommended as being more accessible.

On the tenth night on the scouting mission we were supposed to leave, but we had some trouble. The rescue PT boat's radio wasn't working and they couldn't hear us, so it went back to its base. That night the Japs started shelling where they thought we were and we played a deadly game of hide-and-seek. We won. The next night another PT came out, the radios worked, and we got off. I'll never forget the joy of being back aboard a U.S. vessel after thinking that all was lost.

On December 26, 1943, the First Marine Division under General Repertus made a successful landing at Borgen Bay.

Our other scout party, headed by Australian captain John Murphy, was not so lucky at the other end of the island. They were ambushed by a Japanese patrol, captured, interrogated, and tortured, and all of them were shot. Another of our scouting parties headed by Aussie Captain "Blue" Harris was captured in Hollandia. They, too, were killed except for two men who survived and later told what happened.

I spent six weeks in the hospital, and lost thirty five pounds from malaria. Then I was assigned to the Aussie ship *Westralia* to take pictures of the beaches for Naval Intelligence during the Hollandia landings.

Later, I made the landing at Leyte Gulf, Philippines, on October 22, 1944. It was there that my ship was hit by a Japanese kamikaze. Thirty-five of our scouts were killed and a like number wounded. After twenty-seven months in the southwest Pacific, I was sent back to the U.S.A.

Dr. Bernard C. Wildgen, MD, USNR (MC)

NO SPECIAL TRAINING was given me and no medical instructions were provided with the orders I received to join the Special Service Unit No. 1 and the Seventh Amphibious Scouts.

On arrival I found the medical facility to consist of a native-type grass-roofed shack. One medical corpsman was present. I don't remember his name.

Medical supplies were limited. The sole antibiotic was sulfanilamide, tablets and powder. Penicillin was unavailable.

Atabrin, the antimalarial, was dispensed daily to the troops. This held the disease in check nicely—if it was taken daily. It was not curative for *Plasmodium vivax* malaria, for which quinine was needed but was not available for our unit.

Commander Coultas warned us regarding hookworm infestation and the necessity of wearing shoes to avoid contamination of the feet. I do not remember any such cases in the unit.

One Australian from Melbourne, First Lt. Allen Lylne, AIF, developed extensive skin ulcers of the forearm. Warm compresses and sulfa powder brought no improvement. He was examined by an Australian from Goodenough Island. That doctor recommended a popular treatment: "Leave the tropics." He was sent back to Melbourne.

When I was starting to cut away the bandage dressing on Lylne's arm, the Australian doctor asked me to stop. Then he unwrapped the purulent dressing. He would have it washed and sterilized, then use it again. We didn't have this degree of supply shortage in our unit.

I had the good fortune to serve on the USS *Fulton* for six weeks with a group of older doctors. One was an accomplished dermatologist who taught recognition and treatment of skin disorders of the tropics. This served me well for the Fergusson and Milne Bay areas.

One stubborn problem was the fungus infection of the external ear canal. Local swelling would completely close the ear canal orifice. Warm, hypertonic compresses were required to reduce the tissue fluid, then allow medication to enter the ear canal where it was effective. A number of men had this problem, some with a tendency to recur.

In Brisbane I found and purchased a medical text of tropical diseases, authored by an Australian physician. This was an aid in understanding malaria, dengue, hookworms, and yaws.

Dengue was not a problem in the New Guinea area. I had treated such patients in Nouméa, New Caledonia.

These patients were quite ill during the course of the disease; however the mortality rate is almost zero.

Yaws, a spiroaste disease, was present in the natives. One large, strong black who was the "property" of an Australian plantation owner was left in my care because he had a large skin ulcer on his leg. The U.S. Army hospital on Goodenough Island did the laboratory work to determine the diagnosis of yaws. He was started in treatment, with favorable results.

About hygiene: The bathing facility consisted of a dammed-up stream, producing a pool possibly three feet deep. We would enter this and scrub with soap and rinse with the stream. This was probably a mosquito paradise. The water was refreshing, whereas the seawater left one sticky.

The toilet facility was a tent that contained two or three stools. Each consisted of two gasoline barrels with the ends removed. Deep holes were dug to stack two barrels end on end, with the upper barrel extending chair height above ground level. The seat was made of boards with the customary hole.

A daily event was when the New Guinea blacks would pour a cup of aviation gasoline into each of these holes and then cast a lighted match into the barrels. The resulting explosion and flame eruption was often heard throughout the camp. This eliminated the fly population and gave the men a necessary fast sprint out of the tent.

Things were changing. On October 1, 1943, Admiral Daniel E. Barbey ordered a new kind of beach party be formed and trained at the Milne Bay area. Their job would be to go ashore with the assault boats, put in buoys, fix channels, erect markers for incoming craft, handle casualties, take offshore soundings, blow up beach obstacles, and maintain voice communications between troops ashore and incoming boats and nearby ships. It was to be a new type of beach party to include machinist's mates, pharmacist's mates, boatswain's mates, NCDU (Naval Combat Demolition Unit) men, scouts, and beach masters. Beach Party No. 1 served at Arawe in December 1943.

Special Service Unit No. 1, Navy 323, was a highly classified unit of the Amphibious Scouts that trained and operated with select volunteer officer and men from different services. They overcame extreme obstacles and provided the intelligence that contributed to the successful assaults of the first phase of the road to Tokyo.

About this time the unit began to wither. The Australians requested their personnel be returned. The other men from the Army and Marines returned to their outfits. In late December 1943, the remaining officers and men of Special Services Unit No. 1 were returned to their respective services. The U.S. Navy men went on to a continuation of their duties as the 7th Amphibious Scouts, where many of them continued operations to the end of the war.

The Army's Alamo Scouts

About the same time that the Special Services Unit No. 1 operated, another group of men trained to do the same job came into being in the Sixth Army forces fighting in New Guinea. Lt. General Walter Krueger needed a continuing supply of preinvasion intelligence for his whole campaign to thrust into New Guinea.

In November of 1943, Krueger was disappointed with the lack of cooperation and the slow distribution of preinvasion sketches, maps, and data from the Navy, so he formed his own special group to do that work. Officially they were the Sixth Army Special Reconnaissance Unit, called the Alamo Scouts. He modeled them after the best such elite groups in the military, including the Scouts & Raiders, the Rangers, and the Naval Amphibious Scouts.

The Alamo Scout Training Centers produced eight classes during the war, including 250 enlisted graduates and 75 officers. Of that number, only 117 enlisted men and 21 officers were selected to be in the Alamo Scouts and go on missions.

By June of 1944, the Scouts had been on fourteen missions—including preinvasion recon on Los Negros, Hollandia, and Biak—without a single casualty. Now the Sixth Army was ready to invade the Vogelkop Peninsula on New Guinea, and the general needed specific and detailed intelligence about possible invasion beaches.

It started June 17, 1944, when Lt. George S. Thompson and his team of Alamo Scouts boarded submarine *S-47* at Seeadler Harbor and headed for Waigeo. It was a multiservice group and included the G-2 officer from the Scouts and men from the Air Force and the Allied Intelligence Bureau. Lt. (jg) Donald E. Root and Coxswain Calvin W. Byrd, both of Navy Special Services Unit Number 1, were included. Both had been on the Cape Gloucester and Gasmata missions with the Special Services men. Two men were also along from the 836th Engineer Aviation Battalion.

Their mission was to land on the west coast of the Vogelkop near Cape Sansapor and determine if the airstrip was large enough to accommodate two fighter groups and one light bomber group.

They arrived on site June 23 in the submarine and spent the day patrolling the coastline, checking through the periscope to locate a good landing point to put an advance party ashore. On midnight of that day, the advance party went ashore in rubber boats and found that the mission could continue.

On the night of June 25, the main party went ashore, led by Lt. Root. They hid the boats and the next morning divided into two teams. One team went inland searching for enemy troops and estimating their strength. The other team, under Lt. Root and including Coxswain Byrd, worked the coastline, looking for possible landing beaches to survey.

On the afternoon of June 29, Lt. Thompson made contact with Lt. Root and the two teams reassembled. There was no enemy activity on the beach, so Lt. Root and Lt. Byrd collected hydrographic data and drew detailed sketches of the area. After dark, the men dug up the boats and radio. They contacted the sub for pickup and then sat in the rain for six hours, waiting. The pickup was set for 0200 on June 30. After some close misses with Japanese barges, the two rubber boats met the sub and were safely taken onboard.

The joint Alamo Scouts and Navy Special Services Unit and others mission was a huge success. It gave the Allied planners detailed hydrographic, terrain, and enemy-troop-strength data.

It also showed that the partially cleared area was a large garden and not fit for a potential landing strip for aircraft.

The Alamo Scouts functioned during most of the war and were often teamed with other units in multiservice operations. They worked with the Scouts & Raiders on many occasions.

The First World War II Use of a Demolition Unit

In the fall of 1942, the Allies formed plans to invade North Africa. The military specialists working on an invasion from the sea to North Africa realized that they would face problems that they had no solutions to. What about obstacles placed on the beach to hinder and stop landing craft? What about mines and other dangers in the water that could tear apart the light boats that took the men to the shore?

The Navy had its Bomb and Disposal squads, and the Seabees had certain units to do such clearing jobs from beaches and harbors. However, they were small groups, and detonation work was not their primary duty: Their main job was supporting the U.S. Marines. Seabees constructed bridges, pontoons, airfields—whole camps—and put up buildings and created floating docks for the Marines.

Intelligence warned the planners of a serious problem. The landings called for an attack up the Sebou River on French Morocco. The invading Army forces would proceed up the river and circle in back of the Port Lyautey Airfield, attack it from the rear, and capture it. This plan had one mission-killer drawback: The Sebou River was walled off with submarine nets held in place with a thick steel cable across the mouth of the river. Somebody had to go in and cut the cable and release the nets so the landing craft could get up the river to attack the airfield.

Frantic messages went out, and in mid-September 1942 seventeen men were selected to go to Little Creek, Virginia, to train for the job. They had an accelerated course in underwater demolition, cable cutting, commando skills, personal attacks, and defense techniques. The seventeen had been chosen from trained Navy divers from Hawaii who had been working to raise and salvage ships and materials from the waters of Pearl Harbor. These men were at home underwater.

On November 8, 1942, the seventeen specially trained men in an open Higgins boat powered over a heavy groundswell and headed for the blacked-out Moroccan coast. All was quiet. The special-unit men did not know that the Vichy garrison had been alerted and knew their boat was coming. Their small craft crept forward and then was pushed toward one of the jetties beyond the river mouth. A heavy rainsquall pounded the little boat and crew.

One of the men on that first mission in the Higgins, William R. Freeman, tells his story. . . .

William R. Freeman, USN

WE WERE PICKED up by a breaking groundswell that shot us forward like an express train. A red flare fired from shore when we passed the end of the jetty. Enemy fire began as we were hugging the south shore, proceeding slowly toward the net. We were illuminated by searchlights from the casbah and immediately kicked on full power and zigzagged in an effort to lose the light.

We were taken under fire by 75mm artillery but were not hit. An American destroyer fired on the casbah, and guns there countered with the main battery of coast artillery. Our game was up for the night, as the operation was based on surprise. The order was given in the time-worn phrase *Let's get the hell out of here!*

That held up the landings along the Moroccan coast. On November 20, just after midnight, our seventeen men tried again, with our landing craft bulging with explosives, two rubber boats, wire cutters, and two light machine guns. This time we passed the jetty through rugged surf and got into the quiet waters without being detected. We reached the net in total darkness.

A one-and-a-half-inch steel cable held up the nets, with a smaller wire on top of it. We used cable cutter explosive devices and set off the charge. It severed the cable on the first try. That also cut the smaller wire. The supporting boats holding the cable in the middle of the river sagged and then were swept downstream taking the heavy submarine nets with them. At the same time firing began from the casbah. The small wire on top had been a warning device, alerting the defenders.

Our Higgins boat raced downstream with the two machine guns returning fire at the cliffs. Bullets slammed into the wooden boat. At the end of the jetty we met monstrous thirty-foot breakers. We threw everything overboard that would move, including one of the machine guns. We made it through the waves and at last got to our mother ship. Not a man on board had been hit by enemy fire, although two suffered bruises from the battering by the waves.

The way was now clear and the assault boats rushed up the Sebou River, attacked, and captured the airfield, paving the way for a successful invasion of French Morocco in North Africa.

The Navy's first underwater demolition men had completed their first mission. The seventeen men returned to the United States to help train more demolition units.

The Navy Combat Demolition Units

Before the name *Naval Combat Demolition Units* was coined, a group of men gathered at the Naval Amphibious Training Base at Solomon's Island, Maryland, on Chesapeake Bay. There were thirteen volunteers who were almost finished with their training in the Dynamiting and Demolition School at Camp Perry, Virginia. Other Navy demolition men and eight officers joined them to take on a specific job. Lieutenant Fred Wise, lately of the Seabees, was named the officer in charge.

They took a crash course in working from rubber boats, placing explosive charges on underwater obstacles, and blowing open channels in sandbars with hoses filled with TNT. There were twenty-one men with Lieutenant Wise when they finished their brief training and sailed for Sicily. They came off cargo ships near Scoglitti, Sicily, early in the morning of July 10, 1943, ready to do any demolition work that needed to be done.

The invasion went smoothly and the demolition men were not needed. But they went to work for two days salvaging stranded boats and marking channels through the sandbars with buoys. They also surveyed other beaches. Their work done there, the twenty-two men were shipped back to the States.

A month before the Sicily invasion, Admiral J. King,

commander in chief of the U.S. Fleet and chief of Naval operations, sent out urgent directives to establish permanent Naval Combat Demolition Units for the Atlantic Fleet and to establish training for permanent units to be assigned to other amphibious forces. The directive also required that men be provided for this work.

Admiral King recalled Lieutenant Commander Draper L. Kauffman to Washington. He had been founder and head of the Navy Bomb Disposal School. His new job was to launch the Navy's Combat Underwater Demolition Units.

Lt. Cmdr. Kauffman was an interesting choice. He had graduated from the U.S. Naval Academy but, due to poor eyesight, was not commissioned. He went to France and became a driver with the American Volunteers Ambulance Corps. He was captured by the Germans, spent some time in a prison camp, but was at last freed with a few other American drivers. He went on to volunteer for the mine disposal teams with the British Royal Navy Volunteer Reserve. His bravery and skill in disarming those bombs for the British soon attracted the notice of the U.S. Navy, and he was at last commissioned in the U.S. Naval Reserve in 1941.

It was June of 1943 when the first class arrived at Fort Pierce, Florida, where the camp had been set up. Most of those twenty-one men who had been in the Sicily invasion stayed at Fort Pierce working as instructors. Men for the units came from three main sources: the Seabees, the Bomb Disposal School, and the Mine Disposal School. These men were already familiar with explosives. The rest of the men were drawn from volunteers from many Navy areas. The Navy had chosen the Fort Pierce site because it offered beaches and swimming and temperatures that would allow water activities year-round. The presence of the Amphibious Forces close by and in training allowed interaction with them. Also, the area was remote enough that demolitions could be carried out without endangering Navy personnel or civilians.

The first men to arrive there found no buildings, only lots of sand and fleas. They would be housed in tents pitched directly on the sand. Later groups had wooden floors and sides for the tents.

At first there was no clear idea what the mission of the NCDUs might be. There was no training program set up.

Not even the officers knew what type of obstacles they might be asked to blow up, what routines or practices might be needed, or under what conditions the men would be called on to work. The men needed practical clothing, obstacles to destroy, a solid training program, supplies of explosives, and adequate housing.

The first class at Fort Pierce had ninety-eight men and officers when training started. The men spent eight to twelve hours a day in physical workouts, rubber-boat drills in the ocean, and Primacord knot time. One of the men in the first class said that the sand flies, the mosquitoes, the heat, the bad food, and poor living conditions made every week "Hell Week."

The training came down to one officer and five enlisted men to one rubber boat. The number was set arbitrarily, since that was the capacity of the rubber boats. Many men washed out during the training, and when it was over, Naval Combat Demolition Units 1 through 4 were established. The training conditions, instructors, and facilities improved greatly over the weeks, and the classes after the first came out extremely well trained.

By June of 1944 there were dozens of the six-man units in England continuing to train and get ready for the invasion of France. They would work on both Omaha and Utah Beaches.

On Omaha the clearance on the assault phase was by the use of a two-pound Hagensen pack. Each man carried twenty of these charges along with safety fuse and detonator assemblies. They continued working until the rising tide prevented further clearance. After the tide receded, tank dozers, Caterpillar tractors, and salvage explosives were used to finalize the clearance.

On Utah Beach, all obstacles were out of the water when the NCDUs arrived. The enemy gunfire was not as intense there as it was on Omaha Beach, nor were there so many obstacles to clear. Electrically fired detonators were used instead of safety fuses, which gave much better control over the firing timing and obstacle removal.

There were casualties: On Omaha Beach, thirty-one NCDU men were killed and sixty wounded, a casualty rate of 52 percent. On Utah Beach there were six dead and eleven wounded. All casualties were the result of enemy fire and none was reported from improper handling of the explosives.

Many NCDUs were sent to the Pacific Theater, where they worked numerous invasions. Midway in the war, the NCDUs were decommissioned and the men had the option of joining the more recently formed Navy Underwater Demolition Teams, who did the same general type of work but included more reconnaissance and mapping of proposed beach landing areas.

Bos'n's Mate First Class Terry "Tex" Givens
Livermore, California

I WAS IN the very first Navy Combat Demolition Unit down at Fort Pierce, Florida. I joined the Navy in March of 1943 when I was seventeen and took basic at Bainbridge, Maryland. One day an officer came in and asked for volunteers. He said it was for a brand-new unit that hadn't even been named yet. We would be out of touch with friends and family for long periods of time on secret operations and it would be highly dangerous work. I volunteered. They sent us to Fort Pierce.

Since they didn't have a name for the outfit, we had a contest to see what it would be. The winner was the Navy Combat Demolition Units. There were about ninety-eight of us in that first class. We were broken up into teams of five enlisted men and one officer. In our team we had six enlisted, since we needed a rated enlisted man and he was added to our group.

After training, our team went to Europe. We were in action all the way from southern France to Florence, Italy. I remember that we lived in the soccer stadium at Salerno. We were on the center beach in southern France. We didn't do any swimming in those days: We were on an LCM that was outfitted with racks of rocket launchers. These were set up in thirty or forty tube groups that fired the rockets. The only trouble was the range on them was only three hundred yards, so we had to be in that close to shore to do any good. The rockets fired out in salvos, I forget how many at a time.

After we fired the rockets, we beached the boat and worked from the beach while the infantry charged ashore and went inland. After that, we loaded the wounded and dead onboard the LCM and took them out to a hospital ship. At one point there were a lot of prisoners that we had to transport. At the time I had a .45 automatic on my hip and an Ml rifle on my shoulder.

Once in a while we got up into the main lines of fighting, where we weren't supposed to be. We usually got out of there quickly. On this particular landing we stayed on the beach for five days.

At Salerno we did a lot of research and development with the Navy. We experimented with small boats loaded with explosives and radio controlled. We put the explosives on the boat, then tried to direct it by radio into the target on the beach. It had been done without live charges before, but not much with the boats loaded with explosives. The idea worked pretty well for us. We rammed the boats into the beach, then set off the explosives.

Some of the experiments didn't work out so well. One of the boats run by another crew wouldn't obey the radio directions. It turned and headed back for the mother ship and had to be detonated quickly before it hit the friendly craft.

We did experiments where we poured oil on the water and then set it on fire, trying to make an effective smoke screen. It never worked very well. If we tried that today, the environmentalists would go crazy.

Another experiment we did was to load telephone poles with explosives, tie them alongside our small boat, and charge in toward a beach with sandbars that prevented the landing craft from getting onshore. The poles would be released when we got up to speed and they would surge into shore and stop. There we triggered a scuttling device by radio that let the pole and its weight of explosives settle to the bottom on the sandbar. The scuttling also set off a mechanical timing device, and after so many seconds the explosives were set off and the sandbar disintegrated so the landing craft could enter.

The idea worked well, but the Navy never let us use it in a combat situation. The Navy asked us what suggestions we had, and we always told them the rockets we fired needed more range. We were vulnerable to enemy fire when we had to get in so close to the beach.

After that, our unit was sent back to Fort Pierce for further training: this time, how to function in the wet evaluating beaches and removing obstacles. In 1945, I was sent to the Pacific. By that time I missed most of the landings. Our team did work some of the beaches on Japan that would be invaded if the war had continued: We swam in and checked out the beaches and looked for sandbars or other obstacles before the occupation forces went into Japan.

Just as the war was over, we were doing reconnaissance on beaches on Hokkaidō, the northernmost Japanese island. We swam in to do the job and sent the report back. After the war was over, some Japanese came out to us and asked to surrender and to turn over to us a prisoner-of-war camp they had there. We told them that we were not set up to do that but that the Army would be along soon and they would take care of it.

Gunner's Mate First Class Harold Wilson
Greenville, South Carolina

I JOINED THE Navy in Baltimore, Maryland, on March 27, 1943, and went to Bainbridge, Maryland, for my boot camp. I signed up for electrician's school, but before I was assigned, recruiters came and touted a new group that would train in Florida. I volunteered. I was picked as one of forty-two out of more than five hundred who volunteered.

We went by train to Fort Pierce, Florida. Our new home was not a motel but rather barren sand, where we erected five-man tents. We placed our cots on the sand with standards on all four corners. At night we draped mosquito netting around the standards and tucked it in under the mattress. No mess hall existed, so we ate powdered eggs, dehydrated potatoes, and K rations that cooks prepared in another tent. We had an open-air dining hall.

We were told we were in the Navy Combat Demolition Units, and the reason we were needed was the disaster of losing thousands of Marines in the Tarawa Island invasion in the South Pacific. We were in the Navy's plans to make reconnaissance prior to any beach landing and recommend landing points. Any obstacles were to be removed to allow access to the beach by landing craft.

At the new camp we met thirty-six Construction Battalion Navy men from Camp Perry, Virginia, and nineteen Mine and Bomb Disposal men from Washington, D.C. That gave us ninety-seven enlisted men and one officer for each five-man unit. We trained that way, five enlisted and one officer. I was assigned to Lieutenant Commander Draper Kauffman's boat crew for the entire training period.

Training started at five A.M. each morning with running on the rock jetty. It consisted of huge rocks that were covered with moss with the ocean washing over them. It eliminated a number of men, who ended up with broken bones when they fell on the jagged rocks. Following the run, we had thirty minutes of calisthenics and then we had our powdered eggs.

Our training included a three-and-a-half-mile run around palm trees and across the sand. We had training from Scouts & Raiders on the obstacle course. We swam a mile or more in the Atlantic Ocean. We paddled a rubber boat after carrying it over the jetty and then taking it out into the ocean five miles before turning around and coming back in. Some days we had demolition training where we set off explosives.

We had night problems. One was to take our five-man team and paddle up five miles along the shore, come in at a selected spot, and bury our boat. Then we tried to infiltrate an abandoned plantation house where sentries had been posted. Four sentries patrolled the perimeter. We had to infiltrate into the house, pick up a candy bar, and return to our boat. If we got caught, we had to sit in the house and let the mosquitoes eat us up until the exercise was over. If our five men all returned, we would dig up our boat and paddle back to camp, arriving about three A.M. Then we had to get up for the new day two hours later and do it all over again. We did this for two months.

Standard gear for water exercises included swim trunks, a cartridge belt that doubled as a lifesaver belt, swim fins, coral shoes, a swim mask, and a knife. For land work we had jungle greens or dungarees. We might also have detonating caps, Primacord, and a rifle or pistol.

I was there before they established "Hell Week." In my experience every week seemed like Hell Week.

By the time our training was finished, ten five-man teams made it through. Seven units went to the Pacific

Theater, two to the Mediterranean, and one to England. The seven units, including mine, NCDU No. 4, went to Treasure Island, San Francisco. After a ten-day leave, we sailed on November 9, 1943, on a merchant ship, the *Cape Sand Blast*, and zigzagged across the Pacific to New Caledonia. The town was Nouméa. We landed on December 3 in what had to be the worst hellhole the Navy could ever use. This French-owned island was an active leper colony. We were three thousand men waiting for assignments.

One evening, the meal was so tainted that all the men developed dysentery. It was mass confusion trying to get three thousand men to the twelve-holer outhouses.

Three weeks later we boarded the same merchant ship and went to Guadalcanal, where we had Christmas on board. From there we went by landing craft to Turner City on Florida Island in Tulagi Bay, where we stayed until July 1944. Turner City was a staging area for sailors that allowed troops to bivouac until needed. Both my NCDU Nos. 4 and 5 were there with a hundred tons of explosives with which we had trained. Tulagi was a deep bay that accommodated any size Navy ship. It was set up with warehouses for restocking ships.

We trained on an island called Mandalena, an Australian coconut plantation. We used Bangalore torpedoes, fifty-five pound can charges, twenty-six-foot rubber hoses packed with TNT, and twenty-four-pound tetrytol packs. We experimented blowing channels through coral reefs opening a channel to shore. After each explosion, natives swarmed the area in dugout canoes to pick up the stunned and dead fish. They liked the fifty-pound parrot fish best, which they hoisted into their canoes and disappeared as quickly as they had come.

Our rations were sometimes scarce because of shortage of refrigerated ships that delivered food in the Pacific. We filled out our diet with fish that we caught using the fifty-five-pound cans of TNT. We also caught numerous red snappers.

Some of the men did sport fishing. One speared a big stingray with a homemade spear. It had a cord tied to it and the other end of the cord tied to a bucket. The big stingray escaped. Several days later we heard general quarters had been sounded on the mail ship. They saw what they thought was a periscope. On closer inspection the thing started making tight circles. It was the stingray that had surfaced with a spear still in it and the bucket still attached.

We returned to Turner City and practiced using our Munson Lung, which was the precursor of the current scuba tank. They were good down to a depth of twenty-five feet.

On February 15, 1944 the NCDUs Nos. 4 and 5 made the first operation to Green Island with the New Zealand Infantry. We were aboard an LST with about forty other LSTs in the group escorted by cruisers and destroyers. Green Island was forty miles from New Ireland, a heavily fortified Japanese stronghold. Admiral Halsey's Third Fleet was a hundred miles away, giving us air cover. As we approached the island, there were forty Japanese fighters sent to intercept us. Our carrier pilots shot down thirty-seven of the planes. Three got through and hit our task force. One was shot down by shipboard gunners. The next one was flying upside down at deck height between the LSTs, probably hoping that someone would shoot at him and hit one of our own vessels. I could see his face as he flew by with his little skullcap. He went out to the end of the task force and peeled up. Then our fighter planes shot him down. They also got the fortieth Japanese fighter a few minutes later.

Green Island was flat and shaped like a horseshoe. The teams' purpose was to deepen the channel to the harbor entrance to allow larger ships to anchor there. Due to a very swift current flowing out of the harbor, none of the explosives would hold. We exploded some fifty-pound cans of TNT in an effort to deepen the ledge, but only got a school of large tuna. We gave them to the LST cooks and enjoyed a meal with them. The New Zealand Infantry took the island, but the bay was not used for large ships. The island eventually had a useful airstrip.

We lived on the island for two weeks. During that time we blew coral heads from the bottom of the bay that were three to four feet under the surface and could have been hazardous to our ships.

On the second day of the battle for Green Island, a New Zealand tank rolled out of the fight and down to the safe area near where we were camped. We were surprised to see the tank. The hatch flew open and four tank men came out. They promptly boiled water and had tea. Then they loaded up their gear and reentered the tank battle.

The island was secured in ten days. I walked down from our camp and saw a man on a platform with a swirling device. I asked what he had and he called it "radar." It was the first time I had heard the device mentioned or seen one.

We then returned to Turner City to await our next assignment.

Shortly after the Green Island shoot, we almost got to go on R & R in Brisbane, Australia, for fifteen days.

We were on our way to the dock to get to Henderson Field on Guadalcanal when an officer came up and met us. He said the trip was off: We had another mission.

A transport in Tulagi Bay took us to the Saint Matthias Group in the Pacific. We arrived March 20, 1944. The Marines and Army landed on opposite sides of the island and fought each other for a while until they realized that there were no Japanese: They had abandoned the island. The Navy set up a PT boat base there at once.

Our NCDUs were running short on rations, so we went to the PT base. We were there four days when a Jap periscope was sighted in the bay. The PT boats dropped depth charges in the bay and the sub shot to the surface bow up, then sank stern-first. There were no obstacles for the NCDUs to remove, so we returned to Turner City.

While at Turner City, the twelve NCDU teams there totaled sixty enlisted men and twelve officers. Orders came through to disband NCDU and form UDT Able. Underwater Demolition Teams existed in other locations. All seventy-two men now jointed together as one group known as UDT Able.

We boarded the USS *Noa APD-24* in Tulagi Bay under the command of Lieutenant King. This older destroyer was modified to accommodate UDT teams. Two stacks were eliminated and the space used for troop compartments. We went to Palau Island for the landing on September 12, 1944. At five A.M. the teams were planning to make reconnaissance on the beach when suddenly we were hit in the aft engine room by the USS *Fullam* (DD-474), a U.S. destroyer. Over 125 feet of the *Noa*'s starboard shaft with propeller went completely through the destroyer's bow, which flooded three of their compartments. The *Noa* lost all electric power and had to spread the word to abandon ship by word of mouth. We grabbed what we could and went topside. The entire deck was awash with water up to the main deck door. We started to crank down landing boats by hand. We noticed that the end of the boat had been damaged by the destroyer as well. We were standing waist-deep in water now.

During that time Ed Murphy decided to go below and retrieve $1,200 he was holding for a shipmate, Del Pizzo. We told him it was too dangerous, but he felt obliged to get it. Down in our quarters he saw Chief Petty Officer Jerick still sleeping in his bunk. Murphy woke him and warned him to get a move on, the ship was sinking. Then Murphy grabbed the money and was gone. When Murphy was halfway up the ladders to the deck, Jerick flew past him running barefoot and wearing only his shorts. When Jerick saw the situation topside, he dove overboard and swam to a rubber boat.

Our boat wouldn't drop down, so we had to bum a ride with the landing craft ahead of us. We overloaded it, but made it to the USS *Pennsylvania*, which was anchored nearby. We had no loss of life when our ship sank.

Since our landing craft was lost, we didn't participate in the reconnoitering of the beach. Other teams found a significant number of obstacles and barbed wire, which they destroyed. We had ringside seats as the Marines stormed the beach and at last overwhelmed the defenders.

We were transferred to the battleship *Maryland* and taken to Manus Island. We waited there for two weeks then were transferred to the Hawaiian Islands. There we got a nine-day leave. We were stationed on Maui.

Our UDT Team Able was disbanded and the men distributed among UDT Nos. 11, 12, 13, 14, and 15. Fifteen Able men went into UDT No. 14 on November 30, 1944. I was one of them.

We soon learned our next objective was Lingayen Gulf in the Philippines. Not knowing what to expect in the Philippines, they gave each man nine medical shots. Some of the men were sick for a couple of days.

On November 30, 1944, UDT No. 14 boarded the USS *Bull*, which was heading for the Philippines. Going through the Philippine Straits, we saw a low-flying airplane. No ships were firing at it, so we assumed it was a U.S. scout plane. Then all of a sudden we realized it was a Japanese kamikaze. It dove in and crashed on the deck of a small carrier, the *Ommaney Bay* (CVE-79). The plane hit Navy aircraft on the deck, causing them to explode, and the fire moved to the hangar deck and the powder magazines. Multiple explosions took place on the ship. Men were jumping overboard and the ship was listing badly to starboard. About 850 men were rescued by nearby destroyers, but 450 were lost. This all took place a hundred yards behind us. When the ship was no longer thought to be salvageable, the task force commander ordered a destroyer to sink the carrier.

This was a huge task force. It was ten miles wide and fourteen miles long. There were 1,450 ships, including craft of all kinds. The task force arrived in Lingayen Gulf on January 6, 1945. The UDT teams made reconnaissance of the bay the next morning for the landing and found it easily navigable, with no obstacles.

On January 12, 1945, several ships left Lingayen Gulf for the Ulithi Islands. On the way through the Mindanao Sea, we were asked to locate a downed pilot.

We searched the area and found the pilot was on the beach with twelve Filipino girls. The pilot had two broken legs and a broken arm. The ship's doctor examined him after we took him on board. We blew up the aircraft and gave the girls an American flag. Before we left, they had it flying from the tallest palm tree.

We left from Ulithi, heading for Iwo Jima. We arrived February 17, 1945. Our landing craft trailed the destroyer we were on by about seventy-five yards. Suddenly another LCI was hit by a mortar shell on the deck and disintegrated the boat. More mortar shells rained down.

We took evasive action, zigzagging our landing craft parallel to the shore, dropping off UDT swimmers while our LCI, destroyers, cruisers, and battleships shelled the island to give the swimmers cover. Carrier planes began strafing the area in front of our swimmers. We were given time limits to recon the shore, take our notes and check for obstacles, and then swim back out and be picked up by our landing craft.

Because of cold water, we used grease to cover our bodies to aid in holding in our warmth. When we got back to the big ship, we got a miniature medical brandy to drink.

The next day we directed the Marines as they made their amphibious landing on the beaches. The second day after the landing, all types of landing craft were broached on the beach from the high surf. This made them useless and cluttered the beach and did not allow ships to land supplies and men.

From February 20 to 28 we cleared the beaches. We blew up the first two craft, but that resulted in casualties to our men, so we put cables on the other boats and had them pulled out to sea, where we sank them.

During the time we were clearing the beaches, we

saw the Marines raise the flag on Mount Suribachi there on Iwo Jima. We also saw a damaged B-29 land on an unsecured bomb-cratered air strip. The airmen came piling out and ran for safety. Maybe they saw the flag and thought this was a safe strip.

The USS *Bull* and other ships proceeded back to Ulithi. We were resupplied and then gathered a large task force and went to Okinawa, arriving on March 29, 1945. D-day for the invasion was set for April 1. Our UDT Team No. 14 was assigned to decoy work. We set up explosions on the beach that would cause a distraction. It was designed to look like a landing would take place at this location. The real landing would be on a heavily fortified, walled area sixty-five miles to the west. On April l, ten UDT teams blew the walls in the water and opened passage ways for the landing craft.

Later we were dropped off on the USS *Wayne*, a transport, and taken five miles to a bay that was used for damaged ships. We were sent to a merchant ship loaded with ammunition, which needed to be unloaded. It was dark and the bay was full of ships. It took us a while to find the right one. They asked us for the password. Our coxswain had forgotten it, so they shot at us with small arms. We had to go back to the ship and get the right password.

Then we spent the rest of the night unloading fourteen-inch projectiles and black-powder bags. We were interrupted by air raid warnings and sat in the pitch dark several times. There we were, sitting on an ammo ship during air raids. That ship would have made one great explosion.

From there we were sent to Hawaii, where we boarded a ship for Treasure Island in San Francisco and a thirty-day leave. After that, we were sent to Maui.

We were ready to go back to the war when the second atomic bomb dropped. That was the end of it. UDT No. 14 was dismantled at the training base at Maui and we returned to Oceanside, California. The team was decommissioned in October 1945. I stayed in the Navy until March of 1946, spending my time back where I had started, in Bainbridge, Maryland.

Lieutenant Commander Carl R. Noyes
Billings, Montana

IN JUNE OF 1943, I was inducted into the Navy Reserve at Helena, Montana, as a warrant officer, carpenter, on inactive duty. Then on July 16, 1943, I reported for active duty at the Navy training center at Camp Perry, Virginia. In September of that year I was sent to New York City to attend stevedore's school. After that schooling I went to Camp Perry, Virginia, for further training. In February of 1944 I went to Fort Pierce, Florida, to the amphibious training base. In May of that year I was sent with NCDU No. 132 to Appledore, Devon, England, and then to Instow in Devon.

Two weeks later we reported to Lt. Cmdr. Herbert Peterson at Salcombe, Devon, for further training and preparation of explosives for the invasion of France. We added more men to our No. 132 team.

June 4, 1944, I reported with team and weapons to an LST for transport to Utah Beach, Normandy, France, for the invasion. We made the landing on the morning of June 6, D-day.

Our mission on Utah Beach was to clear underwater obstacles. The above-water ones would be taken care of by the Army demolition teams. This is to provide unimpeded landing of the VII Corps of the U.S. Army.

We were set up to clear four gaps, fifty yards wide, at 250 yard intervals through the seaward band of obstacles on each beach, then widen gaps to the left until the entire band of obstacles was cleared.

Our entire force made the landing 1,500 yards south of the intended location. Even so, we had to clear the obstacles there:

- Scattered wooden ramps looking like large letter *A*, the feet resting on the sand while the members slope upward. The timbers were ten to twenty-four inches in diameter.
- Three sparse bands of wooden and concrete piles mingled; wooden piles as on Omaha Beach. The concrete piles were reinforced with half-inch bars at each corner. The piles were irregularly spaced on thirty-five-foot centers.
- Eight unconnected "bays" of Element C, scattered to seaward of other obstacles.
- "Hedgehogs" of the same type as on Omaha, but some reported as welded throughout instead of partially bolted. These were mostly at the northern end of the actual assault area in a well-defined band to landward, spaced fifteen to twenty feet apart. In some instances a single strand of wire was strung between each two hedgehogs, perhaps to foul screws of landing craft at high water.
- Tetrahedrons, made of six equal preformed, reinforced concrete limbs fitted to form four equilateral triangles capable of resting on any of them by having a pin thrust hinge-wise through the projecting loop ends of the reinforcing bars at each end.

- Standard steel antitank-type tetrahedrons.
- Teller mines: not many in the actual assault area but dense in the intended assault area.

All of the NCDUs touched down within one or two minutes of their scheduled times, H hour minus three hours. The units were not in the order from right to left as originally planned; instead they spaced themselves out, but this made no difference in their work.

Officers reported that, with few exceptions, they were hardly aware of the enemy fire until they were through and took cover. However, machine-gun, artillery, and rifle fire left six NCDU men dead and eleven wounded.

All units went to work laying charges and blew their first gaps—generally more than fifty yards clear through from the waterline to the barbed wire at the seawall—in five minutes. They immediately wired and fired their second and many of them their third shots, widening the gaps leftward as per plan. By 0800 of D-day, Lt. Cmdr. Peterson saw that the entire beach in the assault area was clear of enemy obstacles. The infantry arrived right on schedule and was able to go straight across the beach and over the seawall with no obstacles to worry about.

The Army Engineer Demolition Teams hit the beach a little late and went to work breaching the seawall exits and clearing minefields behind it. Some of the Army men remained on the beach and breached gaps edge to edge with the Navy gaps.

In all cases the NCDUs used hand-placed prepared charges of either composition C-2 or tetrytol: for concrete posts, either one or two charges were placed at the base of the post; for tetrahedrons, two charges at the apex and one at the foot of each leg; for wooden posts, either two or three at the base. For the ramps, two were placed at the apex and in some cases one at the base of a leg. In the case of element "C," from eighteen to twenty-two charges were placed at the various welded joints. In each case the charges were connected to a trunk line of Primacord. Electric firing was used exclusively.

There were a few cases where shell fragments penetrated the prepared charges and one instance of a Primacord lead being cut by shrapnel. In these cases the explosive did not detonate from the shell fragment.

The NCDUs used the Army's Ml ammunition bag and could carry thirty-two pounds of explosives suspended from the shoulders and still work easily while carrying that load.

We were on Utah Beach until June 12 and then took an LST from the beach to quarters in Fowey, Cornwall, England. In July we went to Salerno, Italy, then to Oran, Africa, then back to Naples, Italy. On July 30, eleven men and I were assigned to the LST 659. Then, on August 15, 1944, we made the southern France landing.

After the landing I was sent to Corsica, then to Naples and Salerno. On September 11, I took the USS *General George O. Squier*, a troop transport, to Lido Beach, Long Island, New York. After a leave I reported to Fort Pierce, Florida. Soon I was in San Francisco. From there I went to Guam for a month, then on to Iwo Jima, and then a month later on to Okinawa. On September 4, 1945, I was the officer in charge of Detachment Twelve in Okinawa.

I took a ship back from Okinawa to Seattle, where I arrived December 12. The next day I was released from active duty and headed for Montana. I remained in the Naval Reserve until January 24, 1950, when I retired and was promoted to lieutenant commander.

Code Name: NEPTUNE
Operation Order No. 1-44
Portland, Dorset
31 May 1944: 1200

The Naval Combat Demolition Group is associated and working with an Army Demolition Group consisting of two battalions of Combat Engineers attached to V Corps. One NCDU together with one Army Combat Demolition Unit forms a gap assault team.

Tankdozers embarked in LCTs will land at H hour and proceed against obstacles as directed by the army combat demolition unit officers. All paths cleared through minefields will be marked by personnel of the Army Demolition Units with a standard minefield gap marker, five feet high.

NCDU sections two and one will form part of assault group C-1 and O-2 and will function under the commanders of those groups.

This group will clear and mark sixteen gaps, fifty yards wide, through the seaward band of obstacles on the OMAHA Beaches; two on FOX GREEN, six on EASY RED, two on EASY GREEN, two on DOG RED, two on DOG WHITE, and two on DOG GREEN.

The NCDUs will widen the gaps in the seaward band of obstacles until the entire band is cleared. They will assist the special Army Engineer Demolition group in clearing gaps through other bands and removing all obstacles from the OMAHA Beaches.

NCDU Section One will land as directed by Commander Assault Group 0-2, and clear eight gaps through the seaward band of obstacles on beaches DOG GREEN, DOG WHITE, DOG RED and EASY GREEN in accordance with the table set forth.

NCDUs will land at H plus three minutes. If the seaward band of obstacles is Element "C," ten men from the Army section of the gap team will reinforce the NCDU to assist in removal of the obstacles. The two powder men of each NCDU will launch the rubber boats with reserve explosives from the LCM at the time of debarking and tow them ashore.

When the boats reach shore, one man [is] to remain with the boat while the other proceeds inshore to the highwater mark with a white, triangular range marker, two feet wide at the base, and eight feet high. The man proceeding inshore with the marker will place it on the beach above the high water mark on the center line of the gap cleared by the combined Army and Navy teams.

When the depth of water prevents further clearance of the seaward band of obstacles, the NCDUs will mark the extremities of the cleared gaps by green flags mounted on buoys, and then assist the Army team in clearing obstacles in the inshore bands.

Support NCDUs will land as directed to assist or augment the assault NCDUs Unload reserve explosives from the support craft. Retract and remain on call, to be unloaded as directed by NCDU Section Commanders.

Reserve craft [are to] remain afloat on call to be unloaded as directed by NCDU Section Commander.

Indicate intention to explode charges by a violet smoke grenade lighted when the fuse to the charge is ignited. Unless otherwise directed, use a two-minute delay fuse for all charges.

Second Class Bosn' Mate James M. Brown
Punta Gorda, Florida

As AN NCDU man, I went in with my unit to the French coast shortly after H hour on June 6, 1944. We followed in the wake of the first wave of assault troops. We knew there was a wide "wall" of anti-invasion obstacles on the beach. These had to be removed so the landing craft would be able to get to the beach and pour out men and machines.

We spent five days aboard an LCT, landing craft tank, before we actually got going. We ate K rations and slept under tanks on the open deck. On the sixth day we transferred to an LCM and soon started our run into the beach. A few shots hit our craft but they weren't serious and didn't worry us much. After we disembarked, we really ran into the hell-and-high-water scene. All around me men were falling. Some cried out in agony. We had to continue going in or swim back to England. We all went in and tied our charges to the beach obstacles. We each carried twenty, two-pound explosive charges. These charges were fastened to the obstacles and connected by cables strung to a position clear of the explosion area. Then they were set off electrically. This blew gaps in the wall so the landing craft could get ashore.

Some of these deterrents were made of heavy, standard railway tracks propped pyramid-fashion. They were ten feet high and eight feet wide. Most were mined. The tops of the tracks were sharpened to impale craft approaching the shore. Obstacles extended from a position still underwater, despite the low tide at H-hour, to a line far up the beach even at high tide. We crawled on our stomachs under the withering Jerry rifle and machine-gun fire from one objective to the next.

Sometimes we had to delay setting the charges off because assault troops were taking cover behind the obstacles. We shouted warnings to the troops, who then moved out of the areas.

Bodies of men killed in the assault floated in the shallow water around us. It wasn't a nice sight. Some of the dead were our buddies, who we had talked with just a few minutes before.

A large shell hit a rubber boat we were using to go into the beach and destroyed the rifles and pistols we had brought with us, so all we had left were our knives. They were completely useless against the long-range rifles and machine guns facing us.

Those of us who were not hit finally finished blowing the gap assigned to us and got to dry land. What a relief it was to see the reinforcements pouring through our gaps and up the beach. Many of our NCDU men had been wounded by shrapnel, and everybody was dazed and shaken. Somehow we managed to crack a joke occasionally to help cheer up the boys who were wounded. Army and Navy corpsmen gave field first aid to our casualties and they were soon evacuated out to hospital ships offshore.

I had made it. I had lived through "hell and high water."

Chief Machinist's Mate Jerry N. Markham
Jacksonville, Florida

BEFORE I JOINED the Navy, I worked in Jacksonville in a large paper company with a self-contained power supply. We made our own electricity and steam and used both in the process of making paper. My job was operating the steam center for the plant, which ran continuously.

The job was exempt from the draft, so my prospects of joining the service through the draft were remote. However, I maintained an active interest in the world situation. I followed the Franco-Spanish war and what his Fascist friends were doing to rebels there by reading papers and books.

I kept up on the Chamberlain fiasco over Hitler, and the invasion of France and rape of Poland, and the emergence of Churchill. I knew about the FDR Lend-Lease program where he gave fifty destroyers to England to aid them in their defense against Germany. Then Pearl Harbor exploded in the Pacific. I was twenty-one years old at the time. A lot of my friends had volunteered to join the services. I was only a spectator listening to reports on the radio.

Finally one day I decided I'd join the Seabees and put my experience as a power engineer to good use. I also had experience in construction there at the plant. So I joined the Navy's construction battalion. I waited to be inducted in the service in New York City, where my mother was living. So I joined the Navy Seabees in NYC. We reported to duty and several hundred of us went to Pennsylvania Station and were put on an old troop train. I remember my first Navy duty, on our way to Camp Perry, Virginia, a Seabee base at that time. A chief came into the car and pointed at me. He said, "There are forty-one men in this car. You're responsible to see that there are forty-one men in the car when we get to Camp Perry, Virginia." Every time the train stopped guys would jump out the windows and run across the road and get candy bars and come crawling back on the train. I got concerned about keeping a head count in my car. I took a count and came up one man short. I went through the cars on both sides of mine, but they had no extra man. I couldn't find him. The chief came in and asked how it was going. I told the chief I was missing one man. The chief scowled at me and made his own count. He got forty-one. I'd forgotten to count myself.

At Camp Perry we all drew our blankets, gear, and uniforms. Starting the next day, we were introduced to our boot training. It was the usual: reveille, line up for early morning muster, chow, close order drill, obstacle course, etc. Boot lasted six weeks. Then we would be assigned to a construction battalion and a specific work area. After a week of boot camp, they sent me to a water purification school, due to my work history. I got out of a lot of the boot camp KP and guard duty.

I finished the six weeks training and knew I'd probably be assigned to some island and be in charge of water chlorination and have to run a plant to turn salt water into fresh water. That just didn't appeal to me. One day as I waited for my assignment, I had messenger duty, and I saw a notice go up on the board asking for volunteers for dangerous and hazardous work. Must be ages 19 to 27 and have experience with small-boat handling, swimming, diving, and explosives. This appealed to me, so I signed up for it. Deep-sea and shallow-water diving had always interested me as a boy. I had read *Twenty Thousand Leagues Under the Sea*. I used to dream about walking underwater. So I volunteered for the NCDUs, a special-forces group. I reported for duty on the same base.

There were ninety of us in that group. They lined us up the following morning and forced marched us four miles to a drill field. Six Marines were there waiting for us. They told us their job was to separate the men from the boys. They put us on a modified Marine raider training program. This proved to be strong on physical fitness, for endurance as well as responding to discipline. Those Marine drill sergeants loved to do this to a bunch of sailors.

After five weeks of this, we were down to thirty men from our starting class of ninety. Men who didn't pass muster on the physical side were quickly washed out. Since this was an all-volunteer outfit, you could volunteer to get out as well as in. Some did.

They shipped thirty graduates to Fort Pierce, Florida, where there was another amphibious base. That was the Naval Combat Demolition Unit headquarters. I and three other guys were held back because we demonstrated some proficiency in shallow-diving gear. They wanted us to serve a dual purpose: to help with the training and leadership for the next group going through. Soon we had another bunch of volunteers show up. When we met the Marines, the sergeant in charge took one look at me and said, "Marko, come here. What the hell you doing here? Not even a Marine has to take the raider twice." I told him, once you have been through that crap, it's a cakewalk. He choked a little on that. We finished training the second group, which was also cut down from ninety to thirty, and sent them on to Fort Pierce. I went with this group. The camp down there was still in the building process. Our first job in Florida was to pour concrete to form a swimming pool near the beach. The idea was to use it for practice setting explosives for certain types of beach obstacles.

Now we went through another series of training. We did the water drills, rubber boats, tougher physical training, landings, and powder work. Then came the infamous "Hell Week": seven days of night-and-day, nonstop swimming, boating, running, swamp dragging, mock attacks on objectives, and setting off explosives. It went on night and day with almost no sleep and little food. It tested us physically and was even tougher mentally and emotionally.

The whole idea was to weed out anyone who could not show the endurance, the ability to do the work, and the discipline to obey orders and complete the mission. If you finished it, you could be proud of yourself. *I* was.

After that, they formed us into combat units. I only experienced it one time in the service, when officers and enlisted men got together on a strictly democratic basis and organized. It started when the officers for each five-man squad held a meeting. There would be five enlisted men and one officer for each unit. The officers each picked out the enlisted man he wanted to be second in command under him. Then that officer went to that enlisted man and asked if he wanted to be in that officer's unit as his second. The enlisted man had the option of being the number-two man in the unit or declining. If he said no, the enlisted man went back in the pool to be picked by another officer. If the enlisted agreed, then that officer and that enlisted selected four other men to be in the unit. Again these men selected had the option of serving in this unit or declining. It made for groups with men who were compatible and who wanted to work with each other. The future would show that the closeness of the group meant the men would put their very lives on the line for each other.

Ensign John E. Bussell was our unit officer. In the team were Henry Samuel Fabich, Carmine Carl Fulgieri, James Edward McHugh, Raymond Rudolph Pienack, and myself.

After the six-man units were formed, we began a training program filled with four to six units working on exercises together. We would go through the process of launching small rubber boats, paddling out several miles and coming back, simulating an invasion and landing among obstacles and setting charges and blowing them. Obstacles had been built on our beaches by Army engineers and were realistic.

We were given a chance to use tetrytol explosive, TNT, Primacord, electronic detonators, and fuses that we didn't have at Camp Perry.

After months of this training, we were used to working together as four or six six-man units at a time. Then we were pulled together and sent to Lido Beach, Long Island, New York, where we prepared for overseas shipment. We arrived there prior to Christmas in 1943, were issued new cold-weather gear, and boarded an LST for our ocean voyage. A group of twelve LSTs made up our convoy to try the crossing in January of 1944. First we had to go to a town in New Jersey because the longshoremen wouldn't handle the explosives in the outer harbor to get them onboard the ships. So we had to load two thousand pounds of explosives on the ships to be used for our future demolition work. After fifteen days at sea in the frigid North Atlantic, we knew we had made a winter crossing. It was so cold that the sea spray froze to the ship and your clothes. On deck you had to wear a mask to protect your face.

Our security was so solid when we arrived in England, nobody knew who we were, what we had been trained to do, or what to do with us. Our first duty was to stand guard at ammo dumps. Our officers were on ward duty until we got squared away at the base to do our own training. We were at Swansea, Wales, and bivouacked there with Army engineers who built beach obstacles and tank traps for more training.

Finally it came closer to D-day. We were not too well informed about what it was and what types of obstacles we would be called upon to blow. We got two lieutenant commanders assigned to us to get some authority to go up in the loop and find out what kind of obstacles we would be facing. We found out that our services were seriously in demand. We each had a gap to blow on the beach in a time slot. We reviewed it carefully and looked over pictures about beach sites. We had Omaha Beach as our objective. It's a crescent-shaped area about five miles long. Our section had ravines and 120-foot cliffs just in back of the beach. The whole area was heavily mined and defended, especially the ravines that led to the top of the cliffs.

We could see that the beach was filled with rows of mines and obstacles of different shapes, sizes, and density. The beach was three hundred yards wide at low tide. There was a twenty-six-foot tide that came in a foot every eight minutes. The water temperature was cold. Our job was to blow an obstacle-free gap fifty yards wide and 350 feet long through the mines and obstacles. We didn't have enough land mines and explosives in our squad to do it, so we grouped with the Army Engineer Demolition men. We had trained with them for six weeks and had five engineers and three untrained seamen assigned to our unit.

These men who filled out our Boat Team No. 11 on Omaha Beach were seamen William Vanfebilt, Elmer Malcolm Drew, and Harold Henry Crocker. From the 299th Army Engineers came Kenneth G. Kassell, Charles E. Ohman, Alvin F. Mosher, Theodore Petoniak, and L. V. Donaldson. The Army men were to join their group at the high-water mark.

So we had units of thirteen to fourteen men for each gap. The Army demolition men had gap teams of twenty-six men. We all went in on the same gap assignment and riding the same landing craft at the same time to blow one gap. That was the plan.

The Army unit would be in the front of our landing craft and would strike out first and go halfway up the beach and blow the obstacles from there to dry sand. We would start at the low-water mark and blow up the obstacles up to the point where the Army men began. This should finish clearing the gaps up to the high-water mark. This way we would have enough explosions to blow the mines and booby traps and obstacles in our area. Then the invasion forces could charge out of the water and across the beaches. That was the plan.

We loaded our Army and Navy units on an LCT and towed a fifty-foot landing craft behind us for use going into the beach. The landing craft, tank, carries three or four tanks and a jeep.

On June 3 we loaded aboard the LCT and slept on the steel decks under and around the tanks. We had no hot water and ate K rations. Soon it started raining. On June 4 we went out into the English Channel and quickly a storm blew up. They called off the invasion for that day and we went back to port to wait. While in the stormy channel, most of us on board became seasick. Conditions on the LCT were horrible that night: no shelter, no good food, no warmth. I figured that only our vigorous training held us together. If we hadn't been in tip-top condition, many of us wouldn't have made it.

The invasion was on again. We started on the night of June 5 from England in our LCT and were two or three miles short of the French coast when I noticed that our LCT was riding low in the water. I went to the captain of the ship and told him. We took a look belowdecks and found we were taking on water fast and we were sinking while under way. I went to my unit officer, John Bussell, and said we were sinking, so we called the small landing craft up and transferred to it. The LCT sank soon after we left it. We went to a transport ship for a while, then got in our small landing craft and came back and got in line for the invasion. We started in for the beach with the rest of the group lined up to begin the invasion. Our gap teams were heading for gap eleven on Easy Red Beach.

We had five support gap teams in reserve waiting just offshore in case there was a need. The Army had five gap teams in reserve as well and two command boats with officers overseeing what was going on and where help might be needed. This was the battle plan.

As we came in to the low-water mark on the beach, we saw our landing sector and dropped our ramp.

That's when we felt the murderous German machine-gun fire. It was cross fire from the left and right and more fire coming from those looming cliffs from hidden guns. Mortar fire began to be accurate, and a round made a direct hit to one landing craft and blew it to hell. We dropped our ramp and the Army unit went out first, pulling their rubber boat with extra explosives. At once they ran into a hail of gunfire and lost half of their men. We followed them with our rubber boat as we hit the beach with the machine-gun fire as heavy as at first. The only cover we had was to hide at the base of the German beach obstacles. We were three hundred yards out from the high-tide area.

I came up in the rear of my unit packing the Primacord and detonators that would tie all of the charges together so they could be fired simultaneously. Coming up at the rear, I saw that most of our unit had got into the water. I was off to the side when a mortar round hit our rubber boat and killed two of our men. I looked down and saw one of my friends with his head blown completely off his body. Our unit officer, Ensign John Bussell, lay facedown in the water where large chunks of shrapnel had taken his life in a second.

It was a tremendous shock to see death so quick and so close to home. Three of our men dead already and the rest scattered all over. I figured the Army unit was worse off then we were. I took over the unit command and we began to do our job, going from obstacle to obstacle and placing charges. I tried to follow close behind our men to tie the planted explosives into one line for detonation. The machine-gun fire was intense. We lost more men. All this time the tide was coming in a foot every eight minutes, so before long we would have to move forward. We were so tied down and took so much time that the second assault wave of infantry began landing in the middle of our work. Then before long the third wave came in and we had to warn the soldiers to get away from the obstacles so we could blow them. Soon the beach was overcrowded. We were only able to blow half of the obstacles in our gap, and some of the landing craft were hitting obstacles on the way in.

The third wave of troops brought total chaos. Later we learned that the assault on Omaha Beach was almost called off. The Air Corps had not hit its targets on the top of the cliff with the 22,000 pounds of bombs. The heavy cruisers offshore were supposed to blast the cliff gun positions, but they didn't hit them. Our Navy's rocket launch ships sent thousands of rockets into the area, but most of them fell short and didn't hurt the German gunners at all.

None of the support came. Nothing did the job. Heavy-gun shells from the sea bounded off the rounded protected bunkers of the cliff guns.

We were strictly on our own. General Bradley was almost ready to call off the Red Beach landing when I noticed that four destroyers came in so close to shore, they almost grounded and fired right into the cliffs and the high-water-level area. They soon knocked out the machine guns and the mortar positions. They pounded the concentrations up the ravines, so the troops could work up them and capture the big cliff guns from behind. Then we could make progress and secure the beach.

The four Navy destroyers saved the day on Omaha. We had high casualties. From 190 NCDU men who went ashore, 32 were killed and 63 wounded—over 52 percent casualties. Over 50 percent in my unit. After our demo work, our most important job was to help the wounded get out of the cold water and up past the high-water mark. Three men dug a foxhole behind a sand dune and a mortar shell landed on the dune and buried them in sand. I was close by and ran over and dug out their heads so they wouldn't suffocate. They said I did good work saving the three men and they awarded me the Navy Cross. Every man on that beach was a hero that day. I put in recommendations for medals for three of our men, but the requests got lost in the red tape and the hectic realities of combat.

Soon we had the beachhead established with the help of the destroyers opening the ravines for the infantry. That saved the day.

How did I feel when landing on the beach? Was I scared? In fear? Yes. It was a mixture of two fears: the fear of simply not surviving and the fear of not doing my job.

Thanks to the training that we had and the closeness of the group, doing the job overcame the fear of survival. That helped me more than anything else. Why haven't I talked about this until now?

Lots of unpleasant memories. Just as the action started, I saw my unit officer dead in the water and a buddy with his head blown off. Younger men riddled with machine-gun fire. The encouragement of the other men was inspiring, so we could get the job done with what we had to work with. I was able to get some units to our right to blow a partial gap adjacent to our area. Our Army demo-men team was pretty well knocked out. Most of them didn't even reach the high-water mark: no place to hide except behind the obstacles.

We have to thank those four destroyers and their accurate gunners, who opened up those ravines for us and really saved the day. Without them there it would have been a total disastrous defeat on Red Beach, Omaha.

We blew five complete gaps and three partial gaps, not nearly the number we had been assigned. Within three days our units completely cleared the beach of the highly mined obstacles. Numerous men in my and other units were given high awards. All well earned. All in all, a difficult job well done.

I spent three days on the beach, clearing up mines and ammo spread all over the place that interfered with the flow of people. On the fourth day I realized that I was passing blood. The medics took me to the aid station and then out to the hospital ship. I had severe internal bleeding from a nearby concussion of one of the enemy rounds. I recovered.

After the invasion, most of our units were shipped back to the States and assembled at Fort Pierce. We were told that the NCDU was being disbanded, and we were given the option of going back to our prime service group or join a UDT team. An officer, Walter "Scotty" Cooper, a boat commander on Omaha, asked me if I would help him as a senior chief to form UDT Team No. 25. I did and we got thirty-three men from the NCDUs who had been Omaha Beach veterans. We had a team that was outstanding.

We trained for six weeks, then we were shipped to Maui, Hawaii, for advanced training. After a few months we were assigned to an APD high speed destroyer. We were now almost totally self-contained. We had our own UDT destroyer, ship's company, small-boat crews, a full load of all the explosives we would need, and a full complement of UDT teams.

We returned to the States in our APD and were stationed off the coast of Oceanside, California, with sixteen other teams waiting for assignment. Everyone knew that we were ready and waiting for the invasion of Japan. I knew that invading Japan would be far worse than Normandy. We would not have air control. Our supply lines would be four hundred miles long. Every Japanese man, woman, and child would be a deadly enemy. Thousands of lives on both sides were saved by those two nuclear bombs. So the war was over. My duty was done.

I returned to the Lido Beach separation center on Long Island in New York and was discharged September 18, 1945.

Lieutenant James M. Sprouse (deceased)
Alexandria, Virginia

WHEN WE WENT to war in 1941 I was working as a civilian for the Navy as a hardhat diver. I couldn't get a release as a civilian employee of the Navy until they got somebody to take my place where I was working in Bermuda. That took until June of 1942.

I joined the service in June of 1942. Because of my diving work I went in as a Chief Bosn' Mate in the 11th Beach Battalion.

Soon I was in the Navy Combat Demolition Units at Camp Perry, Virginia. We were all volunteers and about 90 percent of these were Civil Engineer Corps officers and enlisted men drawn from the construction battalions at Perry. This was a natural, since many of these men had been hard-rock miners and construction workers familiar with the care and feeding of high explosives. Where else could the Navy find men with a high degree of improvisation necessary for such an undertaking? Many of the mechanical devices the NCDUs used were conceived and developed by CEC engineers.

I joined NCDU in February 1944, following a short period of training at Camp Perry that consisted of PT, obstacle courses, swimming, and running until I almost collapsed. Soon I reported to the training base at Fort Pierce, Florida. I was a member of Class Five that went through the compound.

The Fort Pierce school, under the extremely capable and demonic direction of Lieutenant Commander W. F. Flynn, had one of the most rigid physical training programs ever used by the Navy. A normal working day ran from 0600 to 0l00 the following day, unless there was some special project to be performed, in which case the working day extended through the next day. The training was rigorous and concentrated, with the major emphasis on physical conditioning.

Each happy day began with either a three-mile speed march or an invigorating swim. The length of the swim was gradually extended until each graduate was able to swim two miles. The course lasted eight weeks, and the number of trainees who were dropped from the program was high. Many failed physically, some lacked the necessary ability for working almost constantly in water, and a few volunteered to quit. I recall one man was dropped because he was too reckless: He was apparently unable to develop the high degree of respect always due high explosives.

To complete the course we went on an all-day and all-night problem. Then the class was divided, with part of the group going to the advanced base in Maui, Hawaii, and the rest of the men going to advance bases in England.

I went to England with fifteen six-man units. The time was short. We were flown to London via Newfoundland and Scotland. We arrived at the base at Appledore, North Devon, on May 9, less than a month before the Normandy invasion. Recent aerial reconnaissance of the target and other intelligence had revealed underwater obstacles on the French coast with which we were not familiar. It was necessary for us in cooperation with the fifteen units already in England, to devise means of demolishing these new threats. After ten days of practice runs in some of the coldest water in the world, we moved to the base at Salcombe, South Devon, to prepare the tremendous number of explosive charges that we would be using. We had tetrytol for concrete, TNT for wood, and C-2 plastic explosive for steel.

It was decided at Salcombe that one officer and five men to a unit was too small. So each unit was supplemented by six enlisted men from the 299th Army Combat Engineers and one Navy signalman, making a total of thirteen men in each unit.

On May 29th we entered the briefing encampment at Plympton, where we were first told just where we were going and when. On June 1 my unit and two others boarded an LST at Dartmouth for transportation to France. The invasion had been set for June 5 but bad weather postponed it until June 6, 1944.

The captain of our LST was apparently a professional poker player in civilian life. No amateur could win so often. He immediately adopted the attitude that we in demolition were going to our certain deaths, and there was therefore no reason why we should have any money when we left his ship. We didn't.

During the night, between midnight and H-hour,

the airborne troops were dropped and ferried in by gliders. General Ridgeway's 82nd Airborne Division and the 101st Airborne were the principals. Then there were God knows how many glider-borne troops. We watched as they passed overhead for two hours. Even late the next afternoon we saw 1,600 C-47s each, towing a glider, pass above us. The glider pilots had a good deal. All they had to do was land a large, unwieldy craft loaded with combat troops in any spot they could find: fields, ponds, woods, grassland, even a highway. Then if they survived, they sometimes walked through enemy lines back to the beach. There they bummed a ride back to England, where they were quickly assigned another glider for a repeat performance. Some of those men shifted their duty from the Air Corps to the infantry.

Each of the eleven teams on my particular section of the beach was in its own LCVP (landing craft vehicle, personnel), which had two thousand pounds of explosives in it. Each man carried forty pounds of powder in back- and chest packs. Of the eleven officers in command of these units, nine were CEC. The other two were line officers from the Mine Disposal School.

The operational plans called for the LCVPs to drop us at the beach, withdraw two thousand yards, and return to the same spot forty-one minutes later. At that time we would unload the remainder of our explosives and our personal gear and weapons. Our boat dropped us, but on the way out it caught a mortar shell, which disposed of the LCVP, the coxswain driving it, the rest of our explosives, and all of our personal gear and weapons.

The Army men would be going on across France and they were without personal gear or even a rifle. I had the only weapon in our group, a .45-caliber pistol.

The Army men on the beach had to scavenge the next few days for equipment. When they found a dead man with a weapon or gear they needed, they took it. So, piece by piece, they refitted themselves for the march across France.

The demolition units were due at the beaches at 0605, H-hour minus 25, which gave them twenty-five minutes to clear the obstacles before the first assault wave began arriving at 0630. The transport area, the point at which we embarked from the LST to the LCVP, was twelve miles off shore. This meant we had to be in the LCVP at 0300 for the run to the beach. The water was quite rough, and with the exception of the coxswain and myself, all hands became seasick.

En route to the beach, it was necessary to check in at two rendezvous areas, where all our LCVPs assembled before leaving for the next rendezvous or for the run to the beach. We were given a compass bearing when we left the LST and another at each of the checkpoints. Oddly enough, the plan worked: We arrived at the appointed time and at almost the right place.

On the way in we passed through the combat portion of the Western Task Force, which was engaged in the softening up of the beaches and the bombardment of targets inland. The battleships *Arkansas*, *Texas*, and *Nevada*, the cruisers *Tuscaloosa* and *Quincy* (CA-71), thirty-two destroyers, eighteen patrol craft, two French cruisers, one British monitor, and five British cruisers were engaged. The *Nevada*, you may recall, was sunk at Pearl Harbor but was now very much in the fight.

To further assist in neutralizing the beaches, an eight-hundred-ton carpet of bombing was made with C-24s transversing the beach in single file parallel to the water's edge. Then some thirteen thousand rockets were thrown in a barrage that was to be lifted thirty seconds ahead of our touchdown time. Rockets in those days were often inaccurate and erratic. I believe that many of our casualties were caused by our own rockets falling short: friendly fire.

In the Mediterranean there's no high tide or low tide; it's about the same all day. If we found underwater obstacles in France, we could go right up to them. In Normandy the Germans figured that we would go in at high tide to get our ships as close to the shore as possible. We didn't do that. We arrived, by plan, at dead low tide, and walked to the obstacles in knee-deep water.

The time of day 0605 was broad daylight, so we could work our twenty-five minutes in the light. Unfortunately this also gave the Germans perfect defensive firing light to nail us down or kill us.

One stroke of bad luck for us. The Germans had brought their 11th Panzer Division up to the beach at Normandy. Normally a German division was eighteen to twenty thousand men. The panzer divisions were thirty thousand men. They had moved the unit to the Normandy cliffs to practice repelling invaders. Guess who showed up at the wrong time—us.

We went in at Red Fox on Omaha Beach. It later became known as Bloody Fox. I can't describe what I saw that morning. You could almost walk from ship to ship across the whole English Channel. Our LCVP could carry about twenty men and one jeep. Going in that morning, the sun was rising, and it was a beautiful day. The big ships behind us were firing shells over our heads. You could see the sixteen-inch shells flying toward the shore. About three minutes before we got to the beach, the Air Corps put down a bombardment on the beach. It was just unbelievable. There must have been a thousand B-25s that went down the beach, dropping bombs. Then, about thirty seconds before we were to arrive, the rocket ships laid down a barrage to protect us but actually killed a lot of our men.

I'll remember that invasion for the rest of my life. I was thinking as I was going in that this was a very great point in American history: *This is the greatest invasion ever staged, and I am part of it. I'm here and I'm a part of it. I'm so happy to be here, I could just bust.* Because I thought that all of my life, if I lived, I would remember being there. I was just so pleased to be there, I would not have been anywhere else in the world. I was just delighted to be in that invasion. Before it was over—and it was a bad day—I was still delighted to be there. I lost 90 percent of my good friends that day and I was still glad to be there.

The Germans, expecting that we would land at high tide, had placed the obstacles only as far as the tide fall. We were therefore able to take the LCVPs in to a point where we had to wade only two hundred yards in knee-deep water to reach the beach and the outer rows of obstacles.

It was a tough two hundred yards. They threw the book at us with their big guns, rockets, mortars, oil bombs, machine guns, and rifle fire. Some of the machine guns had wooden bullets. They were accurate for only a short range, but because they tumbled end over end, they made a large, nasty hole when they hit flesh.

We encountered wooden ramps, several bays of Belgian gates, reinforced concrete posts, concrete tetrahedrons, wooden posts, and steel hedgehogs. Also much barbed wire. Each concrete or wood post had a Teller mine on the top, which had to be blasted.

Military men say that the battle is the payoff for all

of the training. That morning the long and intensive training at Fort Pierce and in England proved their worth. Each man, without exception, worked swiftly and efficiently, despite the intensive opposition, and the obstacles were removed and the gaps cleared for the landing craft. Our NCDU casualties during this battle were 52 percent dead and wounded.

The Germans had jammed our walkie-talkie radios, so we had no communication between teams and with our CO. But this proved to be no great inconvenience.

Once we had blown all the obstacles we could, and the third wave of assault troops were onshore, we dug in on the beach and regrouped. We continued the demolition of scattered obstacles and unexploded shells and mines for several days. We lost a few more men, mostly to strafing planes and air raids. One man's foxhole caved in and smothered him to death.

About three weeks later we returned to England on the same LST, whose captain was still playing poker, and went back to our base. We refilled our ranks to replace men lost and drew new equipment. We were in Milford Haven, Wales, for a time and I saw some of our men who were in a hospital there, including my brother.

Our next assignment was the invasion of southern France. It was between Cannes and Nice, and we did it mostly to placate Winston Churchill. It was a nothing operation. There were no Germans down there, just a few mercenary troops, Czechoslovakians and Poles and Russians. As soon as we hit the beach, they held up their hands and surrendered. I was awarded the Silver Star but I gave it back to them.

They said I had stormed a German dugout single handedly. That was true: I ran up to this dugout, went to a door and threw in a grenade, then threw in another one and rushed inside. There wasn't a single enemy inside. It was empty, and had been all the time. I didn't want a Silver Star for rushing an empty position.

I went back to the States in September of 1944 and reported to Fort Pierce.

For the record, these were my decorations: the Silver Star (awarded later for a real tough assignment), two Bronze Stars, two Purple Hearts for wounds, a Navy Commendation, an Army Commendation, an Air Medal, a European Theatre Operations with five battle stars, and the Far East Operation with two battle stars.

Early in the war an organization grew up called the OSS, the Office of Strategic Services. Many years later it became the CIA. It was a spy outfit but also went behind enemy lines to do sabotage. At Fort Pierce we had an awards ceremony with a band and everything. A Navy captain talked to me saying he was there on behalf of the Chief of naval operations. I went with the OSS because they were looking for somebody to go behind Japanese lines and take out some bridges. He asked me if I'd do it and I said yes, anything to get out of Fort Pierce.

They sent me to school on Catalina Island, off the coast of California, for six weeks. That was the best experience of my whole Navy career. It was a wonderful school. It was cryptography, small arms, hand-to-hand combat, Morse code, and survival. They had excellent instruction. If you wanted to go out and shoot on the range, they had people there twenty-four-hours a day to assist and teach you.

From there I went by ship to Calcutta, India. It took forty-seven days. I was supposed to fly, but I had a bad tooth that kept me grounded. I went to a jump school in Chakala, India. Paratrooper school. I made five jumps and that qualified me. In the States, five jumps wouldn't even be a start, but it was enough there. From there I went to Burma and Thailand.

I made three mission jumps in Burma and one in Thailand behind enemy lines to take out one electrical transmission line and one bridge. That's where I received the Silver Star.

Lieutenant Harold Blean
East Wenatchee, Washington

RIGHT AFTER I graduated from college I took a job in Alaska, putting my architectural engineering degree to work. I spent two years working in the construction of Elmador Field at Fort Richardson. There was no draft in Alaska at that time, and I was in a critical defense job. That's why I didn't get into the service until 1943. I talked to the Navy and they liked my background in construction and they commissioned me an ensign in the Navy Construction Battalion. This was the Seabees, and we built airfields, docks, and housing in the Pacific. After a few months with the Seabees, I had a chance to transfer to the Naval Combat Demolition Units.

I and my class at Fort Pierce endured three months of extensive physical training, working with explosives and with rubber boats in and out of the ocean. There were a lot of problem-solving assignments. One was to go into the woods to find and bring back a specific item or blow it up. We worked also to destroy obstacles on the beach and in the surf. We learned how to blow up different types of obstacles made of steel, wood, and concrete. After the training was done, my unit, NCDU

No. 137, was held on after training to work on survey damage from the various experimental efforts to remove beach obstacles.

The men in my No. 137 NCDU were Edmund Buffington, MM l/C; James Brown, Coxswain; Gilbert Luttrell, MM 2/C; James Patrick, GM l/C; and William White, Chief Boatswain's Mate.

When that survey duty was done, we were some of the last Groups of NCDUs sent to England. That was in April of 1944. We flew over with stops at Gander, Newfoundland, and Prestwick, Scotland, and then on to London. It was the first time most of us had ever been in a plane big enough to fly across the Atlantic.

Our first housing in England was on board an LST in the harbor at Ilfracombe while they finished building a base for us. It was our first exposure to the ship aspect of the Navy. Soon we were heading for France. We were taken at night to a warehouse and I was asked for a list of the men to go aboard. I gave the officer my copy of the list and the officer said I'd have to have seven copies of it. J. O. Patrick and I sat on crates and printed out seven copies of our list of thirteen men with serial numbers, and we finally got on board.

We knew we had been assigned four gaps of beach obstacles to blow up including steel rails and hedgehogs. We had to go in at H hour and take them out. We were on a 330-foot-long LST. About twelve miles off the French shore we transferred to our LCM, which was fifty feet long, for the run into the beach. My petty officer, Chief White, came up to me and said one of the men had lost his life jacket and White was going to give him his. I had to explain to him the importance of the second officer's safety over that of the member of the unit. He would have to take over leadership of the unit if I went down wounded or dead. We kept checking equipment over and over, yet we knew we couldn't be ready for everything.

We were more anxious when we found out the coxswain driving our boat was lost. He had lost his way in the mist and fog and had no idea where the shore was. Now I had something else to worry about. The heavy morning fog had blocked out everything on shore. At last the coxswain found another ship, which guided our landing craft into the correct formation.

I was the senior ensign in our eight boats in the wave to go ashore at H hour. We got to the circling boats just in time to straighten them out and lead them into the beach.

We arrived on Omaha Beach a half hour before the Army was due to swarm in. We had to get the obstacles blown up so the landing craft could come all the way into the beach to the sand if possible.

We were hit hard by enemy rifle and machine-gun fire but blew all of the obstacles that we could in our gaps.

About six hours into the fight, when the tide was going out, we found a bulldozer. Some of our Seabee guys could drive it. We got it started and found a cable and began to snake trucks ashore that had bogged down in the surf. We stayed onshore for another month working as shore patrol and blowing up any ordnance on the beach that hadn't exploded. One of our jobs was to keep the Navy guys from coming ashore and going up where the fighting was where they could get hurt.

After the Normandy invasion, I went to the Naval Architectural School in Michigan for a year. That led to my being a ship superintendent at Bremerton Naval Yard. I served in the Navy for two and a half years. I was raised with the idea that if you were called, you served. It wasn't something you even thought about. The service gave me any duty I asked for and I was always treated fairly. You did your job as well as you could. We did what we had to do. I can remember the only part of being actively frightened was when we had done everything assigned and we were being forced by the water up onto the beach where the bodies and the human carnage lay. I had to think, *What am I doing here?*

After the war, I returned to the Wenatchee area and became involved in community affairs.

Coxswain Robert E. Ross
Davenport, Iowa

IN NOVEMBER 1944, I finished boot camp in Chicago and was sent to Little Creek, Virginia, for assignment as a crewmember on an LST. While awaiting a berth, we all had work details at the base. One morning at muster we were told that volunteers were needed for distant, prolonged, and hazardous duty. Most of us thought the detail chief was kidding, so some of us volunteered. Back at the barracks we were told we had just volunteered for the American Suicide Corps.

Before we could think much about it, we were on a train going south. We arrived at Fort Pierce, Florida, at three in the morning and were told to get some sleep. The next morning we were assigned to the Naval Combat Demolition Units and started training. I was glad to hear that we would do a lot of swimming. I was just barely seventeen and good at it.

After our NCDU training in Florida we found out the NCDU was being disbanded and we were now all in the UDT, the Underwater Demolition Teams. Eighty-seven enlisted men and thirteen officers were formed into UDT Team No. 25. It was December 1944. We were given ten days' delayed orders and told to report at Treasure Island in San Francisco. We left there in January 1945 and went to a base in Maui, Hawaii, for advanced UDT training. When that was over, the rumors said we were going to one of the Japanese-held islands farther west in the Pacific. This didn't happen and we were sent to San Diego Amphibious Base for several months.

In August 1945 the war was over and we shipped out for Japan for training on the windward side of Japan in thirty-foot surf. After several months there we were sent back to San Diego, where we spent a year. The team was eventually decommissioned and I was assigned to UDT No. l, for more training and eventually discharged in October of 1947.

I, like a lot of other UDT men, were highly trained and ready for the call to action that never came.

Clarence "Mullie" Mulheren, Gunner's Mate Second Class
Pearisburg, Virginia

BACK IN FEBRUARY 1943 my best friend Ustus Taylor and I discussed the possibility of joining one of the branches of the armed services. The event that did it for me was the first Saturday in March when we went to see the movie *Wake Island*. I couldn't tell you who played in the movie, but the depicting of the brave and heroic defense against insurmountable odds by the Marine garrison and the Navy airmen left a tremendous patriotic impact on this teenage boy.

I had already turned eighteen and had registered with the draft board. This was March 1943 with basketball season winding down. At that time, being of draft age, if you wished to enlist in one of the military services, it was necessary to go through the draft board. So, after basketball practice that second Monday afternoon in March, I headed for the draft board office. I conveyed my wishes to join the service, either the U.S. Navy or Coast Guard. I was immediately scheduled for my physical, which I passed, and was assigned to the U.S. Navy as the monthly quota was filled for the Coast Guard.

Woodrow Wilson High School in my hometown of Charlton Heights, West Virginia, had a great basketball team that year. I was the sixth man. At the end of the regular season we won the sectional tournament and went on to the regional tournament. Our team walked through the regional, winning all our games. So we were set to go to the state tournament at the field house at West Virginia University. That was the same week I was supposed to leave for boot camp at Great Lakes Naval Training Center.

I hustled down to the draft board to ask if it would be possible for me to delay my boot camp until the first of April. They knew me and supported our local team. They delayed my departure for the Navy until 14 April, 1943. Our team lost in the semifinals, but what a great experience.

I entered boot camp on 21 April 1943 as one of 112 apprentice seamen of Company 530 in Camp Porter at Great Lakes. Boot was ten weeks, and it was a great experience. A great amount of time was devoted to physical fitness. I made the company basketball squad and was a member of the company color guard. I loved the marching. I loved the singing when we were marching.

I loved the rifle, PT, and standing guard. I recall my company commander, Chief Bricky. He had played football for the University of Purdue and on the Great Lakes football team. He was about six two, weighed in at 215 pounds, and had a face that looked like a Mack truck had run over it. No face masks in those days in football. I admired him, and for those ten weeks he was my idol and mentor. I made an effort to be the very best and do the best in everything he directed us to do.

After boot, we all got ten-day leaves. The girls at home loved my uniform and I wore it all the time. My parents were proud of me and I was proud to sit in Sunday church with my family in my dress whites.

Returning from my leave, in the first part of July I received orders to report to Camp Perry, Virginia, a newly opened Seabee training camp along the south shore of the York River. That was just a few miles northeast of Williamsburg. When I arrived, the camp was a raw environment: not the permanent-looking base as at Great Lakes. There were dirt streets and rustic wooden barracks. Everything seemed so makeshift compared to Great Lakes.

I was assigned immediately to mosquito-control command in this fighting outfit. I soon learned it was anything but an elite fighting unit. We weren't fighting the Germans or the Japanese. We fought mosquitoes. I was one disappointed young sailor. In the bogs and swamps of Camp Perry there was lots and lots of water but no ships.

Camp Perry was built along the south side of the York River, a tidal river on swampy, boggy land. They were in the process of draining a portion of the swamps so the camp could be expanded.

The second day in camp I was issued my weapon, a

backpack in which I carried a five-gallon can of oil, with hose and a spray nozzle. My orders were to invade this swamp and search out the enemy mosquitoes and kill them and destroy their habitat.

After a week of wading through the swamps and fighting the enemy, I was wounded. Yep, I became covered with poison ivy blisters. No Purple Heart, but five days in sickbay. I was one miserable and unhappy sailor. I wasn't fighting the enemy and I was missing my high school prom and track season back home.

When I returned to duty, I was given command of Tide Gate No. 1, taking the tide readings and keeping the gate free of debris so it would open and close freely: soft duty, sitting in the sun, getting a good tan, and I had a big shade tree nearby where I set up my sentry post.

Not long after I worked the tide gate, I became aware of a group of men who came by on the road, either going to the dock area or coming back to the barracks in Area E. Man, did they look tough: bronze from the sun, wearing cutoff dungarees, white hats, no shirts, and combat boots. Always jogging with their Enfield rifles at port arms. They looked mean and lean. What outfit was this? They truly looked like a seasoned fighting unit and I wanted to know more about them. I wanted to become a part of that unit. I asked around and found that they were a volunteer training outfit known as the Demolition Unit. I did not know what the training consisted of or what they were training for, but the fact that they looked tough and were always on the move intrigued me. I wanted to be a part of them. Besides, I was ready to join any outfit that would get me out of mosquito control.

One morning near the end of July, before I went on

duty, I gathered enough courage to go over to command headquarters of the Demolition Unit. I walked in and requested to speak to the officer in charge. I was invited in and talked to Lt. George Marion about volunteering for his unit. This was without asking the type of outfit or for what they were training. I wanted in. I told the officer that I was interested in joining the unit. After listening to me, he asked what my present command was. When I told him Mosquito Control, he slapped both hands on the desk. "I'm sorry, sailor, you are frozen in that command," he said. "I don't think I can get you a transfer."

It was then that I really made a strong plea, told him I was a good athlete, good swimmer, that I was a tough West Virginian Mountaineer and physically fit. If accepted, I would stay with it. I wouldn't quit. The only way he got me out of his office was to tell me that he would see what he could do about getting my release from Mosquito Control.

Ten days later I was under my big shade tree down at Tide Gate No. 1 when the chief petty officer pulled up in his pickup truck. He got out, walked to where I was standing, and threw some papers at my feet. "Mulheren, who the hell do you know?" I was puzzled until I picked up the papers. They were my orders to report to the Underwater Demolition Unit.

When my relief came that same morning, I rushed back to the barracks and began packing my gear in my two seabags. I thought I needed a name other than Clarence. It wasn't a tough-sounding name. The name Moe popped up in my mind. I put the name on all my shirts and it became my World War II name. I used a wheelbarrow to haul my bags to Area E and the Underwater Demolition Unit barracks. I was one happy sailor.

Then I was issued my rifle, combat boots, and a bolo knife. They told me to cut a pair of dungarees off, as that would be the uniform of the day.

In a few days I was with the new training unit, I was now one of those tough-looking trainees. How happy I was when I jogged past my old station under the pin oak tree. After a day of physical fitness, though, I wondered if I had not made a mistake, for it was tough. Especially hard under the nose of three rugged U.S. Marines, Sully Manson, Connolly, and Johnson. They made us live hard and they did their best to dehumanize us. Their sole purpose was to make life miserable for us. "Let's keep going there, sailor. You got two minutes to get rid of that charley horse."

Those were two of the toughest weeks I ever spent in my life, from close-order drill with fixed bayonets in plowed fields to the Marine rifle PT. The last activity before going to evening chow each day was tackle football in only cutoff dungarees and field boots. Sully would call, "We don't quit for the evening chow until someone bleeds." Many of us bled many times. After football we still had a three-mile jog back to Area E and the chow hall.

We wore out the obstacle course, doing it over and over. "Quit complaining, sailor. Bust the blister and keep on going." Another favorite fun activity was when twelve of us at a time put on boxing gloves and formed a circle with arms over each others shoulders. A Marine blew a whistle, and you had to protect yourself from all sides. Many times a blow would come out of nowhere and knock me right on my can. Unless you were knocked out, you had to get up and go again. We were on the go every minute of our fourteen-hour day, and sometimes it was a twenty-two-hour day. Meals were such a joy, but even then they hurried us through. Before noon chow they put us in the swimming pool to cool off and clean up. Rifle inspection came every morning and we were expected to keep them functioning at all times, but we never fired them.

There was never a full night's rest. I slept in my dungarees for every night the Gyrenes would let us get to sleep, which didn't take long for me. But then the Marines flipped on the lights and gave us three minutes to hit the grinder and go off for a forced march with our Enfield rifles. Then we had a couple of hours of rifle PT or some crazy night problem.

During the weeks with the Marines we received training in judo and knife fighting. Each morning I would say to myself, *I will try one more day*. I remembered that I promised the officer that I would not drop out. Plus I didn't want to go back to Mosquito Control.

After the Marines, these training periods moved on to diving using a deep-sea rig in the York River. Then we had explosive training and small-boat work. Even with these phases of training, a portion of the day was spent in physical fitness. I hated rifle PT. It seemed like hours without the rifle hitting the deck. This took place in an open field and sometimes in plowed fields. In these phases of training the average day was still twelve to fourteen hours. We did many night operations. Our explosives work at night shook up the entire camp. Soon they put a limit on how much explosives we could use at night.

We had to make our own bangalore torpedoes by breaking open sticks of dynamite and packing the powder down a gutter downspout. Residue of the dynamite remained on our hands. If we forgot and wiped sweat off our brows, and breathed the fumes after the "fire in the hole," it would set off the most gosh-awful headache ever. Our heads seemed to explode with every step. I've never had such bad headaches before or after.

In November 1943, after eight weeks of training at Camp Perry, our class boarded the train in Williamsburg and rolled down to Fort Pierce, Florida, where we received eight more weeks of advanced training. Here we were introduced to "Hell Week" and "So Solly Day." We also were introduced to the 350-pound six-man rubber boats that we were married to. Everywhere we went, these boats went with us. We soon learned that handling these unwieldy rubber boats taught us teamwork. Each man had to pull his weight. At night, midnight black, we had to launch the rubber boats through the heavy winter surf and many times a huge wave would come out of the dark, pick up the boat and crew, and toss us back onto the shore. The cry was always, "Hang on to your paddle!"

We made many night portages, launching our rubber boats through the surf, paddling a couple of miles north until we saw a light on the beach where we were to bring in the boat and portage across North Island to the Indian River. We always wondered what was in the muck besides snakes and alligators.

Several miles down the river our course took us back across land to the ocean and the most dreaded of all launchings, getting our boat off from the North Jetty. It's just a bunch of piled-up large boulders. Many a time a huge wave tossed my boat and boat crew back on the rocks. Our unit had no serious injuries, but several trainees in other teams were badly injured. Some men had their boats land on top of them, all 350 pounds.

Physical fitness always took top priority. Log PT

was a favorite of the instructors, but not with the trainees. Combat with the sand flies while pumping air into our rubber boats was an every-morning ritual.

Hell Week was pure torture as we lived and slept with the boats for five days in the swamps, ocean, and river during boat PT. One fun exercise was bringing our boats from the sea at night, hiding them, and camouflaging them. Next we sneaked past sentries five hundred feet inland to a small light hanging over a pile of Hershey bars. Not only did we have to be aware of the sentries but also booby traps armed with cherry bombs, and small-arms fire.

We were also harassed with small explosive charges. If we made it to the light without detection, we received a candy bar but then had to sneak back unseen. Our boat crew made it in and out each time without getting caught.

A great deal of our training time at Fort Pierce was spent blowing obstacles that the Seabees were constantly building on the beaches of North Island. There were all kinds, from hedgehogs to tetrahedrons. Then, when our team got to the South Pacific in the real war, the only kind of obstacles we found were six-foot square concrete cubes. To clear these various obstacles at Fort Pierce, we loaded our rubber boats with explosives, brought them out through the surf, attached the dynamite to the obstacle, activated the fuse lighters, and returned to the shore through the surf.

After ten weeks we graduated as Naval Combat Demolition Units made up of five enlisted and one officer. I was in NCDU No. 36 and assigned to the Central Pacific. Some of the units went to the European Theater, some to the South Pacific.

After graduation we had twenty-one-day delayed

orders to show up at Treasure Island in San Francisco. That gave me sixteen days at home. We flew to Hawaii to Waimanalo, a small Navy Air Base. Then we took an LST (landing ship, tank) to Maui. On 1 March 1944, we new recruits, along with some of the Frogmen returning from the Marshall Island invasion, were commissioned as Underwater Demolition Team No. 3. I was now a full-fledged UDT man: The NCDU designation had been swallowed up by the UDT program.

I took part in the UDT work at Saipan, Guam, and Leyte in the Philippines, and reconnoitered the beaches at Nakayama Island of Honshū, Japan, where occupation troops went ashore after the war.

When the Korean War started in 1950, I requested active duty from my reserve status and was a frogman again mainly on the training staff at the UDT at the Coronado Naval Amphibious base at Coronado, California. I am proud to have served my country as a member of the most elite combat unit in the military up to that time. It was a great experience and created bonds with other UDT men that have lasted for almost thirty-five years.

The Reverend John A. Dittmer, Chief MM
Crawfordsville, Indiana

WE LEFT OUR training base in Fort Pierce, Florida on March 17, 1944, and flew to New York City, arriving about 1500. It was cold and foggy and darkness started to settle in. In the harbor was a convoy of eight ships anxious to get under way. NCDU No. 127 was quickly loaded on board and the ships weighed anchor and headed toward the open seas. Soon we were doing sixteen knots and blinker lights were talking to each other all over the convoy.

My unit, NCDU No. 127 was headed by Lieutenant J. G. Padgett, CPO Raymond Wihrwohn, and petty officer Myron Walk, SF l/C, Elmer Powell, CM l/C, John Dittmer, MM l/C, and John Dunford, S l/C. We had three untrained seamen with us, Lewis Dube, Bill Duberson, and Ed Falsetto, and five attached Army demolition engineers.

After fifteen days at sea on board the SS *Warrior* we docked at Cardiff, Wales. We were billeted in a British barracks for the night. The next day we took a train north to a U.S. Navy base near Glasgow, Scotland. We waited two weeks while Lt. Padgett tried to sort out who sent for us and why we were at this base.

The spring weather was wet, cold, and nasty. We were assigned temporarily to shore-patrol duty. The enlisted men went on duty about seven P.M. and were assigned to some night spots. We were issued a nightstick, white canvas leggings, an SP armband, and a badge. We got back to our warm barracks about two A.M. after all the city buses and boats had made their last runs. Our job was to get all Navy personnel aboard and separated from the aggressive girls who often hid under the sailors' peacoats in the blackout conditions.

Finally, Lt. Hund got our orders through and contact with him made some sense as to why we were sent to Britain. I had been trained in the States to install Mark IV shallow-water minesweep gear to small wooden ships. I went through about two weeks installing the gear on four small wooden British ships that worked out of Dartmouth harbor. I was billeted during this time at the spacious but empty and cold Royal Navy College building at Dartmouth.

Each evening I would eat with the crew as we sailed from sea back to port. I was put off at the docks near the large college buildings. Then the ships secured for the night inside the long submarine net that kept them safe from German U-boats. After all the ships had been equipped with the Mark IV, I was sent back to my NCDU outfit.

Back at the NCDU, we were waiting new orders. We had plenty of chow, but the British did not. Most of their buildings were cold or only partially heated. Their food was rationed and conditions were harsh for them.

Come spring, the weather improved. Early in May we were taken to a tent-city marshaling area behind a barbed wire fence with sentries to keep us in. We were given no liberty to meet British military people and no recreation at all. We could only read, write letters home, and wait on orders. It was just before the invasion and they were taking no chances on leaks.

Elmer Powell had written a long letter to his wife that was uncensored and gave it to a merchant marine sailor on the SS *Warrior* to be mailed when the ship returned to New York. The sailor got drunk and was arrested in New York. He was jailed and held for several weeks because he was carrying this uncensored letter. He was finally released when his story had been double-checked and compared to Elmer Powell's story. Both men learned the hard way that the laws on censorship were very real and were meant to be strictly obeyed.

The marshaling area was near Dartmouth, Devonshire. We were bored and nervous, and kept in the area. Then, on the second Sunday of May 14, 1944, I told some of the men it was Mother's Day. They went to Lt. Padgett and told him their plan. Five of us got the okay to go to a British church to celebrate Mother's Day. Our orders were we were to go together, stay together, talk to no one, and come directly back. I was to be held responsible for getting everyone back.

We chose a Friends church nearby. We passed a cottage with a nice flower bed in front. Everyone wanted a flower to wear to remember his mother. I made the request. The woman of the house wiped tears away and complimented us for honoring our mothers. She said her boy was a British soldier but she hadn't seen him in two years and didn't know where he was. We went to the church and back to the marshaling area without incident.

On Saturday, June 4, we boarded our LST. We were to move across the English Channel to our assigned beaches and land at H hour, June 5. The first night out the skies darkened, and a cold wind made the seas turbulent. Early the next morning we received a communiqué that we were to stay in formation and under way but our landing would not take place until further notice. It was delayed for twenty-four hours. We'd go in at 6:30 on June 6.

Some of the men were seasick. Some grumbling. I was content to keep my cool and wait it out. I found a place of prayer in a small enclosure forward of the forward winch and just above the great doors on the ship's bow. I wanted to be alone where I could pray as loudly as I needed to and unburden my soul.

The Presence of the Lord settled heavily upon me. I dared not lift my eyes, fearing the Presence would leave me. When I did lift my eyes, I saw an opening in the dark clouds, like a window into heaven. Jesus was standing in that opening and He stretched out his arm toward me. I thought it was just a formation in the clouds, so I bowed my head and then lifted my eyes to look again. It was Jesus.

The twenty-four-hour delay worked in our favor. The weather took a turn for the better. My heart reveled in this beautiful experience with Jesus for many days. On that morning we were aroused at two A.M. and given a meal of canned chicken. The ship's crew was busy manning the davits that carried four LCVP boats. These were lowered and put into the turbulent sea. We were in total darkness but managed to get down the cargo nets and find our places in the landing craft. It was dark as an oven and the seas were still very rough. When the order to cast off came, our motor roared and we went off in the darkness. There were six NCDU men, three seamen, and the coxswain with all of our gear. We had 4,400 pounds of explosives in the center hold and a full tank of diesel oil to power the boat. That meant we were overloaded and riding low in the water.

We carried very little personal gear, only a few tools to place our explosives and fix our detonators on the charges. Our bedrolls would follow us later in the day.

Our gallant lieutenant was into the medical brandy without delay. He was wearing a grin and a red nose. The other men followed suit and soon became talkative and boisterous. Then a bright flash from the direction of the beach came, and a low rumble. They told us a bombing run was being carried out on the beach. Tracer bullets above our heads reminded us the war was still on and heating up.

A squadron of B-25s changed position in their formation. The lead planes moved a little lower in the formation than those in the rear. One of the bombardiers apparently got nervous and touched his release button while still well out to sea. The falling bombs hit the plane below him and exploded on impact. The plane that was hit exploded into fragments. The whole crew was lost.

That was our first sight of actual combat. That scene has never left my mind. As we got closer to the beach, we could hear the scream of the German 88 artillery rounds passing over our heads. We were stationed along the gunwales, both port and starboard. My position was forward on the starboard side, just aft of the steel ramp. The orders were that when I left the LCVP, the others would follow me. The steel ramp opened. My departure was the signal for all the rest to disembark. I stood in my corner and said another prayer.

When my feet hit the sand, the first thing I saw was a good shoe with a white man's leg extending from it, floating in the water. My stomach turned over and I thought I would vomit. A trail in the sand could be seen where the now one-legged man was crawling toward the sand dunes and higher ground. There was a twenty-eight-foot tide at this location and the water was rising rapidly.

One of our Army men screamed. He had taken a 20mm round in his back. The red-hot slug was lodged in his lung. I heard later that the wound nearly killed him but he did survive.

I could hear machine-gun bullets whizzing near my ears. A good verse came to mind: "A thousand shall fall at thy right hand, but it shall not come nigh to thee . . ." from the Psalms.

A disemboweled German colonel lay nearby, still conscious. I spoke to him and offered help. He cursed me vehemently. John Dunford came up to me and said, "Dittmer, what should I do? They have hit me in the ass." I looked at him. His bloody trousers were ragged and bloody in back. A piece of shrapnel had done the bloody work. When I looked at the German colonel again, he had been covered up by the rising tide.

I made my way to the gathering point, where Army doctors were administering first aid. The first wave had already moved onto the higher ground and their wounded were being brought back. The doctor called for litter carriers. Our lieutenant had got lost in the confusion. So I began carrying wounded men aboard the LCMs as they unloaded, but they said they couldn't wait and be a target for the 88 shells coming from the German guns.

The wounded men were piling up as we worked hurriedly loading as many as we could on the LCMs. Then suddenly the little first-aid point disappeared before we could make it back to carry another litter. We looked at one another, amazed. The doctor, the medics, and perhaps a score of wounded men had been obliterated by a wicked 88 artillery shell.

By that time our lieutenant got his bearings and was rounding up his men. He ordered us and Myron Walsh to dig in, because by now the tide was nearly full and too high to do any blasting. Our obstacles to be taken out were several Belgian gates of very heavy angle steel; also some concrete pyramids with protruding pointed steel railroad rails, aimed seaward. Both types of obstacles were quite difficult to deal with; however, some of the crews had removed enough of them by blasting to make an opening and set marker buoys to guide the incoming traffic of ships and LCMs. Myron Walsh and I finished a short slit trench in the sand. We dug it snug up by the seawall.

We found some short pine logs and some tin and

boards for a cover and then shoveled two feet of sand on the top. This made us a good bunker for a dry and safe place. It was wide enough for two to sleep side by side at the bottom. We used our inflatable life belts to suspend a litter-bearer hammock. Walsh and I decided that the lower level was the safest. This was our residence for eight days. Lieutenant Padgett took the hammock and the three of us could sleep safely and dry.

On D-day the LCMs and the LSTs were swarming ashore. The second wave was starting to come in. The Beach Battalion boys were scurrying around with big crawler tractors to pull ashore any truck or tank that became waterlogged. From the doorway of our newly built sand bunker we watched it all happening.

A large Allis Chalmers H-D14 was busy just out from our bunker, pulling trucks out of the water. The operator was working as fast as he could. A few of the German planes were finding openings in our air cover and we were getting some incoming machine-gun fire. But all in all it appeared that things were moving on schedule. We were waiting for the tide to recede so we could tie our Hagensen packs on the obstacles and proceed with our work.

I was watching and admiring the Cat operator as he pulled in the heavy vehicles the short distance from the LSTs. Suddenly a burst of machine-gun fire stopped his work and ended his life. I was shocked and saddened at the sight. Those helping as swampers and hook-on men scurried around the big Cat. The operator's limp body was lifted off and carried to the above-water line near our bunker.

Several men tried to start the big diesel engine. As the operator had slumped forward he grabbed the throttle and had stopped the engine. No one knew the right combination to restart it. An officer bawled out an urgent call for anyone who could start the Cat.

I kept silent. Lt. Padgett asked, "Dittmer, can you do it?" I didn't answer. "Dittmer, answer me: Can you start that cat?" I told him I could. I wiggled out of my bunker and walked to the machine. The officer ran toward me and asked if I could get it started. I nodded. I climbed up on the track and into the seat. I felt like I was exposed to Berlin and Hitler was pointing all of his 88s right at me. I put the levers in position and touched the starter button. A black cloud of smoke roared from the exhaust stack. I started to climb down. The officer said, "Hell no, sailor. Get this truck out of here for us." I set the gears and used my clutch and tightened up on the heavy winch cable, and the Cat moved backwards. The stuck truck followed me like an obedient puppy. The truck driver ground in his gears, and the motor on his truck started and made slack on the cable. The swamper unhooked and I pulled out of the way. The officer was waving wildly for me to return. Another truck was moving out on the ramp, and I could see more coming toward the open bow doors of the LST.

I was no longer at ease in my good, safe bunker. There were several more LSTs to unload.

After several hours there was a lull and I pulled the big machine over to one side. The officer in charge came over, hopped up on the track of the HD-14, and thanked me. "Mate, take this Cat up near your bunker and put the key in your pocket. We'll need you again for the next wave." Lt. Padgett was watching. He asked me what the officer had said. I told him. He said, "You stand by for them, John. We can get by without you for now." Apparently there was no possible replacement for the fallen operator in his beach battalion. I continued as the standby for a couple of days. I looked in the fuel tank; it was still almost full. I knew that I was stuck with the job.

The ships and LCMs were moving up and unloading for the most part without me. The spasmodic machine-gun firing had stopped. Only once was I called on to fire up the big Cat again. Two officers walked up and asked who the operator was, and I told them that for the present it was me. They wanted me to taxi them down the beach about a mile to pick up ten boxes of C rations. I consented and we went to the point where the rations were being distributed. They piled the boxes on the operating deck with us. I delivered them, then I parked the Cat.

When I looked again, the fuel was getting low, so I could honestly say to anyone who asked that she was too low on fuel. I did not know who to call for fuel. Eight days she sat there, and when the NCDU boys pulled out on the evening of the eighth day, the big Cat was still there. It represented an item that cost the U.S.A. about $50,000. It was an expensive war.

On the fourth day a lone German plane slipped by the antiaircraft guns and dropped one bomb before an AA gun brought him down. I saw no more and assumed that the incident was over. A man named McGeary of our NCDU outfit had been hit with a piece of shrapnel from the bomb. It penetrated his heart and killed him. He was a nice quiet fellow and we were all sad for him and his family. For years I thought that his name was Helfritch until my good friend Chotas set me straight recently. On D-day Elmer Powell from Miami came screaming up to Walsh and me, thinking he had been hit. We unbuttoned his shirt to find the wound, but found nothing. He was complaining loudly of the pain. We sent him to the hospital ship along with John Dunford. I never did learn the fate of either of these two men.

While I was carrying wounded men on the LCMs I became acquainted with some of the ship's company. Periodically they got warm, fresh bread from one of the larger ships. Sometimes they shared with me. One time while on board we were strafed by a German plane. We dove under the table as bullets hit the deck above us. Our movement tipped over the big coffee pot and the hot coffee spilled on one of the crew. He screamed that he had been hit. We quieted him and showed him it was only coffee on him, not blood.

I had a special Bible tied in with my bedroll that would be brought in on a ship near the end of D-day. But the ship bringing in our goods was hit and sunk and the goods mostly transferred to another ship, so my bedroll and Bible were missing. We checked the salvage pile to see if we could find it. No luck. Later we decided to take another look. We had to cross a twenty-acre field to get to it. We went across and this time found my bedroll and my precious Bible. When we started back across the open field, we found Army engineers going over the field for "bouncing Betty" mines. They had already found over a hundred. They said the place was littered with them. They had safe paths marked, which we used this time.

We had used no special technique to cross the minefield the first time, just sauntered along. We were blessed. "The Angel of the Lord encampeth round about them that fear Him and delivereth them." God himself was our Good Shepherd, and our Guardian Angels gave us safe passage that day. We learned a lesson: Never go into war without a close, personal contact with your maker.

As darkness came down on the Normandy coast one day well after the area was secured, two American planes came over after bombing work at the front lines. One plane jettisoned its auxiliary gas tank. Someone asked what he had dropped. The answer: his gas tank. As the word passed along through the troops, it changed to "gas attack." Everyone put on gas masks, making it hard to communicate.

The other plane circled back to check on his buddy. In the darkness the AA crew spotted a plane coming in and began firing. They hit his plane and he had to bail out over the beach. As his parachute opened and he floated slowly down, the green recruits on the beach kept shooting at him with their rifles. He kept yelling at them to stop shooting. He made it to the ground without being hit. He cursed everyone he could see, saying he would rather bail out over Berlin than over such a bunch of greenhorns.

After our beach work was done, our unit was returned to Fort Pierce. There I volunteered to go to Japan. By the time my new unit arrived there the war was over, so I saw no action there but did some cleanup work.

Lieutenant Commander Donald M. Walker
Cherry Hill, New Jersey

I ENLISTED IN the Navy on 13 December 1942, and was allowed to finish my education at Philadelphia College of Pharmacy and Science, graduating in February of 1943. This degree qualified me for officer training. I entered the Navy full-time on 9 March 1943, at Northwestern University Graduate Campus in Chicago. I served as an apprentice seaman for a month before being sworn in as a midshipman. During the final weeks of midshipman's training I was interviewed and accepted for Bomb Disposal School. I received my ensign commission on 1 July 1943, and was ordered to the American University in Washington, D.C. for three months of bomb disposal instruction—no mistakes allowed. As the war progressed, it was determined that obstacles had to be manually removed prior to landing troops on enemy beaches. I volunteered for an interview and was accepted for Naval Combat Demolition Unit training at Fort Pierce, Florida. I completed the three months of vigorous physical and mental training, including what is now referred to as "Hell Week." This was in preparation for preinvasion beach reconnaissance and subsequent demolition of obstacles with explosives.

As 1943 drew to a close, my Naval Combat Demolition Unit No. 13, one officer and five enlisted men, was making preparations in San Francisco for debarkation to the South Pacific.

We left San Francisco on a Kaiser-built ship at dusk. The ship's deck cracked just forward of the bridge as the fully laden ship labored through the land swells. Fortunately it held together and we were able to return to the bay area, where we were investigated/inspected by officials and cleared for transfer to a second ship. This time we were onboard the USS *West Point*, formerly the SS *America*. We took a zigzag unescorted trip to the Solomon Islands. We arrived at Guadalcanal in the Solomon Islands on 28 January 1944, with final encampment across the slot at Tulagi. From Tulagi we worked and trained with men of the U.S. Marine Corps. We conducted demonstrations for Navy and

Marine brass and worked with the Bureau of Ordnance to utilize rockets with solid fuel for preinvasion beach saturation. These rockets were later mounted in the wells of LCIs for preinvasion beach saturation.

In mid-May 1944 our NCDUs were assigned to temporary duty with UDTs 3, 4, 5, and 7 for landings at Saipan, Guam, and Tinian. My NCDU No. 13 had orders to serve with Lt. Carberry's UDT 4. After returning to Turner City from the Marianas in August, the NCDUs and boat crew recruits from personnel pools were informally assembled as UDT Able for the invasion of Peleliu aboard an old World War I four-stacker, the USS *Noa* (APD-24).

There was no formal commissioning. Joining the preinvasion task forces at Eniwetok for final preparations and briefings, we proceeded to Peleliu as a screening ship. On 12 September during the predawn maneuvering at about 0515 in total darkness and total radio silence, the *Noa* was rammed in the stern by another screening destroyer, the USS *Fullam* (DD-474), which resulted in the slow sinking of the *Noa*. We lowered enough LCPRs to get survivors off the ship, and there were no losses. We were taken to other ships in the area. Since all of our gear was lost, we witnessed the remaining preinvasion bombardment, air strikes, and the invasion itself from the deck of the USS *Pennsylvania*. As I recall, UDT 6 was assigned to reconnoiter our beaches, since we were totally out of action.

When the Peleliu operation was secured, Team Able was transported to the rear area for clothing and needed supplies. On 12 October 1944, orders were cut sending UDT Able to the States for "survivor's leave." However, our demolition group was ordered to disembark at Pearl Harbor for transfer to the UDT Advance

Training Base on Maui. The only man in our team to make it back to the States on that ship was our CO, Lt. King, who had his appendix removed the day before we hit Pearl.

At Maui, I became the executive officer of Underwater Demolition Team No. 13, which had received only basic training at Fort Pierce.

UDT No. 13 trained for the invasions of Iwo Jima and Okinawa with a departure date in January 1945. Both were islands that had to be captured for the United States. We witnessed the now famous Mount Suribachi flag-raising at 1020 on 23 February 1945. Things became tougher and tougher, including kamikaze attacks as we neared the Japanese homeland. Shortly after successfully participating in these two invasions, I was detached as XO of UDT No. 13 for duty with the Experimental Division at Fort Pierce.

While at Fort Pierce, I received the Silver Star medal for action at Iwo Jima. This award allowed me to apply for release from active duty in October 1945 and return to civilian life as a pharmacist and to continue in the Naval Reserve as an inactive member until 1959.

Electrician's Mate First Class Harold Benjamin Ledien
Topsham, Maine

MY NCDU TRAINING began in July 1943 at Camp Perry, Virginia. At the end of our basic training, a call came for volunteers for hazardous duty. They wanted large, rugged men. I stood up and volunteered. I was five feet six inches tall. They took me. I went to Fort Pierce for more training. The first phase was physical with obstacle courses, swimming, and running. The mess hall was three miles from our tents, and we had to cover the space in twenty minutes.

We had training with rubber boats going in and out of the surf on landings. We trained in demolition using live explosives. Deep-sea diving with the heavy suits and helmets was another part of our training.

To be a frog, we had to be physically, mentally, and emotionally fit or we did not survive the course. We became naked warriors who wore a pair of trunks, a face mask, and a pair of swim fins. We carried a knife, a pencil, and a plastic board to write on underwater.

After our training we left for England, then after a wait we shipped out on June 5 for the big Normandy invasion. We crossed the channel on an LCT. Eight men and an officer made up our team, called NCDU No. 138. Army engineers on our boat had a similar-size team.

Men on our team were Ensign John Allen, Darcy Francis, Joseph Dennis, Stanley Dracz, Edward Greenfield, Arthur Hickey, Dean Kirkpatrick, and Herman Munson.

As we approached Omaha Beach we were covered with planes, rocket launchers, and boats, all firing at the beach and cliffs. The shore was being devastated and I thought that nothing could be alive on that beach because of the bombardment. As we got closer to shore, the firing stopped from our side. As we were about to embark on the shore, we came under heavy mortar, artillery, and machine-gun fire.

What we didn't know was that a German Panzer division of thirty thousand men was holding maneuvers on the land mass above the cliffs. We walked right into them. We left our landing craft and towed our rubber boat with us. It had all of our extra explosives to use to blow up the obstacles on the beach.

As we ran down the ramp into the shallow water, a mortar shell landed next to us and hit Greenfield, the man just ahead of me. We put him back into the landing craft but he died a few minutes later. The Army team on the other side of the landing craft also had a mortar round land beside them, and one man died there as well.

There were two rows of obstacles that had to be taken out. Ours was closest to us, while the Army was to remove the ones a hundred feet closer to shore. The Army set explosives on the obstacles that were assigned to us. I spoke to Ensign John Allen, our officer leader, and asked him if we were going to go take out the Army's obstacles. He said no. The first wave of the Army had landed and our unit was scattered all over. We crawled up on the beach and looked for cover. There was none. I asked the Army lieutenant if he wanted to blow the obstacles farther up the beach but he said no, since there were too many soldiers hiding behind them. Our team had separated and we moved up to the dunes. I was saying the Lord's Prayer and the twenty-third Psalm all the way to the dunes.

A Ranger unit had landed earlier behind the enemy lines. The paratroopers had also landed, and eventually they drove the Germans off the cliff so we could secure the beach. It had been an exciting day.

Petty Officer Second Class John Gee
Chesterville, Maine

I TRIED TO join the Army in 1943, but the local quota for the Army was full, so they sent me to the Navy. They sent me to Swanson, New York, for five weeks of basic training, and then gave me a ten-day leave. I reported back to the Navy at the Brooklyn Navy Yard in New York for assignment. They sent me onboard the luxury liner *Queen Mary*, which had become a troop transport. There were two thousand sailors on board along with fifteen thousand soldiers.

On April 15, 1944, after a seven-day voyage in which we dodged German U-boats, we landed at the Navy base in Helensburgh, Scotland.

When the Navy officers looked at my orders, they told me that someone had made a mistake. Most of the sailors were supposed to go to Florida for underwater demolition training.

So I sat there waiting for orders. I saw a notice on a bulletin board looking for volunteers for an underwater demolitions unit. The Navy chief told me it wasn't very dangerous. He lied. He said we'd go in after the invasion to blow down buildings and things that were not safe. He stretched the truth again.

Among the incentives offered for this duty was that the men would be excused from mess-cooking duty and would be able to get out of the Navy as soon as the war was over. That is, if we lived—but he didn't say that.

I volunteered and was given a railroad pass to the Naval Combat Demolitions Unit training site in England, near Plymouth. I had five weeks of training there until June 1, when the unit was sent to a site to await boarding ships for the Normandy invasion. The training had included work on explosives and hard physical conditioning including long swims before the days of scuba gear.

I was assigned to an LST (landing ship, tank), and we'd be in the first wave on the beach. We were waiting orders to proceed to Utah Beach. We even did some training on the LST using models of the beach obstacles we would be facing.

On June 6, at about 2:30 A.M., we went down the landing nets from a bigger ship into the LST with our explosives. I carried a carbine. The big ships were shelling the beach and we circled the landing craft twelve miles out until 5:30 A.M., waiting for the orders to head for the beach.

To a young man who had never even been on a train or outside of Maine before I joined the service, it was a great sight to see. The shelling and bombing of the beach came in the darkness, and it looked like a gigantic fireworks display.

There were twelve NCDU men and eighteen Army demo men on each LST. Just before we landed, rocket ships fired thousands of rockets onto the shore area.

At 6:30 sharp we approached the beach at low tide. The coxswain dropped the ramp in about a foot of water. There were incoming mortar and artillery shells. Our area to clear of obstacles was 150 yards wide, and the ten other units were assigned similar areas.

We lost two of our twelve NCDU men killed while setting charges on the obstacles about six hundred feet from the sea wall.

The obstacles encountered in the Normandy invasion included wooden sloped-ramp barriers designed to flip over landing craft; Element C, or Belgian gates, large metal structures with vertical prongs designed to rip out the bottom of larger landing craft; the "hedgehog," composed of three metal beams welded together, designed to rip a hole in the bottom or side of a boat; angled stakes designed to punch holes in landing craft; and concrete or steel pyramids designed to pierce the hull of any boat and rip it apart if it tried to pull away.

The most common obstacles on Utah Beach included ramps, Element C, steel pyramids, and wooden posts. On that beach in France the tide comes in fast, rising a foot every eight minutes. By the time the second or third wave arrived behind us, the water was chest-high, so we had to work quickly to remove the obstacles.

Removal involved attaching Primacord and C-2 plastic explosive or tetrytol explosives and blowing them up. By eight A.M., all major obstacles had been removed across Utah Beach.

The second wave was made up of infantry that was supposed to secure the beach. It was amazing: I never got near any shrapnel or bullets. After attaching explosives and blowing the obstacles, we charged up to the seawall and dug foxholes behind it.

We stayed there for about two weeks, watching the complete invasion force come ashore from five thousand ships. The Germans kept shelling the ships and beach with their .88-caliber artillery from five miles inland.

One day, almost at dark, five American planes came in low over the beach and one was mistakenly shot down by antiaircraft guns thinking it was a German plane. The pilot parachuted safely.

While running for cover one day I scratched my arm on barbed wire. I thought I'd get a Purple Heart for it but was told it had to be from enemy fire. I decided I didn't want to get a Purple Heart after all.

As I recall, our NCDU teams on Utah Beach suffered 30 percent casualties. On Omaha Beach it was much tougher: The rate there was 52 percent.

While on the beach, with our work all done, we took wounded men out to LSTs, which transferred them to the hospital ships offshore. Some of them were men from the 82nd Airborne who had parachuted into France behind the German lines.

We got our food rations from Navy ships, since there were no facilities onshore in those first days. We took turns going out to the large ships, whose crews would pass rations down to us in knapsacks.

It was terribly exciting. I was young and craving an adventure. It was also unbelievable to be in the middle of the whole invasion.

The infantry secured the beach and began moving inland. We saw some of the gliders land. Some crashed into the cliffs, but we'd see the men come piling out. A lot of those men were lost. Landing craft and amphibian vehicles continued to pour ashore after the beach was opened bringing in more men and supplies.

After the Normandy invasion, my unit was returned to England and later shipped out on the battleship USS *Texas*, heading for Naples, Italy, to participate in the southern invasion in August. We found similar beach obstacles there but did not come under enemy fire. No one in my group was wounded. I hitched a ride in an Army jeep to see some of the Italian countryside.

I returned to the U.S. for thirty days' leave and then was assigned to a UDT unit for six months in Hawaii. My unit participated in the last invasion of the war in 1945 in Borneo. It was different there. We had to do a lot of swimming like modern-day SEALs do. We went in on rubber boats, towing our explosives behind. We encountered Japanese mortar fire but sustained only a few casualties.

After that, we went back to the States for cold-weather training to get us ready for a November invasion of Japan. The two nuclear bombs ended the war and our invasion plans.

We were flown to Tokyo via some Pacific Islands and were in Tokyo Bay when the Japanese surrendered to General MacArthur on board the USS *Missouri*. Later we had to board Japanese warships and blow up their guns and destroy shore emplacements. I was mustered out a petty officer second class, the same as a sergeant in the Army.

Our NCDU officer was Carl Noyes. Other men in our 132nd NCDU were John Flynn, Ray Levine, Floyd McQueen, Richard Olpp, and Orville Wakefield.

Author's Note

FOR MANY YEARS, and in many books and articles, the Navy's NCDUs have been given almost total credit for blasting apart the obstacles on Normandy's Omaha and Utah Beaches just prior to the famous amphibious landing in World War II.

There were twenty-one NCDU teams on Omaha Beach with the task of blowing sixteen gaps fifty yards wide. Those teams were made up of 183 naval personnel and 107 Army engineers.

Besides these Army engineers, there were also twenty-four Army Combat Engineer gap assault teams with twenty-six men on a team and twenty-four Army Engineers on three gap teams without NCDUs. A total of 773 Army Engineer demolition men worked Omaha Beach on D-day along with the 183 NCDUs, which means there were four times as many Army demolition men working on clearing the gaps as there were Navy men.

Two weeks before the assault, the command of the operation including the NCDUs was turned over to the Army engineers. Right after the landing, the NCDUs were returned to Navy control.

Here is what one Army demolition veteran of the Omaha landing says about the operation. . . .

Lieutenant Wesley Ross, U.S. Army
Hillsboro, Oregon

GENERAL LEONARD T. GEROW, commanding general of V-Corps, had been picked to spearhead the landing on Omaha Beach. He was concerned that the 288 men, both NCDUs and Army engineers, was too small a group to blow enough gaps through the beach obstacles, which had been greatly increased in numbers by the Germans.

The revised plans called for sixteen fifty-yard gaps to be blown through the antiboat obstacles located landward from the mid-tide line. The 146th Engineer Combat Battalion, the 299th Engineer Combat Battalion, and the NCDUs who had initially been assigned this task were selected for the job. They would land on Omaha at 0633.

The three 246th ECB line companies returned to the ATC in mid-April for the antiboat obstacle demolition training. They were taught by U.S. Navy experts. They were joined by the 299th ECB, which had arrived by ship. The men had just completed an extensive demolition training program at Fort Pierce.

The operation was taken over by the V-Corps Provisional Engineer Group on April 30 to revise the Omaha Beach obstacle demolition mission. This included taking over the command function from the navy for its NCDUs. The goal: form twenty-four gap assault teams from Army personnel and to set them and the twenty-one NCDU teams to blow the sixteen fifty-yard gaps in the obstacles.

One tankdozer was allotted to each of the sixteen primary gap teams to be used as needed in demolishing the beach obstacles.

I was the officer in charge of Boat Team No. 8, which included NCDU No. 137 with Ensign Harold P. Blean as its leader.

The day before we were set to leave our training area at the marshaling area, one of the five Army engineers assigned to my boat, Melvin Vest, was killed in a training accident: A quarter-pound block of TNT exploded in his hand. We had been using five-second fuses to gain TNT familiarity. One of my NCOs decided to use a fuse lighter instead of a match as we usually did, without taking proper precautions to make certain that a spark did not flash outside the three-inch-long fuse directly into the blasting cap, and set it off immediately.

We bundled up Vest and hustled him by truck to a nearby hospital, but he died of shock four hours later. He had suffered extensive damage. He was our boat team's first casualty.

Our Boat Team No. 8 was part of the group to clear fifty yard gaps through the obstacles on the western section of Omaha, so the battalion landing teams of the 116th Regiment, 29th Infantry Division, could be beached on the dry land from their LCVPs.

Originally we had only one medic attached to our Team No. 8. Then they put another one with us shortly before D-day. This should have been a warning that this would not be a walk in the park.

About June 1, we moved to Portland Harbor and our team met our LCT (landing craft, tank). It was 112 feet long and had a drop-down ramp. It could carry four Sherman tanks and our gap team. Our fifty-foot LCM (landing craft, mechanized), with five hundred pounds of explosives in our centrally positioned rubber raft, was towed behind the LCT. The raft also carried Primacord, blasting caps, and Bangalore torpedoes. Each man would also carry forty pounds of explosives.

At last we were ready, embarked, and later scrambled down the heavy rope landing nets into our wildly bobbing LCM. We left for our assembly area several miles off the beach. We circled for over an hour, waiting for the signal to move in.

Then we straightened out and headed for the beach, partially hidden by the fog and mist. We saw the battleship *Texas* firing salvos onto shore. Her fourteen-inch guns must have all fired at once. The flame and smoke was quite a spectacle, but the blast was almost unbelievable and would have blown off my helmet if my chin strap had not been fastened.

As we approached the beach, I began to see splashes in the water from the mortar, artillery, and small-arms fire. A detonation of our explosives by this fire would have been devastating. As we came close in, our Navy gunner on the landing craft began hosing down the beach ahead with his twin .50-caliber machine guns. It was a morale booster we needed, because as we came up to the beach we saw several dead GIs floating facedown, bobbing and rolling in the surf.

Our coxswain promised me an easy wade ashore and he gunned his twin Gray Marine diesels, driving the LCM hard aground before dropping the ramp. The water came only to our knees. We saw no tankdozers or infantry ahead of us as we left our LCM. But we had landed three hundred yards west of our assigned spot, and the infantry may have hit the right spot. We landed on Easy Green Beach, slightly west of the fortified house near the mouth of Les Moulins draw.

Most of Boat Team No. 8 ran inland 150 yards to our foxhole, a huge bomb crater, and then spread out and began tying on charges to the obstacles. Several of us slid the rubber raft out of the LCM. I grabbed the wire reel containing the Primacord ring that had two strands of Primacord friction taped at two-foot intervals to a small rope, and took off running for the obstacles.

I ran in short dashes and hit the ground often to make a hard target. I ran the Primacord loop clockwise around the wooden obstacles, and Sergeant Bill Garland ran his around counterclockwise. We met and square-knotted the ring mains on the Primacord coming from each charge on the obstacles. That way by lighting the fuse on the long line around the obstacles, they would explode simultaneously.

We were under heavy small-arms fire almost immediately, and machine guns, mostly unseen, were tracking our movements. I saw three riflemen slinking to the left in defilade behind the natural sandbank seawall above the high-water line. They were heading east toward the fortified house. They were our infantrymen.

We took casualties soon after landing. Our medics were unbelievably efficient and began taking care of our men where they lay. Many of the less seriously wounded didn't even bother calling for help. Minden Ivy, a rugged little Texan, took a bullet through the wrist, resulting in a compound fracture, but he kept right on shooting and refused aid. He did accept occasional help in reloading his M1 rifle.

Soon we had the satchel charges all placed on the hedgehogs and were ready to blow them. Just as we were attaching the forty-five second detonators, an infantry landing craft hit the beach a hundred and fifty yards seaward and directly down our gap. I knew how deadly explosive-driven steel fragments can be, and in forty-five seconds those men would have been in and around the hedgehogs we were about to blow. I agonized about the delay, but I waited. The hedgehogs were destroyed by the members of Team No. 8 when the tide went out in the afternoon.

As the incoming tide began lapping at our feet, we carried our wounded past the three-foot-deep runnel (a channel of sea water) to an area in defilade below the natural sand seawall. Then I saw Sergeant Roy Arnn lying on the sand. He had severe wounds from an artillery round that had landed close by. He couldn't move, so we began pulling him forward in the sand. As we neared the runnel, a machine-gun burst splattered sand in our faces, so we slid him behind a nearby hedgehog. It still had the tetrytol attached. Soon the German machine gunner found a new target and we got Arnn into the water and crossed the runnel with just our noses sticking out. The medics took care of him.

After our sector was cleared, I headed eastward for more orders. I had gone seventy-five yards, stopped, and twisted to my right to look back at my crew, when a mortar round hit the hard rock eight feet in front of me. If I hadn't stopped, that round would have been in my back pocket.

There were small shrapnel fragments in my right big toe, foot, instep, and calf, both knees, and in my left mid-thigh. I knew there would be more rounds coming, so I hopped inland above the shingle just as two more rounds dropped into the area I had just left.

I dug a foxhole with my hands and my helmet and crawled in out of the line of fire. Max Norris found me and we enlarged the sand hole to fit two. He tied up my thigh and gave me a shot of morphine.

For the rest of the morning and until the afternoon, I was a wide-eyed spectator as the battle unfolded.

That afternoon Lt. Caldwell had me round up enough men to tie charges on the remaining obstacles. We were tying on the last charges when we got hit with German 88s. Bookout, Long, and I were wounded, and Alvin Last was killed. I had a wound on my head and a wound through my right leg just below my knee.

Late in the afternoon of D-day I was taken to the aid station and then out to a hospital ship, where they cleaned up my wounds and treated them. That's when they found the shrapnel in my feet and legs. I was released from the hospital in mid-July and went through Lichfield Barracks for the second time. It was the U.S. 10th Replacement Depot in an English army camp twenty miles from Birmingham.

I boarded a train on 20 July and the next day loaded on an LCI on the way to France, where I joined my old outfit, the 146 ECB, which was bivouacked in the nearby Cerisy Forest.

So, the NCDUs did a great job on Omaha Beach, just as the Army Gap Assault Teams did. In this landing the NCDUs were attached to and under the command of the Army Engineer demolition men, who outnumbered the NCDUs four to one on the beach.

The U.S. Navy's Scouts & Raiders

Since the late 1930s the Navy had been working on amphibious training. It proved to be much more complicated and difficult than had first been expected. Fleet landing exercises were held in various areas. Then number seven in the series of landings was held from February 4 to 16, 1941, on Culebra Island, about twenty miles off Puerto Rico. Both Marine and Army troops were used in the landings.

The Army troops used the new thirty-six-foot Higgins boat, but the Army also used older and smaller landing craft that were not as practical. The outcome showed the leaders that there was a serious lack of equipment, but boat training and the supply functions had worked out well.

The first Joint Training Force was put together on June 2, 1941, and more landings were set for the New River, North Carolina, training area. The next exercise, held there from July 25 to August 6, 1941, showed that more training was needed.

One of the areas lacking was a reconnaissance capability. Experiments were made with ten-foot rubber boats with outboard motors.

Training continued with boat crews coming from the boat pool at the Amphibious Training Base at Solomon's Island at the mouth of the Patuxent River

The Navy ordered more boats for the operation.

They obtained thirty-six-foot landing craft, personnel (LCP), landing craft, personnel, large (LCPL), landing craft, personnel, ramped (RCPR), and the fifty-foot landing craft, mechanized (LCM). The smaller ones could all carry thirty-six combat ready troops or a small vehicle.

A call went out for personnel to fill the spots for small-craft operators. Many men were sent from the Navy's Physical Training Program, headed by boxer Gene Tunney.

Many of these men were well-known former professional and college football players, including one who would become a legend in underwater work, Phil H. Bucklew.

A new camp was soon established at Little Creek and construction went ahead. The area had dirt streets and World War I housing, with no floors and minimal plumbing. Forty sailors came to Little Creek from the ATB School at Solomon's Boat Pool, and soon more volunteers arrived for the first class of what was soon called the Scouts & Raiders.

The first ten men assigned to S & R were Phil Bucklew, Jerry Donnelly, Robert Halperin, Big John Tipson, Robert Herrick, John Johnson, Grant Andreasen, Kenneth Howe, Joe Wood, and Jack Bryon.

They assembled on August 15, 1942, and the commander, Lieutenant Lloyd E. Peddicord, U.S. Army, told them this was a joint Army and Navy venture.

It was emphasized that this was an ultrasecret operation. Not even their families should know about it or what it was called. Their job was to work at night to locate a designated landing beach for amphibious landings and report any obstacles and then guide in the landing craft.

The first Scouts & Raiders Training Base had been launched.

Sergeant First Class Charles H. Johnson Jr., U.S. Army
Tulsa, Oklahoma

I ENLISTED IN the Oklahoma National Guard in 1939, never dreaming that I would almost wind up in the Navy or in a Navy secret operation. Our unit was mobilized in 1940 and I began my infantry training. Late in 1942, two men were selected from each company and told they were going to Fort Pierce, Florida for a secret operation. I was one of the men from my company to go.

We arrived in February 1943 at Fort Pierce and I remember the huge difference in the temperature: from frozen New England to balmy and usually hot Florida. It seems we arrived a little before they expected us. There were few facilities. Our tents were not on platforms with sides but twelve tents pegged directly into the sand.

In my unit we had eighteen enlisted men and three officers. We settled in and began our army Scouts & Raiders training. It involved a lot of physical conditioning, tons of swimming, and a lot of paddling a small rubber boat in and out of the breakers there in Florida. We did a lot of boat work, and soon they would drop us off a ship five miles offshore and we paddled back and raced in with the breakers to practice a quiet, covert landing on a "hostile" shore.

Our first mission was going to be the landing in Sicily. Our boat crew was on board ship during the invasion, but for some reason we were not used. Either the sea was running too high or the way to the beach was already clear. We sat out the invasion there.

Soon after that I was returned to my old outfit, the 45th Infantry Division, and served as part of the backup force on ships offshore during the invasions of Salerno and Anzio.

So that was the extent of my experience with the Scouts & Raiders. The tough training served me well when I went back to my Army outfit. It was a little strange, though: After all those months of training in boat handling and shoreline evaluation and some explosive instruction, I never got to use those skills on an actual mission as a Scout & Raider.

Lieutenant Emil Reutzel Jr.
Coronado, California

AT THE UNIVERSITY of Nebraska at Lincoln, I was enrolled in the Marine Corps Reserve and was called up in the summer of 1943. They sent me to Northwestern University in the Marine College Training Program. I was there for two quarters. By then the Marine program was oversubscribed and I was offered the chance to transfer to the Navy and go to Midshipman's School at Cornell University in Ithaca, New York. I took it and was commissioned in May of 1944. While at Cornell, a recruiter came around looking for men to go into the Navy's Special Warfare units, which he described as hazardous duty. I signed up and was accepted.

I received orders to report to Fort Pierce in Florida and was warned not to say where I was going and above all not to mention Scouts & Raiders, which was still a secret operation. So I couldn't tell my wife. The strange part was, as soon as we hit Fort Pierce, they gave us our mailing address: Scouts & Raiders, Fort Pierce, Florida.

I remember lots of sand fleas, and they bit. We were covered pretty well with mosquito repellent and we slept in tents with wooden frames and floors and mosquito netting. One thing we had to get used to was a bunk full of sand. The training lasted about four months as I remember, and it wasn't too hard. We did a lot of swimming and running, but I was already in pretty good shape.

Some of the UDT men trained across the Indian River from us. Some of the men I had been with at Cornell were assigned to the UDT group. As Scouts & Raiders, we trained for the specific jobs of surveying the beach to see if it was suitable for making an amphibious landing, and then some would mark the route on the beach or in small boats, waving the landing craft shoreward along the specified area. Our men did this first in North Africa. What we looked for was water depth, suitability for landing, reefs, man-made obstacles, and beach slope.

After Fort Pierce, I and some from Class 7 were sent to the Naval Intelligence School in New York City, based in the Henry Hudson Hotel. There we studied photo recon and different kinds of planning for invasions. That was late in 1944. In January of 1945 they sent me to the Amphibious Base in Coronado, California, where I took part in the UDT training. It wasn't the usual "class" training. We were mostly working in classrooms on intelligence situations.

I went out to Pearl Harbor in late January 1945, where plans were being made for the landings on Okinawa. There I was in the Amphibious Forces Command and assigned to a ship delivering troops to the islands. I worked on the Okinawa Safety Operations Plan. I flew down to Guadalcanal and then on to Okinawa on April 1, 1945. The expected difficult landing didn't materialize. The Japanese had pulled back from the beach to concentrate their defenses in hills and caves, and it turned into a tremendously bloody battle.

The first mission I worked on was Okinawa, late in the war. The S & R men had mostly been taken into UDT by that time, since many of the facts the S & R obtained could be found out by photo intelligence. If not, the UDT men were equipped to do the same type of recon, and they could also blow up any barriers or problems they found.

After Okinawa I was sent back to the Amphibious Forces Command in Hawaii, where we worked on the invasion plans for Japan itself, keying in on Kyūshū. There I worked with two other men from Class 7 as we studied photo intelligence to define targets. Shortly after, I was assigned to a battleship as a fire support officer to spot and designate targets for the big guns. It never happened.

The war was over and we were so thankful that the atomic weapons had been used to save thousands of American lives and perhaps a million Japanese lives. I went to Manila after it was captured and it was a total mess. I didn't see how they could ever restore it. Later I went back and they had done very well.

I left the Navy in January of 1946 but stayed in the active Naval Reserve in air intelligence and served my two weeks a year at the Coronado Amphibious Base.

Rear Admiral Richard Lyon, USN (Ret.)
Coronado, CA.

I JOINED THE Navy in 1942 when I was a student at Yale University. I graduated in 1944 with a degree in engineering and then went on to the Columbia Midshipman's School where I became a ninety-day wonder and an ensign. A recruiter came to the school shortly before our graduation and told us he was looking for volunteers who were strong swimmers for a special project. That had my name on it since I'd been captain of the Yale championship swimming team.

That was about all they told us at first. Then we had a meeting for those interested and I signed my name. Right after graduation and my commission, my orders sent me to Fort Pierce, Florida. The facilities there were sparse and we lived in a tent with a wooden floor and sides and given a cot that was to be my bunk. The level of physical training we did soon made that bunk a welcome sight.

I found out I was a member of Class 8 at the Scouts & Raiders school. They told us they picked Florida for the school since the coast and water would be similar to that we would soon find in the South Pacific.

The physical training schedule at the S & R was hard. Much of it was picked up later as a model for the UDT training, and that's lasted all the way through to the current BUD/S Basic Underwater Demolition, SEALs training at Coronado. Our whole class of some fifty men was all officers, most of us raw, untested ensigns, and a few junior-grade lieutenants. Ensign Bell was head of the school, and he was helped by a young lieutenant (jg), Phil Bucklew, who had been with the S & R from their inception. Rank meant nothing during the training, which was true whether the class was all officers or mixed officers and enlisted. Every man had to go through the same rough, tough, and concentrated training, including "Hell Week." The swimming part was easy for me with my college swim team experience. I found it much harder to lie in the sand and weeds without moving for long periods of time. This was tougher because the sand was teeming with hundreds of thousands of sand fleas and other biting insects that swarmed all over the island campus.

Our mission was to scout out beaches and waterways to determine if they were safe for amphibious landings, and then to lead the troops into safe channels to the beach. Since we were not trained to clear a path to the beach by destroying man-made or natural barriers, we had little training in explosives and demolition.

Near us at Fort Pierce was another group training. They were called the Naval Combat Demolition Units. They had transferred there from Camp Perry, Virginia, and were the forerunners of the Underwater Demolition Teams.

After Fort Pierce, our whole Class 8 was sent to the Advanced Naval Intelligence School in New York City. It was located in the Henry Hudson Hotel. There, part of our training was the study and evaluation of photo reconnaissance material. We also studied charts and maps and specialized in Taiwan, so we could recommend where the best spots would be for amphibious invasions. It turned out our forces never went to Taiwan.

After our training, there some members of our class went to China and some were assigned to the European Theater of Operations. I went with a group to Pearl Harbor, where I was in the Administrative Command of the Pacific as a scout officer. Our men were assigned to whatever area in the Pacific needed Scouts & Raiders. I went to the Philippines, where I scouted out beaches around Davao. I conducted scouting operations in the area of the islands with an eye to launching amphibious assaults. I was the scout officer, and the entire crew and I swam in and checked out the waters and the beach. The war ended then, so the landings never took place.

Just after the war was over, I was assigned to conduct recon on the beaches off Wakayama, Japan. We found no obstacles and we landed the Thirty-third Infantry Division safely and they went to work as occupation forces.

The Scouts & Raiders as a group was decommissioned after the end of the war. The UDT men were doing the same work, and with the added thrust of demolition. The S & R men who stayed in the navy gravitated to the UDT teams.

I took my discharge, but later went back in the Navy and went through UDT Class 2 at Coronado and soon was part of UDT 5. I left the Navy again in 1952 and returned to Navy Reserve status. Then, in 1978, I returned to active duty as deputy chief of Naval Reserve, and was there until July 1983, when I retired after forty-one years of service.

Lieutenant (jg) Warren Sullivan
Englewood, New Jersey

I TOOK MY basic Scouts & Raiders training at Fort Pierce, Florida, in Class 7. After that, they sent me to the Amphibious Base in Coronado, California, for demolition school. That was near the end of the war, and the Scouts & Raiders were being disbanded. I took the option of going to Maui, Hawaii, to the UDT training school there. After going through more UDT training, I went into the school as a training officer. We sent two teams out to the Pacific after that, as I recall.

Some of the men we trained were from the Army. General Douglas MacArthur wanted Army specialists to clear the path for his group of ships that would take him back to the Philippines to fulfill his promise of "I will return." We trained them and sent them off. Not sure if they were used to help clear the way for the general or not.

Some of us went to Borneo on a small mission, and then into China. I remember we were in Peking in October of 1945, then they shipped us out to the West Coast, where we went back to Coronado and the UDT training grounds. I joined UDT 8. There were eighty to ninety men in the teams in those days.

Part of my duties in Coronado was to teach Navy flag-rank officers what UDT was and how we operated. Most of them had never even heard of us and our vital work in an invasion. I stayed in Coronado until my discharge number came up. I was discharged as a lieutenant junior grade.

Lieutenant (jg) Alva E. Gipe, USNR (deceased)
Canby, Oregon

FROM JULY 14 TO 17, 1944, our recon team had been behind Japanese lines in Sansapor, New Guinea, for two rain-soaked days. Our team consisted of Lt. John Dove, Alamo Scout; a Lieutenant Colonel from the Army Air Corps; a major from Army engineering; an enlisted

Alamo Scout; and me. This third day had turned sunny, and we were trying to dry out. I told Lt. Dove, team leader, that I would like to take another look at the beach area under near-normal circumstances, as most of my previous hydrographic examination of this beach had been under very unfavorable weather conditions.

Dove said it would be okay, since we were about three hundred yards from the beach and in thickly wooded terrain. The rest of the team would stay put while I took care of the hydrographic data. I made my way to the beach and crawled out to a brush-covered point that jutted out from the jungle and gave me a fairly protected area to observe tidal action and beach conditions without exposing myself.

I took out my binoculars and proceeded to glass the western section of the beach. I then turned to survey the eastern section, and there were two Japanese soldiers trudging down the wet sand toward my observation point. They were about 250 yards from me, close enough to make it urgent that I get the hell out of there. I tried, but I found myself hung up in some thorny bushes. This was it. I rolled over on my side, reached up, and shook the thorns loose. I swear, the entire jungle seemed to be moving as I wormed my way slowly off that prominent area.

I wasted no time getting back to the rest of the team and explained the situation. I told them that I was not sure whether I had been seen or not. We decided the best thing to do was to prepare a defense perimeter immediately, which we did.

As scouts in enemy territory, we had discussed such an emergency and knew what we were to do. We arranged ourselves in a circular formation where each member faced inward and could see the other man across the circle facing him. Thus we hoped that we could see anyone approaching from all 360 degrees.

We remained in this formation for thirty minutes. All of a sudden, the hair on my neck started crawling. Something was coming up behind me but no one gave a sign. I could stand it no longer. I turned my head slowly to the right, then to the left. Bingo. There he was: a skinny, scrawny, half-starved black-and-white fox terrier dog.

I did nothing. The dog did nothing. We simply looked one another in the eye for what seemed like an hour. The dog finally turned and silently sneaked off into the dense jungle.

I broke the silence and whispered, "Did you see that?" We then discussed the situation and decided to move from that area. The nips had not seen me.

The next night, the PT boat that brought us in picked us up. We were all glad to be heading to friendly territory.

Lieutenant (jg) Lloyd J. Palmer
Hilton Head Island, South Carolina

As I was nearing the finish of Midshipman's School at the Northwestern University Chicago campus in July 1944, I received orders to report to Boston for minesweeper duty. This did not strike me as a very appealing assignment, so I responded to a posted notice that volunteers were being sought for the Scouts & Raiders program. I applied and was accepted. Two more from my class there also went to S & R, John Wise and Ed Merrill.

On August 1, 1944, I reported to the Amphibious

Training Base at Fort Pierce, Florida, as a member of Class 7, along with forty-seven other officers. Included was Joe Lee, who had taken the role of historian-archivist of our class and S & R in general. The training was strenuous physically and mentally, but the physical aspect is what I remember, especially the Log PT. This involved doing calisthenics with very heavy palm logs, one officer and a crew of six per log. The exercises became a regular part of our routine, and I don't think a day passed without at least one session and sometimes more.

We also did a lot of open-water swimming while fully clothed and wearing our heavy "boondocker" shoes. One of the exercises was to swim from the beach offshore two hundred yards, then turn and swim parallel to the beach for several hundred yards, which at times seemed forever, before returning to the beach. Wearing the same kind of clothes and shoes, we had to run for fairly long distances on the beach. We were always under the watchful eyes of the training staff. The competitive juices flowed as many strived to finish first. All of us who went through the S & R training agree that we reached our lifetime pinnacle of physical fitness during the three months at Fort Pierce.

While there was heavy emphasis on physical conditioning, we spent more of our time learning the skills that were necessary to perform the job the Navy was training us for. There were hours spent on learning to identify enemy and U.S. planes and ships from silhouettes flashed on a screen; we were taught to identify snakes, especially the poisonous ones, for our own well being. We learned the techniques of sneaking ashore from sea and returning to the sea undetected. We learned methods to silence any enemies we might encounter on the beach. Also, we worked on techniques of using a knife and becoming familiar with guns and competent in using them.

Navy Combat Demolition Unit training was taking place at that time at Fort Pierce, and I believe the transition to UDT had started. Because of the UDT programs, which involved the use of explosives, we received some basic training in explosives and their application to targets. Much of our time was spent in seven-man rubber boats, which were the platforms from which most S & R operations were conducted. We learned how to handle them and especially how to land in the surf from them. Amphibious personnel landing craft were needed to haul boats and their crews to drop points, so we had to learn the basics of operating those crafts as well. This included how to hit the beach and how to retract from the beach. Much of the application of what we were taught was put into practice during nighttime exercises.

Near the end of our thirteen weeks of training, in November 1944, there was a night exercise in which we left Fort Pierce about dusk and headed north in landing craft. There was one seven-man crew in each boat. We exited over the side offshore from Vero Beach with the objective of accessing the Naval Air Station, collecting intelligence and getting out safely. The first night my crew and I crossed the intracoastal waterway and reached the mainland during early daylight. Since we couldn't safely move about, we found an area of fairly heavy vegetation that we thought would provide us cover until we could move again toward dark. Surprise! We had just settled down when a civilian carrying a rifle challenged us, suspecting we might have come ashore from a German U-boat. After some fast talking, we convinced him that we were Americans on a training mission, and he apparently believed us. When he went away, we thought he might be back with the local police or the military, but that didn't happen.

That night we moved in toward the airfield and some of our group became separated. It was a moonlit night, and when we came to the chain-link fence surrounding the field, we were considering alternative ways of accessing the place. While we were just outside the fence, we heard the sound of a sentry on the other side who was getting near. Fortunately there was a small depression where we were, and we lay motionless in it among the weeds and with the mosquitoes. As the sentry neared where we were concealed, we saw he had a leashed German shepherd dog with him. That was going to complicate our efforts. The dog fussed as they neared our position, perhaps suspecting something unusual, but the sentry spoke to the dog and they moved along.

After waiting until we thought they were a safe distance away, I decided the easiest way to gain access was to go over the fence, which was not in itself difficult. Bad decision: As I hit the ground on the other side, the sentry called out for me to halt as he and the dog approached me. Suddenly he began frantically calling the dog because it had become unleashed and was rushing toward me. I crouched while reaching for my knife, anticipating the dog would leap on me. Fortunately the sentry's voice commands brought the dog up short. Supposedly the security forces at the field had been told about the possibility of our exercise and were told not to release their dogs. I had a few choice words with the sentry, but I had been captured and that was the end of the exercise for me and my crew.

After we were interrogated and the exercise was declared over, we were sent back to the beach to recover our rubber boat, which had been hidden in the vegetation and partly covered with sand. What we found was nothing except some ashes. Someone had torched our boat.

We had lived in tents at Fort Pierce for thirteen weeks; now we had a complete change of pace. My class was transferred in November 1944 to the Advanced Naval Intelligence School located in the Henry Hudson Hotel on West Fifty-seventh street in New York City. During our four weeks at the school, we were taught how to read maps, interpret what we saw, and other intelligence basics. Compared to Fort Pierce, this turned out to be quite a low-key sojourn, with plenty of opportunities to enjoy some of the good things that New York City had to offer. We finished there just before Christmas in 1944.

From New York our orders took us to the Amphibious Training Base at Coronado, California, in January 1945, where we continued to do some of the things we did at Fort Pierce. In a matter of weeks we were sent to Pearl Harbor. About that time the Scouts & Raiders program was being discontinued and we were offered three choices of assignments: We could go into the UDT program at Maui where we would undergo further training; we could go aboard a ship as an intelligence officer; or we could become a deck officer aboard an AKA. I chose the AKA. I had to wait several weeks before I received orders to the USS *Brigit*, *AKA-24*. The ship was completed in 1944 but had developed a problem with a propeller shaft, so it was in Pearl Harbor for repairs. The ship had been scheduled for the invasion of Okinawa, but the repairs took it out of that assignment even before I joined it. That shipboard duty took me out of the Scouts & Raiders/UDT, program although those who chose UDT had a chance to continue their training and to use some of their S & R skills.

To my knowledge few, if any, of my classmates were ever in combat situations with S & R or UDT teams. Class 8 followed us at Fort Pierce, but that was the last class. I remained on board the *Brigit* from April 1945 until my release from the Navy in May 1946.

Lieutenant (jg) O. Melvin Kendall
San Diego, California

I WAS IN Class 6 at Fort Pierce Scouts & Raiders school back early in 1945. We finished just about V-E day, Victory in Europe, early May 1945, and the Navy sent the twenty-five officers in my class to the American Museum of Natural History in New York, where we learned to make contour maps.

After a ten-day leave, our group of twenty-five headed for San Diego. We found out what some of the guys did on their leave. John Petoskey got married. John Paul "Pappy" McGraw said he and his grandpappy sat on the porch with a jug between them and chawed tobaccy and spit at the chickens.

My next assignment was to the Amphibious Base in Coronado, California, to the Advanced Intelligence School. This included communication training at Oceanside. One day an Army major walked in and said he was looking for six volunteers to go to the Pacific Theater to work with the Underwater Demolition Teams. We went from the amphibious base to Oakland to a hotel. Our only duty the first few days was to call in every morning at seven A.M. and ask if our names were on the shipping-out list. It took a few days and most of us wired home for money so we could enjoy the sights and pleasures of San Francisco.

Our names came up for a flight and we flew to Pearl Harbor. They sent us on to Maui on the mail boat. The crew hated the run from Pearl to Maui. There are about a dozen currents going all which ways in there and the crew even got seasick on every run. We did too.

On Maui we lived in tents with screens. The first day there we were told we had two hours to decide if we wanted to volunteer for Underwater Demolition Team training. The alternative was no fun, so we volunteered and took powder training: learned how to blow up things.

Tom Crist was the boss. He was a Seabee and tough as old leather. I wound up teaching the men how to swim better, since that was my specialty. Near the end of our training Crist called me into his office and said his executive officer was leaving and asked me to take over the spot. I jumped at the chance and worked on the men's swimming for the rest of my duty there. The other men were assigned to ships as Scout officers. I got to stay on Maui for a year before I took my discharge. It was great duty.

Seaman First Class Edward J. Fazekas
San Jacinto, California

I ARRIVED AT Fort Pierce, Florida, via Bainbridge, Maryland, and Jacksonville, Florida, Naval Air Station in early 1944. I had a choice of three options: Scouts &

Raiders, Underwater Demolition Teams, or Attack Boat Staff. I chose S & R because I was told it had first priority on base. That meant first in the chow line. Initially I was assigned to the training staff. I'm not certain if it was because I was only seventeen at the time or what. I was not assigned to a boat crew until later. Each boat crew consisted of one officer and six enlisted men. Our HQ was called the casino. Possibly at one time it had been a gambling facility. We were told that the training terrain environment, such as swamps, mosquitoes, and snakes, would represent what we could expect to encounter when deployed. They were not kidding. Sand fleas would penetrate mosquito netting and impede our ability to sleep—when that luxury was available to us. I recall the first test we had, and that was to run to the end of a jetty and jump into the water and swim to shore. Swimming was not my forte; however, I passed that test. We had daily calisthenics consisting of running on the beach and then tossing palm tree trunks back and forth while lying in the sand. We also had hand-to-hand combat instructions from an Army expert.

It seemed that we were constantly on the move. One night we marched to Vero Beach, eighteen miles away. We performed some explosives procedures and marched back. We had instruction on handling dangerous snakes. We did a lot of paddling of rubber boats hours at a time to the point of complete exhaustion. You felt like you just wanted to fall over the side. Our gear was minimal: no masks, flippers, etc. Nothing compared to what the modern-day Navy SEALs have.

Part of our training was to make mock raids, and I was involved on the one going into the Fort Lauderdale Airfield. We arrived by small boat from Fort Pierce via the Indian River to the Fort Lauderdale Cost Guard

Station. This raid was supposed to be a five-day operation. All military and civilian law enforcement people were supposed to be on alert. When the fourth day came and went, everyone knew we were going on the fifth day. In the dark we were at sea in our landing craft. I remember a Cost Guard cutter coming within a few yards of us. They did not detect us. We quickly went over the side with our rubber boats and headed for shore. We found a canal and began to paddle toward the airfield. We eventually hid the boat, broke up into twos and headed onward. I was sure that the canal was infested with snakes.

We heard sirens, saw flashing lights, and knew that we were being pursued. One serious mistake we made was judging the distance to the airfield. *Everything appears closer at night* became a byword for us. We drew enemy light when we got to the perimeter of the base. We crawled in the brush too long. Our team split up. I crawled through the fence and began moving in the weeds toward the runway, when I saw a sentry with a dog. There were thirty such guards on duty that night. The dog picked up my scent and began to come towards me. When they got close, I jumped up, dagger in hand, and yelled. "You are my prisoner."

There is no doubt in my mind that in real combat they would have been dead. However, this was a training exercise and the guard immediately shot off a flare and I was captured and taken to the compound.

There were all sorts of stories about what the S & R guys did during these maneuvers. One was about when an Army officer had one of our men with a rifle to his back marching him to the compound. Our guy knocked the rifle away and downed the officer and escaped. Another one was that some S & R guys stole the base commanding officer's car and drove it right out the front gate.

We left the impression that the S & R guys were tough and not to be messed with. I think we were like the Foreign Legion of the U.S. military. Many of our S & R officers were ex–All American football players. These included Marshall "Biggy" Goldberg from Pitt and Cliff Heffelfinger from Ohio State. Cliff has since passed away and I've lost contact with Biggy.

It was my understanding that the S & R men were to be the ones to penetrate enemy lines and scout out the best location for a beachhead. Then the UDT guys were to remove the obstacles to make landing possible. There was some rivalry between the groups during our training. We were being prepared to work on the invasion of Japan when the war ended and orders came to disband the S & R groups. We were sent to the fleet. Some S & R men were already in the Pacific and they probably felt that if necessary they would be involved in the invasion of Japan.

What I liked about the S & R program was that the individual controlled his own destiny. We were basically on our own and our survival would mostly depend on our own actions. S & R teams also were in the European Theater of Operations. Even though I never had a chance to serve as an S & R in combat, I am fortunate to be a part of the current reunion organization. I encourage you to visit the Navy SEAL/UDT Museum in Fort Pierce, Florida.

Gunner's Mate Second Class Bill Spencer
Springhill, Florida

I BECAME ACQUAINTED with S & R after I graduated from Gunner's Mate School in Newport, Rhode Island, and was shipped to Little Creek, Virginia, for amphibious training. Within two weeks after arriving in Little Creek I was not pleased with the training given me. I was painting some interiors of buildings along with ten other hapless sailors. We heard about S & R at eight A.M., volunteered, and were on the train at noon. That's the fastest anyone has ever moved in the Navy. This was in early July 1944. After passing the grade in training at Fort Pierce, we were shipped to Morro Bay, California, and en route tested the shore patrol's resolve to hinder us from enjoying the five-day train ride. We left Fort Pierce in late October 1944.

Our further training at Morro Bay was pretty intense. We were associated with the Marine Corps Raiders during this juncture. It was later said the reason for Morro Bay was the similarity to the Japanese coastline. Maybe so, since our training seemed to indicate this. After graduation from Morro Bay, we enjoyed a five-day leave and then were divided into small groups. We always trained in six- or seven-man teams. We were given our new assignments. Ten of us went to San Diego and reported aboard the USS *Charles Lawrence* (APD-37). A short briefing prior to boarding was to make sure we told no one of our training and who we were. We were to replace part of the "boat crew" as ship's company. We boarded on the evening of February 15, 1945, and set sail for Pearl Harbor the next day. We arrived in Pearl on February 22. We left Pearl on March 5, 1945, and arrived at Funafuti on March 11.

We left there the next day and sailed to Guadalcanal, arriving on March 17. The next day we went to Ulithi Atoll in the Caroline Islands. From there we left on March 23 and went with the amphibious forces and arrived at Okinawa on April 1. We were there just three hours before the invasion started.

We took part in the invasion for the first five days, then were ordered to escort a crippled cruiser back to Guam. From there we went to Saipan and Ulithi Atoll and then back to Okinawa on April 23, 1945. We did a lot of picket duty watching for subs and kamikazes. I believe we had some night recon duty in small boats but what, specifically, we never knew. Here are some notes from my journal I wrote then and still have:

The first was the eerie feeling that gray dismal morning on April 1, 1945. This was my first real action, the first two or three days of the invasion were not that bad. It was during the last half of April and May that the Navy took hell. June wasn't too bad. Fighting had slowed somewhat in our area and a change could be felt. We had burned out a thrust bearing while on picket duty, so we limped to a place called Wise Man's Cove, where we tied up to a tender for repairs.

This was still Okinawa, and the kamikaze planes were very active. There we were, tied up to a tender and defenseless. The first raid came around 1830 when we heard .50-caliber and 20mm fire coming our way. General Quarters sounded and all hell broke loose. Our pickets splashed the plane. There was a lot more that evening, so no sleep and thirty-nine more air raids. A stray shell hit our deck and exploded near our chief quartermaster and hospitalized him and he got a discharge. He lived to his eighties and attended several of our ship reunions.

The hostilities were winding down now and the war's end came. We were in Leyte Gulf in the Philippines when the war was over. We had been preparing for the invasion of Japan and assembling our forces in that area. Not long after that, we were ordered to escort the first occupation troops to Kure, Japan.

Other S & R men onboard the *Lawrence* were Robert Metz, Fred Ruhl, Harry Smith, Clare Chips Carrick, and Randy Snyder, all deceased by now. Robert Barnette, David Fouch, Gilliam Barber, and William Gadd.

Those of us still alive keep in touch as much as possible and visit each other on occasion. I'm proud to have been a part of the precursors of today's Navy SEALs.

Motor Machinist's Mate Second Class Kenneth W. Kachline
Easton, Pennsylvania

I LEFT HOME for Navy boot camp on February 5, 1943. After boot, I went to Naval Training School for diesel engines at Richmond, Virginia, from April 16 to June 19. From there I was ordered to Fort Pierce, Florida, where I volunteered to go to the Scouts & Raiders on October 25. Being a young lad, I guess I was looking for adventure, so I volunteered. Our training was intensive, including hand-to-hand combat, a group lifting of a palm log, the use of rubber boats, nighttime silhouette studies, map reading, and swimming.

I left Fort Pierce on February 14, 1944, and arrived at Lido Beach, New York, on February 16. There we received orders to go to Pier 92 and board the ship

Île-de-France, a passenger liner converted to a troop transport. The ship joined a convoy and set sail on March 13. We arrived in Scotland on March 21. There we were sent to a base in Rosemuth, Scotland. Our team was 5 Scouts & Raiders, and the men on it were Ensign Sidney S. Chapin, Coxswain Robert J. Coppa, Seaman 1/C Andrew B. Connolly, Seaman 1/C Edward J. Coulter, Seaman 2/C Donald J. Carter, Seaman 2/C George A. Castilow, and me.

We were sent to London, then to several staging areas in preparation for the invasion of France. Although our team was left behind on D-day, our officer was assigned to an LCS that already had its own crew.

We received orders to return to the States. After a two-week leave we went to Fort Pierce, Florida. On October 10, 1944, we received orders to report to the 7th Amphibious Force, Southwest Pacific Area, at Oakland, California. We left two days later on the world's largest flying boat at that time, the *Martin Mars*. We landed in Pearl Harbor, then went on to Hollandia, New Guinea.

Our team participated in the assault landing at Lingayen Gulf on Luzon in the Philippine Islands. We spent one night in a foxhole there.

On March 1945, Sid Chapin, Bob Coppa, and myself were sent on a recon mission reporting to the USS *Ingram*. We were picked up by PT boat *490* and escorted to *PT-496* to Impampulga Island in the Guimaras Strait.

Our work was to do hydrographic inshore surveys to the beach. It was about 2300 hours when we put over the side in our five-man rubber boat. Two sailors we picked up on the ship helped us paddle in. We took soundings from three hundred yards offshore to the land. While working our way in, we saw a group of men on the beach. As we swam into the beach, the two sailors stayed with the rubber boat. Our scout crew was met by Filipino guerrillas on the beach. We brought two of them back to the flak boat. After being questioned, the guerrillas were taken back to shore and we continued the survey. A short time later the guerrillas told us there was a Japanese patrol in the area, so we left and paddled seaward. We didn't go very far when one of the sailors broke his paddle. By flashing the prearranged trouble signal, we were picked up by the ICM salvage boat.

About 0200 on 23 March 1945, the survey was complete and we returned to *PT-490* and back to the *Ingram*.

Later I participated in the preassault recon of Zamboanga and Brunei Bay and the assault landings at Zamboanga, Tarakan and Brunei Bay.*

Chief Boatswain's Mate Ray King
Johnson City, Tennessee

I JOINED THE Navy on February 14, 1941, at the ripe old age of sixteen years, and went through boot camp at Norfolk Training Center. I was stationed at the Navy Airfield in Norfolk for about a year and then I asked for a transfer. They sent me to Providence, Rhode Island, to train to run bulldozers to build airfields. Not liking that, I got a transfer to the amphibious base at Norfolk, where I learned to run landing craft. After this training

---

*Author's note: Kenneth Whitfield Kachline was awarded the Bronze Star medal for these actions against the Japanese forces.

they sent twenty-five of us to Solomon's Island, Maryland. There we spent the spring of 1942 teaching boat crews to operate landing craft. In July of 1942 they sent three hundred of us back to Norfolk.

There they told twenty-four of us to pack up and get on a truck that took us to Little Creek, Virginia. There we were told by a Navy ensign and an Army lieutenant that we were new volunteers for the Scouts & Raiders. We all looked at each other and asked what the heck that was. All of us they picked for the S & R were pretty rough guys.

We called the officers the Tunney fish because they were given the rating of chief and all had been professional ballplayers. Tunney was in charge of the operation.

They came into the Navy to teach physical fitness training. We did the training there at Little Creek, including all-night problems, until the end of October. Then we boarded ship for the North African invasion. We hit the beach in our landing craft and then went back to the ship. My three men and myself were waiting to be hoisted aboard the ship when the captain asked if we would take a load of guns back to the beach. My crew quietly said we were not going. I asked them if they got paid that month and they said they did. So I said get your asses in the boat and earn your money.

Before we could get under way, we had the stern of our craft blown away by an enemy round. The next day we lost an LCM with a tank and a load of ammo on board and seven men KIA.

After the invasion we were sent back to the States, where we drove twenty DUKWs to Fort Pierce, Florida. Took us three days. DUKWs were amphibious vehicles, land to water. There we helped start the

Scouts & Raiders and the UDT programs. I was only there a short time when they sent two officers and eight of us enlisted back to North Africa, where we trained our own men and left the others behind in Florida.

After twenty months there, they flew the ten of us back home. The men we trained did landings in southern France, then came home to the states by ship. We were only at Fort Pierce a short time when the skipper told me to pick eighteen men who I wanted to take with me on a mission. I picked people I could trust. I was about to get mashed up by the fifty who didn't get picked. We were sent to China, where we went behind the Japanese lines to record the beaches of South China for possible amphibious landing locations.

Lieutenant John S. Ferry
Washington, New Jersey

I JOINED THE Navy when I was a freshman at Lafayette College and was then put in a program to train future officers at Swarthmore College. A year later I went to the University of Notre Dame for naval officer training. I figured they were sending us to different schools to force us to grow up a little. Most of us were nineteen or twenty by that time. I was commissioned and volunteered to go to Scouts & Raiders. I was in Class 7 with fifty-two mostly brand-new ensigns. Now that I think about it, we were all well educated, athletic, and adventuresome trailblazers.

They sent us to Fort Pierce, Florida. It was *hell*. It was the home of twenty thousand sailors and six thousand civilians. The accommodations for the demolition trainees consisted of a few rows of units with wooden floors and sides and canvas tops. This was true resort living. The first week was programmed to meet the sadistic needs of the training crew. "Hell Week" separated the men from the boys. It just proves when you are young and full of piss and vinegar, you don't realize what your limits are.

After Hell Week we were divided into crews. Each crew consisted of five enlisted men, one chief, and one officer. My Navy Combat Demolition Unit was No. 95. Later it was changed to UDT 6 when the groups were combined. We became highly trained and physically fit demolition specialists. Many of the men were volunteers and graduates from the Navy bomb and mine disposal school. Our object was to blast the obstacles from beaches where the Allied forces would land. These could be man-made or natural obstacles.

During training our first objective was to develop into strong swimmers. In a short period of time we could all swim one mile before breakfast. We also did a lot of training on how to use small rubber boats to launch through and return through the ocean surf. Our daily uniform was swim trunks and canvas swim shoes. We soon were introduced to the use of face masks and swim fins. It was a special treat one day when we were allowed to go into town in a suit and tie. We were sick of swim trunks.

We learned new methods for a speeding boat to pick up a swimmer in the water. During the process we developed a lot of sore arms and shoulders. Some of the physical training consisted of raising a palm log over our heads and doing movements with it up and down and to the side. If you couldn't do the log lift with your crew, you were history.

We were called Navy Scouts & Raiders. By the end

of World War II we numbered about 3,500 men divided into thirty large teams.

After two months of training, about twenty-five of us were cut from the units and sent to the Advanced Navy Intelligence School in New York. There we were trained in reconnaissance, charting, and surveying. We also were drilled on silhouettes of Japanese planes and ships and our own aircraft. They told us that later we would be sitting at the mouth of Japanese ports to spot enemy ships and figure out their destinations.

After completing Naval Intelligence School, I was sent to San Francisco and then on to Maui, Hawaii. Eight weeks after leaving New York, I was sent back to San Francisco, then to Washington, D.C., where I met with some young Chinese officers. Shortly after the meetings, we flew to Calcutta, India, via Europe. There we were assigned to drive into China over the Burma Road. On the way I stood on the Sphinx and crawled into a pyramid. In Calcutta we were trained in driving trucks. We were stationed at Camp Knox. After a few days they told us to drive the Burma Road with trucks filled with supplies. Once there, they said we would meet with our Chinese friends and be coast watchers, reporting enemy ship movements.

When we got to the border of China they told us that Japan had surrendered and the war was over. We unloaded the trucks, which were filled with supplies for the POWs, and loaded them up with the POWs and took them back to Calcutta for medical help.

Even though the war was over, our work wasn't done. We had to clean up the many ammunition dumps left in India. India was breaking free from Britain and the English didn't want them to have the arms that were on their land. When we finished that, we sat around waiting to be sent home. But it gave us time to see the sites such as New Delhi, the Taj Mahal, and burning ghats.

Matthew W. Kaye
Madera, California

IN THOSE DAYS of training at Little Creek, Virginia, it seemed that we did hours and hours and days of endless circling in our LCVPs, landing craft vehicles, personnel. We lined up with the thirty-six-foot-long boats and on signal dashed for the beach. Weeks later we were transferred to USNATB at Fort Pierce, Florida.

Different training? Much the same, only this time in we tied up at a cargo net on a vertical wall before we made our circles and run for the beach. One night we read the bulletin board and saw a small announcement that caught our attention: WANTED: VOLUNTEERS FOR EXTRA HAZARDOUS DUTY. Four of us from my boat crew signed our names. The next morning they marched us down to the end of the road to the Scouts & Raiders area by the old casino. We met Ensigns Bell, Tripson, and Herrick. Also "Shorty" Buchanan, Ponds, and Kaylor, all members of the ship's company.

We didn't need training in small-boat handling but caught everything else from bodybuilding to hand-to-hand combat, demolition, gunnery radios, and stealth. We were divided into boat crews and assigned an LCP(R) (landing craft, personnel, ramp). I had made friends with the harbormaster and he told me which boat was the fastest. We got that boat. Ensign William G. Morrisey III was our crew officer.

As with any military unit taking realistic training,

we had our share of accidents. Sergeant Zimmerman of the U.S. Army lost his right arm when a faulty grenade exploded. Montaign, a Scout & Raider, died from an "unloaded" gun accident.

After graduation we left Fort Pierce for the Brooklyn Navy Yard. A few days there and we boarded the USS *Tarazed*, a troop transport. As soon as we were under way, Ernie Chyz and I groped our way topside for some fresh air. The ship was being tossed about and I thought we were running aground or being thrown against a mountain. The mountains turned out to be massive waves on both sides of the ship. It was a rough Atlantic winter crossing.

Two days out of Gibraltar we picked up our escorts to get us through the dangerous seas ahead. We hugged the coast of North Africa and pulled in at the port of Oran. We saw a lot of French warships that had been abandoned when the Navy men refused to scuttle them. Fight or leave, they were told. They left.

At Algiers we left the ship and stayed in some French-built barracks. Then we boarded an LCI (landing craft, infantry) and moved along the coast to Tunis. The channel to the docks was littered with dozens of ships either sunk or scuttled trying to block the port. Our ship worked through the maze slowly.

We saw ships with the bows missing, one on its back with the keel in the sunlight, a sunken sub with a third of its bow pointing toward the sky. Masts stuck out of the water, dock cranes were twisted into weird shapes, roofs were blown off. On the buildings not a single unbroken windowpane was to be seen.

Our stay in Tunis was short. After a few days in another French barracks we sailed to Bizerte. From there we took trucks south and east to a former French base called Ferryville. Quarters? A row of tents. In the center of each tent was a makeshift stove fashioned from metal ammunition cans. When facing a roaring wood fire, your front roasted while your back turned blue from the cold. The nights were bitter cold in Tunisia.

We went to work as instructors of paratroops and Rangers, teaching them Scouts & Rangers skills we had learned at Fort Pierce.

One day we were each issued automatic pistols with fifty rounds of ammunition. We took the weapons to our tents to unpack them and clean off the Cosmoline. Twenty minutes later I lay on the floor, shot through both legs. Erick, one of my closest friends, had been checking the ejector of his gun. He forgot that the slide stays open after the last round. He squeezed the trigger after miscounting. It felt like someone slammed a crowbar across my legs. It wasn't fatal. Later I was shaken awake by a gowned surgeon and told that I would be all right in six weeks. He said the wounds just had to be cleaned and bound in order to heal. They did and I was back with my unit.

Electrician's Mate First Class Warren DeMerritt
Lafayette, California

I WAS DRAFTED into the Navy and took boot at San Diego, then was assigned to Naval Training School for electrical at St. Louis, Missouri. After training I went to Little Creek, Virginia, where I volunteered for Scouts & Raiders in Fort Pierce, Florida. It was a twelve-week program that included extensive and intensive physical and mental conditioning.

We graduated 125 men and twenty officers. We

were probably the best-conditioned men in the world at that time. One of our daily routines was to swim above and below water. This was before the advent of modern scuba equipment and fins. Years later someone discovered an old Spanish galleon that had sunk in that same area where we did our swimming.

We shipped out in May of 1945 from San Pedro, California, on the USS *General Collins* and landed in Calcutta, India, where we were part of the China-Burma-India theater of operations.

Our primary mission at that time was to get much-needed supplies into China. We drove the 6 x 6 Army trucks from Calcutta to Assam over into Burma and finally into Kunming, China. We drove over that marvelous piece of engineering called the Ledo-Burma Road.

On the road one day I heard a loud commotion behind us and thought that the Japs had engaged our rear. I was relieved that it was the U.S. Army Cavalry on horseback driving a herd of mules over the road heading for China.

The highlight of my military career was when I had a reunion with my brother in the jungles of India. He was in the 502nd MP Battalion, Company B, China 22nd Division, 5303 Regimental Combat Team, attached to Merrill's Marauders at Chzbua, Assam, India. My brother, Grantville DeMerritt, was in the Army and I was in the Navy and we met in India! It was a happy reunion.

Later our troops were surprised when we found in China a strange accumulation of tanks, trucks, and artillery pieces. We found out all of the war equipment was stockpiled for the anticipated civil war that was coming in China. General Stilwell had it right about the corrupt Chinese government.

When the war was over in Europe, we figured that the China-Burma-India forces would be some of the initial men to attack Japan. Before that happened, the bomb fell on Japan and the great war ended. We shipped out from Calcutta on September 29, 1945. I took my discharge at Camp Elliott in San Diego on December 12, 1945.

Lieutenant (jg) Lloyd Diedrichsen, D.D.S.
Sparks, Nevada

TRAINING IN THE Scouts & Raiders in Fort Pierce was rugged. I really believe that I was in the best physical shape of my life when we graduated. Lieutenant (jg) Cliff Heffelfinger made certain it was strenuous. We all were competent in whatever area we had been trained for, from the rubber boats to swimming, demolition, survival, and the six-man log drill. Talking with other S & R vets and UDTs and SEALs about their training programs, most of us knew we would go through it again—if we were young. At that age a man is gung-ho. Even today that is true. In that training you develop a bond with the others and there is no thought of rank, just respect for each other.

Ensign Oliver Allen, the brother of Ross Allen, who had the Ross Allen's Reptile Institute in Florida, was our nature/survival training officer. He taught us how to live off the land, what plants were edible, and how to make animals we could catch palatable. Snake toasted on a stick was pretty tasty, like chicken. We tried it. His instructions were that if anything bit us, we should catch it and bring it back so it could be identified and proper treatment given. He showed us how to milk a snake for its venom using an old-fashioned Coca-Cola glass. He had a collection of rattlers, cottonmouths, and one small three legged alligator. All were live. Evidently the alligator lost his leg early in life. Allen had an enclosure for his animals next to the barracks. We had the only lawn in the area, about one hundred by forty feet and right next to the Atlantic Ocean and beach. The UDT Teams were just down the road from us. We knew that men who couldn't hack it in Scouts & Raiders moved on down the road to the UDTs. They never agreed with that.

Don Leu, Walt Lowell, and I were just married after getting our commissions and the only married guys in our group. Like us, our wives were from Michigan and Nebraska, so spending a honeymoon in Florida from February 1 to June 1 wasn't all that bad. Don and Ann had a small apartment. Walt and Margaret and Phyllis and I started with a single room. In April we were able to get a small guest cottage. The people who had the other house were commercial fisherman, so we always had plenty of fresh shrimp, turtle, which was in season, red snapper, and many other great seafoods. The weekends were always great, but Monday morning came around too quickly.

We went out one night on a regular four-to-five day training problem into the swamp near Fort Pierce, each group of seven guys to a rubber boat doing battle and paddling through the plush water plants to get to our point of operation. We were to demolish undergrowth and clear an area for a canal or future roadway.

One man in Bob Bosco's boat grabbed a small snake out of the water. Naturally his buddies gave him a bad time for picking on a baby. He tossed it back into the water and Bob splashed the water to get the snake moving. Evidently the little fellow was a bit upset. He nipped Bob on the webbing between his thumb and index finger. According to instructions, they recaptured the snake in a mosquito head cover to take back for identification. It wasn't long before Bob's arm began to swell.

There was always good medical aid available in case someone got injured by the high explosives we used: Bangalore torpedoes, TNT blocks, plastic composition C-2, or dynamite. They rushed Bob back to the base hospital. Bob said it was about two or three A.M. and quiet in the building. A nurse was on duty at the end of one corridor of beds with her back to him and only a small lamp at her desk. On these training trips we were always in camouflage, grease paint on our faces and the big sand shoes. Bob said he walked up and tapped her on the shoulder with his free hand. She turned and saw him and screamed. When things quieted down, they took care of his rattler bite.

Allen added this snake to his collection. He was a full-grown pygmy rattler. Allen had a forked stick and he walked his snakes across the enclosed lawn. Visitors were curious. Some asked about the pygmy snake story. An officer leaned over the pen where the pygmy snake was and demonstrated what Bob had done. The snake got him on the end of one finger. He was hurt, but not bad enough that he couldn't ship out with us.

My unit left Fort Pierce with the following men: Paul Groeschell, our CO; Humprey Noyes, the exec; and Charles Arthur, Robert Bosco, Steve Allen, Arthur O'Brien, Jack Howe, Jack Goephert, Don Leu, Walter Lowell, Bill Stameris, Dick Thompson, Deal Gelwick, Wilber Craig, Fritz Lennox, Robert Green, Lloyd Diedrichsen, and Peterson.

I can recall only one of my group. He was First

Class Cook Paul Molero, my crew chief. He was known by all as Sabu. He was about five five, and an identical twin. His brother was in the Navy as well but somewhere else. His one problem was that in *his* eyes he was six two and about 210 pounds and could handle anybody, including me. He loved to cook. He wanted to be a pastry chef in New York City when the war was over. He was from Brooklyn and thought I had the neatest wife. Wherever we were, he saw to it that we were well fed. On the ship going to Calcutta, he was always in the galley and made a point of taking care of our Navy group attached to the ship, the USS *Bexar*.

We left San Pedro, California, in the first part of June, sailed south of Australia, then to Calcutta, India. Small numbers of Roger II went to China driving 6 x 6 trucks over the Burma Road to Kunming, China. My group was set to be the next drivers when the war ended. Everyone except medical personnel and maintenance men were sent home by the next ship. We came back to New York City. So I had gone around the whole world. We made it back in time for Thanksgiving.

Painter Third Class Jack Smith
Atlanta, Georgia

IN DECEMBER OF 1943, Navy boot camp seemed like a dream to me. Jacksonville Naval Base was on the Saint Johns River and I never was completely warm all the time I was there. After boot we were moved to another part of the base to aviation radio school. I didn't like radio school, and after eight weeks I asked to get out and was sent to the receiving barracks at Charleston, South Carolina.

I don't remember exactly what they said to us, but they were asking for volunteers for the Scouts & Raiders and it sounded exciting, so I signed on the dotted line.

It was the spring of 1944 when I arrived by train at Fort Pierce, Florida, with eight other sailors. Fort Pierce was an amphibious base on the east coast of Florida. It was inhabited by many sailors including the Underwater Demolition Team training base. For each sailor there were about four billion sand flies. After a rain it was impossible to eat without eating more sand flies than food, but that didn't matter because the sand flies tasted better than the food.

On arriving at the base, we mustered in front of a pink stucco building that sat in some coconut trees next to the ocean. It was called the Casino. While standing in a loose formation we listened to an officer telling us we were the sixth team of the Scouts & Raiders. He had great plans for us. He assured us our training would be tougher than any training ever given to any of the Allied Forces. He said it would start at 0800 the next morning at this spot and that Bosn's Mate First Class Maddox and Bosn's Mate Second Class Mason would be in charge of our training.

Everyone was already aware of the two men who stood to the officer's right and just behind him. They were at parade rest with their legs spread slightly and hands held behind their backs. They were dressed in the usual blue dungarees with white sailor caps, both tilted just two finger widths above their right eyes. That was Navy regulation. Their faces were set as if in granite. They were both about the same size, six four to six six, and must have weighed 210 pounds. There was no fat on their large frames and each had a set of keys hanging on his right side, attached to his belt. Their eyes were cold and set as they looked at the men standing in front of them.

"There will be no liberty for twelve weeks, until your training is over, and then I will give you each a two-week leave before you ship out," the officer said. "The crew names are posted inside on the bulletin board. Dismissed."

I found I had been assigned to Crew 13 in Tent 13, so I found my seabag and started looking for that tent. There were four rows of them sitting in the sand just off the beach. When I found Tent 13, three crew members had already arrived. I picked out one of the bunks and dropped my seabag on it. When all six men in the tent had arrived, we were told to go pick up new clothes. They were Marine-green dungarees and hightop work shoes that were called sand shoes. After that, the crew sat around the tent getting acquainted with each other. We were all about the same age, eighteen, except one guy who was twenty and had been in the merchant marine. His ship had been sunk by a German submarine, and when he didn't sign on with another ship, he was drafted into the Navy. They made him the coxswain because of his experience.

The next morning after chow we all mustered at 0800 in front of headquarters. Then they marched us to the beach. Each crew was given a palmetto log about twelve feet long. We were taught how to exercise with it by slinging it from side to side, tossing it into the air, and catching it. If both ends didn't come down at the same time, someone could get hurt. Each crew of six stood far enough apart so we didn't get hurt by another crew's log.

After an hour of nonstop exercise with the logs, we

ran two or three miles down the beach and back, led by the two bosn's mates. After that, we had to climb over rocks and boulders out to the end of the jetty that extended a quarter of a mile out into the ocean at the mouth of the river just behind the headquarters building.

Right after noon chow we were introduced to a rubber boat, big, black, and ugly. We soon found out it was heavy too. The first thing we did was not to put it in the water but to carry it on our shoulders. We didn't walk, which made more sense to me, but ran every step of the way with two bosn's mates pushing us all the way. When it seemed like we couldn't take another step, we were directed to the water with the boat. We still had all of our clothes on. Now we learned to use the ugly rubber boat in the rough water and in the surf. It was nonstop boat work from then on six days a week. They did give us Sunday off.

Our training went on the same day after day. Although I had grown up on a farm and was used to work and at times hard work, it was nothing like this. Soon I became aware that my young body was beginning to change into a much stronger and harder one. I realized that I was not getting tired when most of the others began to lag behind. That was true when we started moving the rubber boats out into the swamps and marshes around camp.

Days changed into weeks. Each crew member was trained in his assigned specialty. We had one machinist, who took care of the diesel engine on the landing craft assigned to each crew. One radioman, one coxswain, and the gunners were trained to disassemble and assemble every small arm while blindfolded. We learned to fire every small arm up to the 20mm gun that the Allied

Forces used—this, even though during training we only carried a knife. We were taught that firing a gun for us was the last resort. We were not supposed to be seen or heard. We were trained to go into enemy territory and search out and bring back information silently. If caught, the only weapon we carried would be a knife. We were trained to kill with a knife and be silent while doing it. They taught us to fight any way we could but in silence. We were told we had to be quick and mean in order to survive.

In a few weeks we changed from working in the daytime to night operations. Then everything was done in the dark. This included wading through the marshes and swamps, sneaking around from here to there all night long. We swam, paddled our boats, and dragged them overland. We always got back to camp just at sunrise. They let us sleep for a few hours, then we had our physical training. We left for another exercise just after dark.

A few weeks later we landed in southern California at Morro Bay, about 180 miles below San Francisco. The California air was far different from Florida: crisp, cold, and no sand fleas. We were housed in a barracks in a state park a couple of miles from the base. After chow at the barracks we were bused over to the base. The land around Morro Bay is beautiful, with rolling green hills and trees.

One day, when we were standing in line for chow on the bluff overlooking the ocean, the huge monolith called Morro Rock exploded right in our faces. It blew rocks and dust all over, and when the air cleared we saw that a large part of the rock was in the ocean.

U.S. Engineers had been blasting the rock to get chunks of it to build a jetty to protect the Morro Bay entrance. They had figured wrong about how much TNT they needed. It became our job to help clean up the fractured rock.

That was the first week in November, and after the warm waters of Florida, stepping into the cold Pacific was a shock to the system. They gave us no new uniforms to wear other than what we had in warm Florida. Landing craft let their ramps down and we went into the cold ocean and loaded rocks out of the water.

When the rocks were cleared out and the jetty was finished, forming a safe harbor for the landing craft, they put us to work in the small boats. We had to learn how to handle the landing craft in the rough waters of the Pacific. A ship sat offshore, and now we began taking the landing craft out to the ship, simulating loading troops and carrying them back to the beach. Back and forth all day. When the weather became too rough for everyone else and they secured, the Scouts & Raiders had to continue in and out of the rough surf, running the craft up on the beach, then backing off, turning around, and going back out to deep water, then back in again.

If a landing craft got caught in a breaker crosswise, it would sometimes get swamped. It was not unusual for some of the crew to get thrown into the cold water or get thrown against the side of the boat or maybe lose the coxswain, who was standing high in the back, steering the boat. When that happened, the crew had to react quickly and take the wheel before the boat was thrown onto the beach sidewise and lost in the rough surf. Our training at this rough time should have stopped, but it didn't. We were young and healed quickly and had few broken bones. We always knew that the "meat wagon" ambulance stood onshore to take care of us if we were severely injured.

One day we were issued green sheepskin-lined jackets. We wondered why. The next day we found out. A Marine captain told us we would be doing rubber-boat training working out through the surf and back in. He told us that in the cold water we would die of exposure after four hours and twenty minutes. He advised us to stay with our boat at all costs. He told us that every fourth breaker was a weak one, that that's the one you pick to launch your rubber boat through. We watched, but we could spot no weak ones in the huge Pacific waves that kept rolling in.

Down on the beach as we readied our boat, the roar from the wind and breakers was so loud, we had to shout to one another. The waves were higher than our heads and they broke with tremendous force. We kept counting breakers, checking the pattern and timing the weak one.

Then we started. I grabbed a lifeline attached to the boat and we ran with the boat down to the water and plunged in. I felt the undertow trying to pull the sand from under my feet. Then the water was knee-deep and I jumped into the boat and straddled the big rubber tube and paddled with all my strength. Our last man was getting into the boat when the first breaker hit us. The bow shot up and came down with a jolt. That was a weak one?

We paddled furiously, trying to put as much distance between us and the beach before the next breaker hit. I could see it building as we raced toward it, trying to reach it before it broke. It was sucking the water up as it rose higher and higher. Then we were climbing up the front wall of the wave with the boat, paddling furiously in the onrushing wall of water. We reached the top moments before it crested, toppling over with a roar, leaving the boat in open water. That brought a sigh of relief from seven wet sailors.

Now that we had reached open water, we had to turn around and go back to the beach. We sat there for a few minutes, resting and looking back at the beach and watching the huge breakers roll in and crash with a roar. It was almost peaceful sitting there with the sound off in the distance and the choppy water rocking the boat. Then it was time to go back into that world of water power, a fury that we had not experienced before in our small rubber boats.

Just outside the breaker line, we sat for a few minutes trying to time the waves and watch for a weak one to ride on into the beach. When the word "Row!" came I dipped my paddle into the green water with all my strength and began paddling with even, strong strokes as the roar became louder and louder. We caught the first wave and rode it in partway, thinking we had it made until the next one caught us in the backwash. Before we knew what happened, the next wave bore down on us. With a roar and a sharp crack like timber breaking, the giant wave slammed down on top of us as it broke.

I paddled with all my strength when it hit. The boat was sucked backward as the wave rolled forward, taking the boat and rolling it over and over. I tried to hold onto the lifeline and the paddle as we rolled, but the line was torn from my grip. In the fury of the churning water, I slammed against the bottom, then was pulled back as I was caught in the undertow. I fought hard trying to reach the beach. Just then the boat slammed into me, pushing me down and rolling me over again. This time when my hands touched the bottom, I clawed for dry land and soon dragged my tired body out of the water and lay there exhausted. Another Raider lay beside me.

"You can get killed out there," I said, and saw only a short nod from the sailor next to me sucking air into his starved lungs.

A week or two later we boarded an LCI (landing craft, infantry) that waited offshore in rough water. As we jumped on board we saw our rubber boats lashed down on the deck.

The next night at about 0200 they woke us and told us to get ready to man our boats. "We're dropping you off on San Nicolas Islands near Ventura" an officer told us. "You will get three days' food supply and we'll come back and get you in ten days."

We boarded our small, ugly black rubber boats on a calm sea with fog hanging on the water. Someone on deck pointed which way it was to land and we began to row. We couldn't hear any surf. If there was land out there, there had to be surf noise. We paddled. The quietness was deafening and we realized that we were alone in a rubber boat in the Pacific Ocean with three days' supply of food and nothing else but cold water, darkness, and fog.

Each crew had a radio but we were ordered to use them only in case of an emergency. We felt as if we had been dropped off the end of the world. Just then a seal surfaced near the boat and barked. I almost jumped out of my skin.

We kept paddling in the dark, hoping we were going in the right direction. It had been some time since we had heard anything from the other boats. Then the coxswain yelled for us to stop paddling.

"Listen," he said.

Off in the distance we heard the faint sound of surf.

We paddled harder then and with more determination. The sound grew louder and soon became a roar as we braced ourselves to hit the beach, even though we couldn't see it.

"Back paddle!" the coxswain bellowed.

Then we could see it: We were being sucked into some rocks. Before we hit the rocks, a huge breaker broke over us, flipping the boat over as if it were a matchbox. We thrashed around in the dark for some minutes, trying to hold on to the lifelines, before the currents began pulling the boat away from the rocks. We didn't know what was in front of us or behind us. All we knew at the moment was not to get lost in the darkness without the boat. Our training kept us alive even though we hadn't worked together for long. As individuals we knew what we had to do and when we were able to do it. Soon we worked the boat away from the rocks and flipped it back over and boarded it. We began paddling again, hoping we were away from the rocks. We turned back toward the surf sound, knowing that the land had to be in there somewhere.

As the sound from the rocks began to fade, we picked up another sound up ahead and knew that had to be a beach. Although no one had told us ahead of time what to expect as far as rocks around the island or what kind of beach we would land on, we figured this had to be a safe spot.

That's when someone said, "Where's Mike?"

We realized we were a man short. It was too late to go back and look for him. We were caught in the pull of the breakers then and heading for the beach in the darkness. We could see a faint outline of land ahead. The roar came louder.

Then, without warning, a breaker caught us, rolling

the boat over and over. I felt the power of the ocean as we were all caught up in the churning water. I could feel the pull of the undertow and then I felt sand under my feet. At that moment we were sucked back out and another wave caught us and rolled over us again. I had lost my grip on the lifeline but I clung to my paddle. Another wave hit us rolling us toward land. This time when I felt the sand under my feet, I clawed for land and safety. Before I could celebrate, something hard hit me in the back and slammed me facedown in the sand as our ugly black boat surged on top of a wave and swept past me.

We crawled farther up the beach and dragged our boat to safety, then flopped in the sand to try to recover. A few minutes later someone began calling. When we got together and counted bodies, we were missing only one, Mike from my crew.

We knew we had to take a boat out and search for him. Time was running out before he would die in the cold water. It was hard to find seven men willing to take the risk of a rescue. The breakers broke almost on dry land, with little beach taper. That gave us little chance to launch a boat. Somebody broke radio silence and called the Coast Guard that we had a man missing at the island. They were sending a seaplane.

We got the last man to volunteer for the search and tried to launch our boat. We had to believe that Mike was still alive out there. The surf was so loud, we couldn't hear his call even if he made one. We tried to launch the boat and we were thrown back on the sand. It was like running into a stone wall. We couldn't get a running start because the breakers broke right on the land. Five feet from shore, the water was over our heads.

We put all of our strength into trying to get through the surf, and when we were thrown back it really took a lot out of us. Each time we failed, it was getting harder and harder to pick ourselves up off the sand and try again. We finally broke through the wall of water on the fifth try and were outside.

We paddled more by instinct than with strength because we had very little left. It was still dark and we started calling his name. We knew his four hours were running out. Minutes passed with no answers to our calls. We would paddle awhile and then stop and yell. It was beginning to get light in the east when we heard the first faint reply to our calls.

We found him in the dim light. He had pulled a lot of seaweed and kelp around him to help stay warm. He began to turn blue and he couldn't lift his arms. He was glad to see us. The seaplane came sliding in then and landed on the water, and we helped them lift Mike into the bird.

It was easier getting back to the beach in the daylight.

We made it through the ten days. Ate a lot of shellfish and seafoods and rationed our water. Some cans of food washed up on the beach, and that helped. We found a gallon can of powdered eggs and learned to eat it even without salt.

We were picked up and taken back to Morro Bay. Nobody ever told us just what part this experience had to do with our training as Scouts & Raiders.

After Morro Bay we went to Coronado, near San Diego, for three days and left on a Navy troop transport heading for Hawaii. It was on this trip that I realized that I loved to stand at the rail and watch the ocean. I never got seasick so I could stand there for hours, looking at the water. I loved to watch the albatross as they glided just above the water, almost never flapping their wings. They came close to the waves and swells but never touched the water in their graceful, effortless glide.

Then one morning we heard a woman singing a Hawaiian song over the PA system instead of the usual bugle call. The ship had picked up a Hawaiian radio station and played the music over the PA.

Later, when I went on deck, Diamond Head sat off the port side about half a mile. Diamond Head. Wow, that was really something. I had seen it in the movies, but now to have it sitting out there in front of me—and Waikiki Beach on the left, and the Royal Hawaiian Hotel in its pink splendor—were really something. Farther down the beach I could see the Aloha Tower.

The ship was standing off, waiting to get into Pearl Harbor. The Navy kept the submarine nets closed across the harbor entrance and would not open them at night. Now we waited and I thought about December 7, 1941. I was fifteen and my two older brothers were home on weekend passes from the military. We lived in a small town in southern Georgia. When they came home late in the afternoon, someone turned on the radio. The announcer told about the attack on Pearl Harbor. The voice made the notice: "All military personnel, report back to your base immediately."

Then the ship started moving again and approached the mouth of the harbor as a tugboat pulled the net away. A destroyer stood by, guarding, watching.

Pearl Harbor was a special place for the men in the Navy, and I remembered a friend who said her father had died on the *Arizona*. The island is flat around Pearl, with the mountains off in the distance. As the tugboat pulled away the nets for the ship to enter, I was not alone at the rail. The whole team was out watching. The harbor is like a river at this point and for about two miles, with the land flat, it was easy to see the masts of the ships up ahead, for the trees there were small. On the right was Hickam Field with Army planes coming and going.

Up ahead was a big red construction crane. Buildings began to appear on the right. Then the harbor opened up and divided, left and right. The large red crane dominated the scenery. I saw more ships everywhere. My ship kept moving slowly. To the right was Ford Island and its concrete ramps and hangars for the seaplanes.

Next we saw a large dry dock with a cruiser sitting high and dry. Then I looked down into the black waters of the harbor. The quietness was almost painful as I looked to the starboard side and the shrill sound of a bos'n's whistle filled the air, sending a chill up my spine. There it was! The Stars and Stripes hung limply just above the black water, mounted on some blackened grotesque piece of steel.

"That's the *Arizona*," someone whispered.

It seemed to me that any sound was much too loud at that moment. The whispering of the men seemed to carry for a long distance. I stood spellbound. I couldn't take my eyes off the flag and the blackened steel. My body felt as if it were frozen and I couldn't move a muscle. Then the bos'n whistle sounded again, unlocking my joints, and I could relax.

Our ship moved on and I saw the flag flutter slightly. The harbor opened up into a bay where many other ships were anchored. A few minutes later we heard the anchor of our ship drop into the waters of the East Lock.

Seaman First Class David Kinner
De Land, Florida

I WAS DRAFTED in July 1943 and chose to go into the Navy. I spent nine weeks at Great Lakes, Illinois, boot camp. After testing for aptitude, I was sent to Norfolk, Virginia, to join the amphibious forces. I took training there at Norfolk, Dam Neck, and Little Creek. Most of this involved learning how to shoot a .50-caliber machine gun, taking it apart, and putting it back together again.

In October of 1943 I was assigned to Fort Pierce, Florida, where I began training with a new Navy group called the Scouts & Raiders. At the camp I was assigned to a sixteen- by sixteen-foot tent right on the beach. Each tent held six guys: That was my crew. It was made up of six enlisted men and one officer. We had a coxswain, radioman, machine mechanic, signalman and two gunners. The crew officer was usually an ensign. I think I was in Scouts & Raiders Class No. 2, the second group to go through training there.

Our training involved a lot of night work with landing craft, underwater demolition, and exercising training. Since I was one of the gunners in the crew, I asked what kind of weapon I would have. They said none at the moment. All during training I didn't see a gun. When I got overseas, they issued me a .45 automatic.

I spent the winter at Fort Pierce training and in February of 1944 I shipped out. The vessel was a refrigerated one carrying fruit and vegetables to troops overseas. We were in a convoy and zigzagged over, taking twenty-eight days to hit North Africa. After a couple of stops to offload cargo in Oran and Algiers, we reached our destination of Bizerte, North Africa, in March 1944. It's a port city. From there we went inland to Ferryville. It was a French ammunition site that was built by the American Seabees. They had little to do for a time and lay around. Somebody found a captured German Kuebelwagen, but nobody could figure out how to get the transmission into gear. One day I found out that if I pushed down on the shift stick, I could get it into gear.

A few months later I and my crew of six were flown to Naples, Italy. Then we went on to the port town of Santa Maria Capua Vetere, Italy, where we practiced additional nighttime landing-craft work before we were loaded on a ship, the USS *Tattrell*, an old World War I destroyer. We sailed to Naples to take on personnel and supplies before settling into the area between Corsica and Salerno. At Corsica the Scouts & Raiders remained on ship while the members of a joint U.S. and Canadian First Special Forces bivouacked onshore. This group had already made sixteen invasions and had paid dearly. They were a tough-looking lot made up of paratroopers and Rangers.

We didn't know where we were headed, but figured we were preparing to invade southern France. This was known as Operation Anvil and later renamed Dragoon by Winston Churchill. The *Tattrell* sailed to two miles off southern France, just off the Îles d'Hyères. The objective by us and the Special Forces back on board was to secure the islands. One big island held a fortress manned by troops from countries overrun by the Germans.

On August 15, 1944, before dawn, I and my crew loaded into two small rubber boats with electric motors and headed to one of the islands. These electric motors were so noninsulated that when the Scouts got in the water, they felt a small shock. The island we hit was either Île du Levant or Port Cros. Most likely Port Cros, as that's the name in one of my World War II books listing all the places and vessels I shipped on. Our job as Scouts & Raiders were to set one man onshore with a light, then pull back 1,500 yards to sea. The man onshore shone a light toward the ship offshore. The rubber boats would align themselves in line and between that shore light and the ship. This provided the ship with a path to send in the troop landing boats. They were twelve-man rubber rafts towed to the 1,500-yard point by a motorized landing craft. The landing craft would work back to the mother ship and bring in more rafts filled with soldiers.

The two Scouts & Raiders boats were used to align two troop ships that night. After all the men were onshore and brought forward, I and my crew would pick up the shore light man and return to sea to a waiting PT boat. Just as we were looking for our man onshore in the darkness, somebody came charging toward us. I pulled out an Italian revolver I had been carrying because the .45 was too heavy. I started to aim at the intruder. My crew officer yelled for me to hold fire. It turned out the man charging up to us was the other crew's shore light man, who had become confused about which way to run for his pickup.

We got offshore and were picked up by the PT boat and went below to warm up. The assault was begun by the First Special Forces. It failed because they had to go up a steep hill and it had a high, thick wall. The Germans saw the attack and used mortar fire and phosphorus grenades on the troops below. The troops took cover in large piles of tree cuttings thrown over the wall after the trees were cut for firewood. The brush caught fire and several men burned to death.

Soon air support and offshore shelling by the heavy cruiser *Augusta* began. They shelled it all day and the next day the troops captured the fortress.

Back on the *Tattrell*, the Scouts saw the ship pick up three Germans from a sunken ship. They were put in the compartment where I was sleeping. Later I realized that my duffel bag with my .45 pistol still in Cosmoline was in there. Then I figured that these guys weren't going to try anything, they wanted out of the war in the worst way.

The casualties from the attack on the fortress were brought back to the *Tattrell*, including those burned corpses in body bags. The smell of the burned flesh was so strong, the bodies had to be laid out topside.

That was about it for my wartime experiences as a Scout & Raider. All that training and shifting around and going back and forth, and then we did one night of work that we had been trained for. We transferred some German prisoners, then went back to North Africa and our ride home. It took only twelve days because we were not in a convoy, where the fastest speed of the group is limited to the slowest ship in the convoy. I did help with a Hollywood film crew back in Fort Pierce, where they were making some training films for the Navy. I filled out the year in various bases in Virginia, Pennsylvania, and Illinois. I was discharged on December 3, 1945.

MOM Mate Second Class Paul Mann
Council Bluffs, Iowa

I WAS RECRUITED into the Scouts & Raiders from the Advance Amphibious Base in Arzew, Algeria. We trained at Porta Dex Poudles, Algeria. In my crew were James S. Maruea, our coxswain; Vernon Martz, our signal man; Mike Marusa, the bowhook; and me as the engineer. Ensign Earl T. Berry was our officer.

Our training lasted about four weeks. Then we were transferred to Admiral Hall's staff on the USS *Samuel Chase* (PA-25), a U.S. Coast Guard amphibious transport out of Oran, Algeria.

We then were assigned to LST (landing ship, tank) 345 for temporary duties in the landings at Gela, Sicily.

We did only two operations in Sicily, guiding Army DUKWs into the beach. In the same operation a group with LST 313 was bombed at the beach. Soon after that, our crew was disbanded and we all returned to LST 345 as members of the ship's company and our Scouts & Raiders' duties were finished.

I remained with the 345 and participated in operations in Italy and Normandy. I returned from England to the U.S. to attend submarine training.

James S. Maruea from my crew remained with the Scouts & Raiders and returned to the States for further training and went into the Underwater Demolition Teams. He won a Silver Star decoration for his work at Normandy.

Boatswain's Mate First Class William P. DeWitt
Ben Lomond, California

WHEN THE WAR started, I enlisted in the Navy and went to Little Creek, Virginia, and then to New York. There I boarded an LST that took me to Casablanca, Morocco. This was so early in the war that the French had not decided which side they were on, so we had to stay on board ship until they figured it out. When they did, we landed and rode north for ten hours, where we were told to establish a camp on a rutty hillside right after a heavy rain had washed half the hill away. We got some semblance of a camp put together with old, rotten hospital tents from World War I. The package of toilet paper they issued us in New York soon ran out, because everyone got dysentery from using greasy eating utensils. Our stay there got so boring that we were anxious for some action.

One day an officer came and asked if we would like to volunteer for the Scouts & Raiders. Needless to say, we jumped at the chance. They loaded us into a couple of jeeps and transported us about fifteen miles up the coast, where we took over some French cabanas for our quarters during training. Ensign Will Noel and Lieutenant Donnal were our trainers. Our uniform of the day was swimming trunks. We went on a different problem every night. We identified sections of beaches from aircraft photos, plus all the rest of the training. We left there after a time and traveled to a town farther north on the African coast called Mostaganem for more training. It was mostly hard physical workouts.

We left from there and were transported to Bizerte in northern Libya. There we loaded an LST with ammo and gasoline in ten-gallon cans for tanks and trucks. Aircraft fuel was brought up by means of another carrier. Nobody on board knew where we were going except the captain and the navigation officer.

We wound up at 0300 in rough seas with huge spotlights zeroing in on us from the island of Sicily. They were giving us pretty heavy fire, but we were throwing it right back at them. We emerged with a victory that could have been a real disaster. General Eisenhower nearly called it off at the last minute, then changed his mind after much consultation.

As soon as it was daylight, we directed ten floating tanks to the beach. Then we helped clear the area of mines on orders of the beachmaster. Even so, several men were severely wounded running their jeeps over mines. One of the assault boats had a line wrapped around its propeller shaft. One guy had to dive in with a knife and cut it loose. This is where a lot of men became heroes.

The next morning we were supposed to go back to Bizerte to get another load of fuel and other supplies but found that we couldn't back off the beach with our LST. We tried everything, unloading our boats and even firing blank charges from the five-inch 38. That is what caused my hearing disability. All this time we were being bombed, and amazingly one of their bombs was our salvation.

The bomb exploded right under the bow and washed all the sand away, so we floated free. As we went back to Tunis to pick up more supplies, we had to be pretty alert for submarines because we had no air cover or any support ships. After this return trip, four of our six Scouts & Raiders crew were transferred by air to Arzew, Algeria, for further Scout & Raider duty.

I was assigned to three antisubmarine boats, two of

which were on patrol at the same time. So that was the end of my Scouts & Raiders experience.

Chief Boatswain's Mate Ray B. Bristol
Piney Flats, Tennessee

I ENLISTED IN the Navy on February 14, 1941, and took my boot camp training at Norfolk. I served on the USS *George Clymer* and then, in the spring of 1942, I was chosen to join a new special-warfare group that didn't have a name yet. I trained under Phil H. Bucklew, who came to be known as the father of U.S. naval special warfare.

We trained in Norfolk and Maryland and learned to load and unload transports and practiced assaults on the beach. We also test-fired some of the first rockets the Navy used.

In November we were sent to North Africa for the Allied invasion. We were to mark the beach at Port Lyautey, Morocco. We went on shore from *APA-57* in advance of the assault troops to recon and bring in the troops on the right beach. After the troops landed successfully we returned to our ship about midday. The captain asked me if I would take a load of gasoline back to the beach. We had over a hundred cans of gas they needed onshore. The Germans were shelling the beach and the landing craft, and before we started to load the gas, our LCS was hit by a 138mm shell on the stern, which wrecked the craft. We got help and stripped all of the guns off the LCS before it went down. We caught a ride on another LCVP back to the APA.

On November 9, 1942, a terrible storm hit overnight and they said the waves were topping out at thirty-five feet. There were no landing craft to be seen anywhere because it was too rough to get them into the water from the mother ship and then the men loaded in.

The skipper of the ship sent for me and said he understood that I had a lot of time in LCMs. This was a fifty-foot-long craft to transport tanks and had twin diesel engines. He asked if I would try to take a load of ammo and a tank in that they needed at the beach. I told him I'd try. It was so rough we almost never got the LCM in the water and loaded. At last we made it. We had twenty-one soldiers on board and one light tank, which meant we were seriously overloaded. They said we were four hundred yards from the beach when we got the signal to start our run shoreward.

Just as we topped a large wave, we were hit in the stern of the LCM with an artillery round. This flipped the landing craft up on end. We jumped from the boat and it dumped all of the ammo and men and the tank into the water as it fell over on top of us. I didn't have a life jacket and almost drowned. I was bashed in the right knee, and it was so bad that when I got onshore I couldn't walk. My three-man crew carried me to a field hospital under a cliff, where they treated me and bandaged my knee so I could hobble around. My crew and I were on the beach several days guarding prisoners until we could catch a ride back to our ship.

Other Scouts moved to beaches as well on Fedala, and Safil. They bulled through the heavy surf on rubber boats, then searched the beach for obstacles and enemy gun emplacements. Then they set up colored lights to guide the landing forces onto the right beach. The landings were virtually unopposed, and the Allied soldiers established a firm beachhead before they moved on inland to find the Germans.

After that it was back to the States. Twenty of the men from North Africa were at Little Creek for a few days and then sent for specialized training to Fort Pierce, Florida, to get into the real Scouts & Raiders work.

In late spring 1943, I went with Ensign Bucklew to Tunisia for secret training for the upcoming landings in Sicily called Operation Husky. The vice admiral there sent the Scouts & Raiders to train with the British Submarine and Combined Operations Base on Malta. There we were introduced to the British use of the kayak in a folding-boat form. We had never seen such things. Wooden skeletons covered with a thin skin of rubber and canvas didn't seem to us to be a good way to confront an armed enemy shooting at us. But after a while we found out they could be useful. They were easy to handle on the water, light in weight at three hundred pounds, stable in rough water, and could hold seven men. They had a low profile and we could approach a shore closely without detection. And they were better for getting through the surf than the clumsy rubber boats and rafts.

First we were paired with a British man to help us learn how to handle the craft. Some of our guys hated them. I loved the kayaks. Somehow I had picked up the nickname of Cowboy in boot camp and it stuck. But I never figured that someday I'd be bobbing along on the ocean in a kayak. At first I thought the kayaks might break apart like toothpicks, but after a while I learned how to handle the craft even in rough water.

By early July we were scouting beaches along the Sicilian coast but still partnered with a Brit. The invasion was planned for January 10, but half a dozen beaches were still virtually unknown territory for the Allies. It was decided that we Scouts & Raiders had to go in and survey those last six beaches. The Navy didn't agree and said that would make the enemy aware of their movements and watch for anyone near the beaches. But the brass won and we were ordered to survey the unknown areas.

Just after midnight I was on board a landing craft as it headed toward our prearranged drop-off point five hundred yards off the southern coast of Sicily. I had a three-man kayak. I was in the rear to navigate. The middle man was along to do any wet water work in the survey, and in front was a soldier with a submachine gun. He was a comfort but not much defense if we got into trouble.

I was checking out the craft, making sure it was ready to sail, when the ship's captain told me we were on station and I should launch. A strong wind blew across the bow, whipping on board froth from the heavy swells. Besides, we were more than a mile from the beach, not five hundred yards. The captain demanded that I launch. I was furious and cursed the overly cautious officer to his face. "If I make it back from this mission, I'll see that something is done about this," I told him.

He outranked me, so I had to launch. The crew started to put the kayak over the side as waves broke against the pitching ship. Before we could get settled in the narrow cockpits, the kayak was slammed against the ship's hull by a huge wave and crushed like an egg. We got back on the ship and tried to launch a seven-man rubber boat. It was difficult, but at last we were onboard and paddling toward our objective, Beach 71. Paddling was difficult in the rough sea for three men in a seven-man boat that was not properly inflated. At

0255 we were about two hundred yards off the right flank of the beach when firing began on the beach. We saw that the Rangers had already landed and, as there was only one place to land on Beach 71, we were not needed. We paddled back out to sea and were picked up at 0815 by LCF 15. We were caught in the searchlights that night several times but we did not take any rounds as a result.

Ensign Phil Bucklew made it to his Beach 72. He used a motorized landing craft instead of the kayak and made it to Green Beach 72. It was one of the six beaches in the landing area. His motor sound drew the enemy searchlights, and the German 88mm artillery guns opened fire as he zigzagged toward shore. Some of his swimmers jumped off the boat and swam to shore so they could mark the beach with lights. The invasion followed and was successful.

Next on the agenda for us was Salerno. Again the admirals and generals didn't know much about the beaches around Salerno and it was our job to find out. We did this in the wee hours of the morning before the invasion.

For this one I was paired with Ensign Bucklew in a two-man kayak. The landing craft dropped us off five hundred yards from the beach, into calm waters and a black sky. There were four crews in four boats set to scout out blue, yellow, green, and red beaches. The size and slope of the beaches was not known, so we had to find it out and report.

It was midnight when Phil Bucklew and I put on our black coveralls and put black grease on our face and hands. It was a flat sea and we concentrated on getting to shore as quickly as we could in our kayak. We had no maps, so we followed our compass course and hoped.

Then the shelling began. Rounds dropped in the ocean behind us and a lot hit the shore ahead of us. Our own ships were walking rounds into shore, not knowing we were there. We were about two hundred yards from shore when a German 88 round hit close to our kayak and nearly blew us out of the water. Bucklew was behind me in the kayak and asked me if I was hit. I said no and he said he lost his britches. He said a piece of shrapnel about the size of his hand cut the belt buckle off his black coveralls.

We paddled on toward shore and Bucklew asked me if I was on fire. I told him I couldn't be on fire: I was too wet to burn. He said I was on fire and smoke was coming up in his face. It was red-hot shrapnel that had hit my life jacket and was smoldering in the lining. We didn't know it then but there were twenty three shrapnel holes in the kayak when we got back to the ship.

We paddled faster and made it through the fire to shore. The approach had no problems for landing craft, and the beach was wide enough for a beachhead. We signaled that to the boats and then set up the lights to point the landing craft to our beach. Despite concentrated fire from both sides on the beach and the land behind it, we guided the troops into our beach. We survived increasing enemy crossfire on our position.*

Then we grabbed our kayak and paddled back to sea. Without warning, a British ship moved in close to

---

*Author's note: For their actions on this landing, both Ray B. Bristol and Ensign Phil H. Bucklew were awarded Silver Stars for "Steadfastly maintaining exposed positions until the hazardous mission had been completed . . ." and "voluntarily assisting in locating and marking a landing beach despite heavy enemy gunfire and bombing attacks and difficulties imposed by complete darkness."

shore and fired salvos of fifty rockets at a time against the enemy positions. We froze in place. The orange glare of the rockets burning trails clearly outlined our kayak on the flat sea. That encouraged us to paddle harder than we ever had before to get out of the light. The sea was lit up like New York City. We had to paddle through that light in plain view of the enemy. As often happens in a bombardment, some rounds fell short and enemy shells came near us, but we got through the hail of shrapnel and all four kayaks made it back to the ship safely.

Later on land we were in an old building, resting on the Fourth of July, when eighty German planes dropped bombs and some hit our sanctuary. The raid wounded seven of our men. I was busy trying to stop the bleeding on one man hit from his stomach to his knees. He looked like he had been hit with a shotgun. He lay on the floor swearing at the German planes. He was furious because he didn't think he could have sex anymore. He lived and stayed in our group. Much later, when we were walking across China, he would drop his pants now and then and pick out another piece of shrapnel that had worked out to the surface. After he got home and discharged, I heard that he had a long life and had six kids.

The rest of the invasion went smoothly and the Germans and Italians were forced to fall back. The Allies were safely on the European continent for the first time in the war.

In mid-September of 1943, Bucklew, Leonard, Martin, L'Heureux, and I got orders to go to England. We made the trip in three weeks in a Coast Guard LCI (landing craft, infantry). Once in Falmouth, we reported to the U.S. Command's Amphibious Craft and

Maintenance Base, where they looked upon us as recon specialists.

One more kayak mission took place on December 31, 1943, that I heard about. Anzio, Italy, was the target, and the beaches needed recon, so two teams of Scouts & Raiders were sent in.

Ensign Kenneth E. Howe and Ensign Carrnen F. Pirro were in one kayak. Pirro said he felt the dread of a deadly premonition just before leaving and told his friends. A letter from his wife told him that she had given birth to a baby girl. He feared he would never see his child.

The second kayak carried Ensign Jerome Donnelly and one other man. Both boats reached their appointed beaches without trouble. Shortly after, the sky erupted with flares and small-arms fire coming near them. This wasn't out of the ordinary. The teams made their recon and Ensign Donnelly and his teammate headed back to sea in their kayak. Pirro and Howe didn't show up at the pickup point. After waiting three hours, the landing boat had to leave. The two men were the only Americans to be lost in action while on a kayak operation.

Scouts & Raiders tried to work with the kayaks, but they were difficult in rough seas. At last they perfected the use of submarines to launch the kayaks fifty yards from shore. The men would paddle to shore, set up the landing lights, paddle back to the submarine, get on board, and submerge. This technique was seldom used.

As D-day approached, I went with our veteran crew with Ensign Bucklew, Martin, Leonard, and L'Heureux on board a lead LST. We joined a convoy in the D-day invasion fleet that was at sea for two days in foul weather. Then at H hour minus 12 on June 6, 1944, our scout boat was launched from the LST. Our mission was to provide covering fire for the Navy Combat Demolition Units and "floating tanks." Then we would set up seaward facing the lights at Red Beach Center and guide in the assault waves.

In the darkness and choppy seas, we couldn't be sure if we were steering the right course. When we were five miles offshore, a beach area ten miles off the starboard bow lit up with machine-gun tracers, bomb explosions, and star shells. It was a Ranger raid at Pointe du Hoc as a diversion. We were still not sure we were at the right beach. Then as we came closer we spotted a familiar church steeple that was one of the landmarks. Omaha Red Beach Center was dead ahead. German shore batteries tried to stop us as we made several passes along the shoreline. One gun in particular located on the second floor of a building on the beach was coming too close to us. Our crew fired rockets but didn't stop the gun. Then I opened up with my twin .50-caliber machine guns. They said I lived up to my Cowboy tag by silencing the German guns.

We quickly ran into shore and set up our beach lights to guide in the waves of landing craft. Then we headed back out to guide in the floating tanks, which were not living up to their designation as "floating." Six in the wave made it to shore; the other twenty-seven foundered in the surf line with the crews struggling to escape. Ensign Bucklew directed cover fire for the NCDUs, fixing charges on Teller-mined "hedgehogs," large underwater obstacles designed to wreck landing craft. They blew gaps in the line to let the landing craft come through. The deadly maze of wood and concrete obstacles became more apparent as it grew lighter. The NCDUs suffered 60 percent casualties at bloody Omaha Beach, but they did their job.

Many of the LCIs unloaded their troops too far off the beach and the soldiers struggled in the head-high water. We did our best to rescue as many of the heavily gear-laden troops as possible.*

After twenty months in Europe, I and most of the other Scouts & Raiders returned to the States to Fort Pierce. Lieutenant Bucklew became our officer in charge. Soon he and the other combat veterans were looking for some action.

After Lt. Bucklew made some inquiries, we received new orders. I went with him and twenty other Scouts & Raiders known as Unit Buck to China for what became guerrilla warfare duty or, as it was officially known, "a different kind of war." We were on a boat for forty days to get to Calcutta, India. From there we moved behind the Japanese lines in China to recon the beaches of the South China Sea for possible landing sites. We lived with the Chinese and got no food or help from our military services. We ate whatever we could find and wore Chinese clothes. Then we were flown deep into China

---

*Author's Note: For his actions on D-day, Ray B. Bristol, Boatswain's Mate First Class, was awarded the Bronze Star medal. The citation:

> For heroic achievement as a Crew Member of the Lead Scout Boat attached to an Assault Group during amphibious operations against the coast of France, June 7, 1944. Cool and courageous in the face of a devastating German barrage, Bristol gallantly carried out his assignments and, despite his own personal wounds and utter fatigue, aided in rescuing and comforting his comrades wounded by the enemy's fire. His complete disregard for his own safety and his unflinching devotion to duty under the most hazardous conditions reflect the highest credit upon BRISTOL and were in keeping with the highest traditions of the United States Naval Service.

and dumped out to make our way to the coast by sampan and by walking over the mountains. The only place we had to take a bath was in the rivers, and they were filthy.

I got an infection in my right ear and thought I was going to die. The side of my temple swelled up and every step I took was like getting hit in the head with a two-by-four. This fouled up my hearing. We were also covered with jungle rot, which did not clear up until late in 1946 and has reappeared several times since on my feet.

When the two nuclear bombs dropped on Japan, that ended the war for us in China as well. We made it to port and were eventually sent home. I was discharged from the Navy on December 22, 1946.

The Reverend Don Hardenbrook
Nampa, Idaho

I TRAINED WITH the Scouts & Raiders in Fort Pierce, Florida. After my training I was sent to SACO (Sino-American Cooperative Organization), Naval Group China, under General Tai Li and Merry Miles. We worked behind the Japanese lines in China.

My part in it came late in the war. I did stay on to shuttle ships to China for the Nationalist Chinese Armed Forces. We were called the Subic China Ship Group. We put U.S. Navy ships back into working order, sailed them to China, and taught the Chinese crew how to operate them. They learned quickly. Then we went out and got into a firefight with the Communists and then turned the ship over to the Chinese. We flew back to Subic Bay, Philippines, and repeated the process over and over for fourteen months after World War II was over. Later I was recalled into the Navy when China sent troops into North Korea to fight the U.S. After that, I got out of the Navy and started preaching the Gospel. I'm now the visitation minister for the Church of the Brethren in Nampa, Idaho.

Seaman First Class Clyde C. Hammer (deceased)
Fostoria, Ohio.
(Millie Hammer, Clyde Hammer's widow, sent this material about her late husband.)

CLYDE HAMMER WAS proud of his part in the Scouts & Raiders operations. He didn't talk much about them but I know he trained at Fort Pierce, Florida, and was later a member of SACO (Sino-American Cooperative Organization), the Scouts and Raiders who worked in SACO during World War II. He joked that they were known as the Naval Group of China and the "Rice Paddy Navy."

Clyde, along with two other men from his home town of Fostoria, were in SACO. They were W. W. Ernest and W. E. Anderson. All played a role in one of the most romantic and dangerous episodes of the war. They were members of a naval group of guerrillas, intelligence agents, and weather observers who worked behind the Japanese lines all over Asia.

The group was formed shortly after Pearl Harbor, at first as strictly a weather-reporting unit. As the needs grew, so did SACO. Soon it was providing the U.S. Fleet and the Army's 14th Air Corps—in addition to the Chinese and U.S. Army headquarters—with weather and intelligence on movements of Japanese ships, troops, and supplies. Near the end it became a dangerous fighting outfit, killing Japanese, blowing up trains, and raiding Japanese outposts. At the end of the war the SACO domain spread from the Indo-China border to the Gobi Desert.

Their information helped the 14th Air Corps to mine coastal waters, forcing the Japanese freighters and convoys out to sea, where the ships were attacked by American submarines.

Weather information helped the Navy to decide when to stage invasions on Japanese islands. Usually the men could get behind the Japanese lines by air. But soon the SACO men became so good at disguises that, when guided by the Chinese, they could slip through enemy lines. Over the entire SACO operation, no member was ever detected or captured by the Japanese.

Seaman First Class James T. McGuire
Chicago, Illinois

IN EARLY 1945 an offer seeking personnel for prolonged and hazardous duty as members of "Amphibious Roger" or "Under Water Demolition" was made to members of the Little Creek, Virginia, Naval Amphibious training base. Having just turned eighteen years of age, this was an offer I couldn't refuse.

Upon reporting to the personnel office as directed, we inquired as to what Amphibious Roger and Under Water Demolition were. In typical Navy fashion we were informed that Roger was for sailors who wanted to play Marines, and the UDT involved swimming. That was all the information they had.

The buddy I was with, Gordon Alva Redmond from

Detroit, advised me that he wasn't the best swimmer, so maybe we should sign up for the Roger group. We did.

Shortly after, we were placed on a train for Fort Pierce, Florida. Upon arrival we were assigned to a tent in the area posted as the Scouts & Raiders Training Camp.

We were assigned to Roger III Group. Training was different from anything we had done before in the Navy. It was very physical but team- and individual-oriented. The uniform was greens, helmet liner, and sand shoes. We wore that outfit at all times in and out of the water.

The equipment was a seven-man rubber boat, which was manned by one officer and six enlisted men, a variety of small arms, a sheath knife, and plenty of explosives. We had blocks of TNT, Primacord, Craterin, charges, etc. When I view today's SEALs, I realize we were bare bones in comparison with today's warfare needs.

But to have been a member of a group of men dedicated to duty, no matter what the equipment or the odds, developed a brotherhood that lives to this day.

Amphibious Roger III included Gordon Redmond of Detroit, Michigan, and William Miller of Chicago, Illinois. Amphibious Roger IV included Ernie MacDonald of Brockton, Massachusetts, and its CO was Lieutenant Commander George Becker.

I began training with Roger III but was hospitalized for a gastric disorder and granted approval to retrain with Roger IV.

Roger IV completed training with a weekend maneuver that resulted in the capture of the Florida community of Okeechobee. The war in the Pacific ended and my unit was dispatched to the fleet. I eventually joined a small boat operation in Hong Kong and became a coxswain of LCVPs and LCMs. I worked my way home on the submarine tender USS *Holland* in July 1946.

Lieutenant (jg) Sidney S. Chapin
Hampstead, North Carolina

DURING OUR TRAINING at the Scouts & Raiders camp at Fort Pierce, Florida, in the fall of 1943, we always had physical exercises. One of our instructors was Big John Tripson who weighed in at about 230 pounds and was at least six four.

One of the games we played was "horse and rider," or more commonly called "bullfights." Thirty of us would run around in a large circle. When a command was given to "Jump on the back of the man in front of you," each of us would speed up until we mounted the back of another man.

My mistake was that I jumped on Big John's back, all 135 pounds of me. The idea of the game was to knock the other horses and riders down. When you were knocked down, you had to do pushups until only one horse and rider was left.

With Big John as my horse, this was a snap, and we were soon the last ones standing. However, then the next phase of the game started. We changed horse and riders. This meant whoever was the horse now became the rider. When Big John jumped on my back, I staggered under the load. His feet scraped the ground, he was so big. As soon as the bullfights started, we were knocked flat and did pushups until the game was over.

Big John Tripson was an all-American football

player at the University of Alabama. He was awarded the Navy Cross during the North Africa invasion and was an instructor at the Scouts & Raiders School. He died on July 15, 1997, and was my friend.

After the invasion of Normandy in early June 1944, I made seven more trips across the English Channel prior to my release from LST 315. Davis, Frost, I, and other Scouts & Raiders boat crews were sent to a rest and rehabilitation camp for R&R called Sandridge near the town of Torquay on the southern coast of England.

As we walked into the camp, we were met by an older man who was working out on a chinning bar. We watched him do a few chins. Back on the ground, he asked me, "How many chins can you do?" I eyed him up and down and said, "I can do one more than you can." Thus the gauntlet was down and he proceeded to do ten chins. Well, I did eleven. He was astonished and said, "You are now my athletic officer and I am Commander Van Alen, boss of this base."

Each morning Commander Van Alen led a one-mile cross country-run with yours truly right behind him. This was a great base with few duties, warm beer, and good liberty available. Commander Van Alen later became known as "Mr. Tennis" and was the man who invented the tiebreaker that forever changed the face of the game. He died in September 1991. It was a pleasure to know him.

In early October 1944 our group of Scouts & Raiders was assigned priority number 1 in San Francisco and designated to fly on the *Martin Mars* aircraft out of Oakland. We had twenty-one men in our group. The *Mars* was the world's largest flying boat and weighed seventy-two tons. It could carry twenty tons of cargo to the farthest spot on earth in five days or less.

Our flight from Oakland to Hawaii took fourteen hours. The plane had two decks. One was filled with double-decker bunks and the other had MacArthur chairs. There was a small galley that seated five and the plane also had a shower.

The wings on the *Mars* were so thick that the crew could enter them to service the engines while in flight. One hundred and fifty fully equipped soldiers could be transported. The cubic content of the giant was equal to a fourteen-room mansion.

If you stood in on one wing, the other wing tip would tower two hundred feet into the air, higher than a twenty-story building. It contained seven and a half miles of wiring, almost two miles of pipe, and twenty-four in-plane telephones. It had flown at one time nonstop from Maryland to Natal, Brazil, a distance of 4,375 miles. It was powered by four 2,200-horsepower engines. We were privileged to have flown on her.

My first scouting mission was in late February 1945 with the 8th Army under the command of Lt. General Eichelberg, at that time on Leyte Island, the largest of the Philippine Islands. I was accompanied by Second Lt. Clarence W. Lowrey of the 41st Division and First Lt. William F. Wheeler from the 8th Army Command.

Our mission was to check out the area around Zamboanga, Mindanao, for possible assault-landing beaches, enemy strength, and the nature of their defenses. Our PBY took off and landed about forty miles up the coast from that city. Three signal fires from the fires onshore let the pilot know it was okay to land his plane.

The guerrilla force was commanded by Captain Don Lacovers. He had escaped from the Bataan Death March. He met our PBY in a dugout canoe at twelve noon. The pilot just about threw us out of the plane, as we were in Japanese territory and he did not want to get caught with his aircraft on the water.

I hiked about fifty miles in the next two days through mountainous country with many streams to cross and water up to my hips. There were lots of leeches to suck our blood.

While the Army guys stayed at Lacovers's headquarters, I was hiking across a peninsula. My group consisted of eight black-toothed Moro natives of the area with shaved heads, loincloths and menacing curved swords attached to their waists. They chewed betel nut, which they kept in a bag tied to their wrists. It made their lips ruby red and their teeth black. This was a group of tough hombres. We stopped our hike on top of the mountains and took time out to rest and sleep. By that time it was midnight.

We had no communications except by hand signals. When we stopped to rest, I had a blanket and a poncho in my pack. The Moros had nothing. With one eye open I watched the group, as I was sure that they would chop off my head. They loved cigarettes and luckily I had a carton. After a long, scary night, we were on the way again at first light.

I had with me some aerial photos of the shore around the city of Zamboanga. I showed these to the natives, who had escaped from the city prior to the Japanese invasion. They responded by telling me the depth of the water in feet in front of their houses.

After returning to the Lacovers headquarters, we coordinated the information I had gathered and then lit three smoke fires as our signal for the pickup plane to land. By now this was my fourth day and I was happy to get out of there. We were the first Americans that they had seen in over three years.

During the assault landing on Zamboanga on March 10, 1945, one of my responsibilities was to deliver a chart. The chart was made from a hydrographic recon of the beach made the day before, on March 9. Making this recon with me were Lt. (jg) J. T. Davis, Bosn' Mate 2/C R. J. Cappa, Motor Machinist's Mate 2/C Ken. W. Kachline, Bosn's Mate 2/C W. J. Ryan, and Seaman 1/C B. Cardwell.

This chart marked coral reefs, which were quite prevalent in the landing area. It also marked where LST ships could land and discharge their cargo. Naturally the beach master and the Army wanted this chart pronto.

Our two scout boat teams had charted the beach in two Australian whaleboats attached to the HMS *Warrego*, manned by crews from the ship. That night, after returning to the ship, we prepared the charts with information from the recon.

We departed the *Warrego* and headed for the flagship of Admiral Royal, the USS *Rocky Mount*, anchored offshore. Upon arrival, we gave one chart to the operations officer and he ordered us to deliver the other chart to the beach master on shore.

As you realize, this was an assault landing, and the shore was not a particularly safe place. There was one building that stood out prominently. Naturally this was to become headquarters for the beach master and the Army. However, the Japs had other thoughts for this building. As they retreated to the mountains, they continued to fire mortars in and around the headquarters area. Guess where we were told to deliver the charts? Well, after we hit the beach about three hundred yards from our objective, all was well. I was with a Sublieutenant Cole from the *Warrego* and we proceeded to our objective just fine. But no sooner did we deliver the chart, when a mortar attack took place. It was scary. You heard a loud whistling sound for about two to three seconds that kept getting louder as it came closer, and then that stopped and a big explosion took place. As I said before, the Japs had this building pretty well zeroed in.

We got out of the target area as quickly as possible, and it's amazing how fast you can run and how far you can go in two or three seconds. Just prior to the whistling stopping, you hit the deck and prayed. After the explosion, you're up again and running. However the sublieutenant with me took off like Jesse Owens and never stopped until he reached his beloved whaleboat.

Several ships, LSTs, LCIs, and LCMs were hit during the morning mortar attacks, but our charts and marking buoys helped in landing nineteen of the twenty LSTs assigned to this operation. We stayed in the area four or five days and did several more recon missions.*

On March 22, 1945 we were assigned to do beach reconnaissance on Pulupandan town and its vicinity on

---

*Author's Note: For his work at Zamboanga, Lt. (jg) Sidney Chapin was awarded the Silver Star medal. The citation:

> For conspicuous gallantry and intrepidity as Officer-in-Charge of Amphibious Scouts in action against enemy Japanese forces during pre-landing reconnaissance of the beaches at Zamboanga, Philippine Islands on March 9, 1945. Despite heavy hostile machine-gun and rifle fire which wounded two of his assistants, Lieutenant, Junior Grade, Chapin made a survey, took soundings and laid buoys immediately adjacent to the enemy-held shoreline, thereby rendering great assistance to our attack and landing forces. His courage and gallant devotion to duty were in keeping with the highest traditions of the United States Naval Service.

Western Negros Island in the central Philippines. That afternoon Bob Cappa, Ken Kachline, and myself were told to find the hydrographic conditions offshore, inshore, and on the immediate beach, and the beach gradient in the vicinity of Pulupandan town.

Our Scout team was picked up from the USS *George W. Ingram* about 1500. We boarded *PT-490* and, escorted by *PT-496*, we proceeded to Impampulga Island in the Guimaras Strait. There we made a rendezvous with Lt. Col. Long in charge of the Army survey team. It was decided that the Scouts & Raiders would do the inshore hydrographic survey on the immediate beach area, while the Army party would do the offshore survey.

With the escort of two PT boats one LCM flak boat, one LCM salvage boat, and one Army picket boat, we Scouts proceeded in an LCVP to the area, arriving off Negros about 2130. Lt. Col. Long and our party, using a portable fathometer attached to the LCVP, started north along the coast, taking soundings from 300 to 1,500 yards offshore. The flak boat gave the survey party close cover with their guns in case of an emergency. The PT boats and the Army picket boat anchored about 2,500 yards offshore.

At about 2300 our team left the LCVP in a rubber boat three hundred yards south of the pier at Pulupandan town and sounded from three hundred yards offshore to the beach. Working our way south with the current and wind in our favor, we observed a group of Filipinos on the beach watching us. After a rather large group had gathered, we landed and brought two guerrillas back out to the flak boat.

After questioning, the guerrillas reported that seven Japs were in the garrison at Pulupandan and ten were at the garrison at Valladolid. They said all the other Japs had fled to the mountains, including six thousand who had been stationed at Bago. After conferring with Lt. Col. Long, it was decided to take the guerrillas back ashore and continue with the survey.

Our scout team landed again about 2,200 yards south of the pier and surveyed the immediate beach area and terrain back to the main road. The guerrillas told us that a Jap patrol was in the area, so we left the beach and paddled seaward. By flashing the prearranged signal, we brought in the LCM salvage boat and we climbed on board. No further survey could be made by the Scouts because of increased current and wind velocity.

At about 0200 23 March 1945, the survey was completed and the Scouts returned to *PT-490*, which remained in the area until morning on patrol. At about 1100 on March 23 we returned to the USS *Ingram* with our report.

Our summary of our survey: The Japs had left the area, except for a few personnel in outposts, and fled to the mountains. These few remaining Japs had several .50-caliber machine guns, a trench mortar, and a few small arms. They might have machine guns mounted on the pier, but no coastal guns or field pieces were known to be in the area. The six thousand Japs who were at Bago had gone to the mountains.

The beach extended from the pier on the north at Pulupandan town about 200 yards south to a large fish trap about 320 yards offshore. The width of the beach varied from 30 feet to 50 feet at low tide to 12 feet at high tide. A sand bar ranging from 200 yards to 400 yards in width ran parallel to the beach from the pier south. It varied from 400 yards to 600 yards offshore at its closest edge. At low tide the shallowest parts of the bar had a depth of 3.5 to 4 feet. With the height of the high water tide ranging up to 5 feet, landing craft could possibly cross the bar.

Inside the bar, the beach gradient was fairly steep, with depths as follows: 140 yards offshore, 11 feet; 80 yards offshore, 8 feet; 50 yards offshore, 5 feet; 20 yards offshore, 3 feet.

The beach itself was steep and composed of coarse, hard sand tending to be granules. It would easily permit the movement of vehicles and troops. Sparse coconut trees and shrubs covered the terrain immediately behind the beach, with scattered holes in the vicinity that was otherwise flat and level. Single strands of barb wire about chest high acted as fences in this area. The main two-lane paved highway lay from 100 to 200 yards inland and was flanked by a drainage ditch 10 feet wide and 5 feet deep.

On June 7, 1945, I and my boat team, which included R. J. Cappa and Ken Kachline, arrived at Brunei Bay onboard HMAS *Lachlan*. That was three days before the Zebra attack was planned. The next day we, with Lt. Starkey and a boat crew from the British ship, did a recon of Green Beach near Brunei Bluffs. The purpose of this trip was to find out if LCMs could land on Green Beach.

We took soundings by use of a fathometer and hand lead lines. Close fire support was available by LCIGs and LCSes, but was not used as no enemy fire was encountered. We finished the recon and sent our details to the TC by radio.

Our soundings were reduced to chart data, and distances offshore were observed from the high-water mark. The length of the beach was five hundred yards and the width varied from twenty five yards at low water to ten feet at high water. The gradient of this beach was gradual and no obstructions were found. The current was negligible and LCMs could beach there easily.

The flanks were marked with white flag buoys seventy-five yards offshore in seven feet of water. A bar with light surf was found thirty yards offshore. In taking the soundings we found that the left flank was one foot deeper than the right flank.

On Z-1 day a recon of White Beach on Muara Island was carried out by the Scouts and Lt. McGee of the British Navy and a boat crew from the *Lachlan*. The purpose was to determine if White Beach had a mud or sand bottom and if LCTs could beach there. Naval gunfire was available for close-fire support craft with direct air cover for spotting. No enemy fire was encountered and a radio message was sent giving details of the successful recon.

There were no obstructions on White Beach and it had a hard sand bottom. Soundings agreed with the chart data and LCTs could easily land there.

Our Scout team further assisted the hydrographic unit from the British ship as needed, and I participated in the successful recon of Weston town on 16 June 1945.

Sid Chapin adds: "One of my team members in the Pacific was Ken Kachline. He was awarded the Bronze Star Medal for his heroic service. His citation:

> The Bronze Star Medal is awarded to Kenneth Whitfield Kachline, motor machinist's mate second class for heroic service as an Amphibious Scout on the staff of commander of the Seventh

Amphibious Force, in action against enemy Japanese forces in the Philippine Islands, from January to September, 1945. Making pre-assault reconnaissance of the landing beaches at Zamboanga, Negros Island and Brunei Bay, Kachline also participated in the assault landings at Lingayen, Zamboanga, Tarkakan and Brunei Bay and, cool under heavy enemy fire, contributed materially to the success of these amphibious operations. His courage and devotion to duty were in keeping with the highest traditions of the United States Naval Service.

Lieutenant (jg) John Macy
Carlsbad, California

I WAS IN the V-12 college officer training program at Northwestern University in Chicago when an officer came through talking about the Scouts & Raiders and asking for volunteers. I signed on in March of 1944 and was sent to Fort Pierce, where I went through the regular Scouts & Raiders training.

I was an ensign at the time. When our class graduated, the whole group was sent to New York to the Hudson Hotel, where we were in Naval Intelligence school for six weeks. In September of 1944 they sent all of us to Pearl Harbor.

The war was changing in the Pacific. There was less need for the Scouts & Raiders and more need for UDT operations. The Navy gave us a choice: We could choose to go into Naval Intelligence and be assigned to a ship as an intelligence officer, or to go into the UDT program. I chose to go with the UDT and was sent back to Fort Pierce. We had received little training in explosives and demolition in the Scouts & Raiders.

So I went through a quite a bit different UDT program with the swimming and physical training and the demolition work. After we finished we were sent to Maui, to the UDT base there, where I was assigned to UDT Team No. 23. We soon boarded a ship and were on our way into the Pacific to participate in Operation Olympic: the amphibious invasion of Japan itself.

We were in mid Pacific when word came about the nuclear bombs being dropped on Japan and then the August 15 surrender. Our ship was diverted to South Korea, where we did some recon work near Seoul. Then we were sent to Tsingtao, China, where we did some more friendly recon work on beaches.

Soon we were on our way back to the States and landed in Coronado in December 1945. The war was over, my duty done, and I resigned from the service and went back to civilian life.

Ensign William C. Sheppard

My Scouts & Raiders team left Lingayen airstrip under verbal orders to proceed to Mindoro on 9 March 1945. We landed at Mindoro on 9 March, 1945 at 1430 and proceeded to the MTB base. We made arrangements with Lt. Hallowell, the CO of RON 16, for us to leave the following morning for Panay.

Our party got under way at 1230, 10 March on board the MTB No. 224 and accompanied by MTB No. 226. Due to rough seas and foul weather, our speed had to be cut down to save fuel, and we arrived late off our objective. We got there at 2400 and our Scout team put off in a rubber boat a mile and a half from the beach. When we hit the beach and verified that it was the correct one, we flashed out the prearranged signal to the MTBs and they pulled back out to sea with instructions to return at 0400 that same early morning.

While approaching the beach and while making the survey, there was constant small-arms fire and occasional explosions that sounded like artillery, mortars, or hand grenades at an estimated distance of three or four miles down the beach east of us. We could see occasional tracers and the glow from one large fire. It was believed to be guerrillas harassing the Japanese.

After hiding the rubber boat in the brush, our three-man party made a recon up the river on the left side of the beach to make double certain that it was the desired beach by identifying the bridge and highway. We observed two men with a small fire by the bridge, but we were not detected by them. We believed they were bridge guards. We then returned to the beach and made soundings in water up to six feet by wading.

It was low tide and the fishermen started coming out to run their fish traps, and it was difficult to evade them while taking soundings. We started back to get the rubber boat to take the deeper soundings and were seen by five Filipinos sitting in the edge of the brush. We were so close when we saw them that we had to keep walking by. One of them stood and said something, but sat back down when we didn't answer. After passing, we slipped back undetected to see if they were following us or going to leave the area. They were still there.

I then took Scouts Coxswain Leonard Hood with me in the rubber boat to take deep soundings and left Gunner's Mate Third Class J. J. Hedderman on the beach to signal where to take the soundings.

Nothing eventful happened until we returned to the

beach to pick up Hedderman and started back out to contact the MTBs. When we were between 250 and 300 yards off the beach, we were fired on by a rifleman from the direction of the river mouth. We went over the side and kept submerged as much as possible and still held on to the boat for about ten minutes and kept moving out to sea all the time.

We flashed the prearranged signal out to the MTBs and were picked up about 0430. We returned to MTB base at Mindoro and sent the desired information by dispatch to Commander Task Force Group Admiral Struble.

The second planned recon was canceled by the commander of the MTB base due to bad weather, rough seas, and long distances to be traveled. We then returned to the USS *Ingram* by air and made our full report to Admiral Struble on 12 March 1945. I reported that both Hood and Hedderman were extremely cool and did good work under trying conditions.

On 16 March, 1945, I joined a Sixth Army Alamo Scout team composed of Lt. Jack Chanley, S/Sgt. Glen Watson, S/Sgt. Allen Throkmorton, Sgt. Bob Walters, and two Filipino radio operators at the Alamo Scout Training Center.

On 17 March the Scout team flew out to Muloc Buloc, which is directly across southern Luzon from Legaspi. We met Lt. Ellsworth and a band of Filipino guerrillas there and paddled down the coast to a barrio called San Rafael, where we spent the night.

On 18 March we paddled on down the coast to a village named Donsol. A different guerrilla band took us up the river to Banuangurang. The river became too shallow to paddle, so we went on native trails to Jovellar, where the Sixth Army had been dropping supplies to the guerrillas. The next day we continued on to Pariaan to the group's headquarters.

On 20 March we sent out trusted guerrillas to find the locations of all large Japanese coastal defense guns and the strength and disposition of the troops with them. They went and came back, and when we verified the locations, we sent the information by radio to Sixth Army headquarters. Shortly after that, the Air Corps bombed those positions. We used grid coordinates to identify the guns' location.

On March 22, I walked to another guerrilla camp for more information. I and some of the other Scouts made more hikes to get information. One long hike took us to Legaspi. We arrived just as our planes were bombing the area and we made a good survey.

Our troops landed onshore 1 April, 1945, and we walked out to meet the 158th Regimental Combat Team, where we made our final report. They told us that of the nine Japanese coastal guns, the Air Corps had knocked out seven using our coordinates.

Lieutenant (jg) Ernest J. Petoskey, D.Ed.
Greenbush, Michigan

MY SCOUTS & RAIDERS training class was number 6 at Fort Pierce, Florida. It was a good group of rough-and-ready type of fellows from three or four officer candidate colleges and universities. Most of the men were in good physical shape when they reported for Scouts & Raiders training. Many had played on fine college teams in a lot of sports.

One day Commander Gene Tunney attended our PT period. He openly stated that our conditioning at that time excelled all other bases that he had visited. That really covered a good many areas, as he was in charge of selecting teams for PT chiefs at Iowa Preflight and other sites.

Our training was much the same as the SEALs do today. We spent hours on hand-to-hand combat, night maneuvers, swimming from seven-man rubber boats, and paddling in heavy surf. There was little sleep for us at that time, as we had a critique each morning following the all-night assignments.

On our days off we swam to buoys with the outgoing tides and returned on the incoming tides. The physical training was exhausting and it prepared us for most any war situation. We became hardened to all types of weather and rough water.

At the Advanced Naval Intelligence School in New York City we took a course in mapping and model making. While aboard the USS *Klein* (APD 120), I used this knowledge to build a model of the landing area of Brown Beach on Okinawa. It was delivered to the AGC or the command ship prior to the initial landing April 1, 1945. The model was used as a study tool for the Army and Marine officers' briefings at the battalion level. Our Demolition Team No. 11 used the model to plan the landing as well. The model was mentioned in a book, *Okinawa: The Last Battle of WWII*. Also helping to build the model were Ensign S. E. Lanier and Seaman 2/C L. B. Lent.

In September 1944 we left New York for a school for beach-master-type training in San Diego under Elliott Roosevelt, a major in the Marine Corps. We left San Diego for Hawaii on the *Kota Agon*, a Dutch transport ship loaded with captured German soldiers. We were confined to the ship at Hilo for a day but were allowed to swim alongside the ship. A group of us swam to the officers' club there and entered in our bathing suits. It was a daring experience.

From Hilo we went to Pearl Harbor, where we were offered billets with the new demolition teams at Maui or as transport intelligent officers. I joined Underwater Demolition Team No. 11 as a replacement officer. Other Scouts & Raiders joined us in later Demo Teams as they were organized and then came with us to the beaches of Okinawa.

After joining the UDT No. 11, I went to the South Pacific and participated in the following operations:

- 29-31 March 1945, Okinawa: Preassault recon and demolition on main beaches
- 2–3 April, 1945, Okinawa: Postassault demolition on main beaches
- 13–15 April, 1945, Okinawa: Postassault recon of eastern beaches
- 8 June, 1945, Brunei Bay, northwest Borneo: Preassault recon of Labuan and Deat islands
- 25–30 June, Balikpapan, southeast Borneo: Preassault recon and demolition of preferred and alternate beaches, Manggar and Klandasan
- 2–3 July, 1945, Balikpapan, in southeast Borneo: postassault demolition operation on Sepinggan Beaches.

On 30 July, 1945, I was recommended for the Silver Star by the Commander Task Unit 78.2.11 for performance of duty on 28 June 1945 on Klandasan Beach, Balikpapan, southeast Borneo. I didn't receive the medal at that time because all the team members, officers and enlisted, received Bronze Star medals for our work at Borneo.

I did receive my Silver Star for action at Okinawa at a review of the Naval ROTC at the University of Michigan in 1946. It was the thrill of a lifetime for me.

Ernest Phinney, USN
Gray, Maine

DURING THE BATTLE for Okinawa, I was assigned to the USS *Roper* (APD-20), undergoing repairs at a facility near Okinawa from damage after being hit by a kamikaze plane. It was May 28, 1945. I was called to the command ship and asked if I would volunteer for a mission into China. They told me it would involve several days' journey through the Japanese lines and back again. I agreed to go.

I was then told that it involved bringing out an intelligence agent. Further instructions were that no one in the group would know any of the others, that we were not to attempt to learn anything about any other member of the group other than first names. Most important of all, we should be prepared to be certain that anyone left behind could not be questioned if caught by the enemy. He meant anyone left had to be dead or, if so wounded he couldn't keep up, killed. Upon seeing the look on my face the captain said, "That's right, there is only one way to be certain. Are you prepared to do that, should the need arise? It must be done, and if it happens to be you, you must be ready to accept it. It is most vital that the enemy knows as little as possible about this mission." I thought that if the others could do it, so could I. I agreed; besides, I guess I didn't think it would come to that. I was wrong.

We boarded the APD on the morning of May 28, 1945, and steamed out to sea. That night we transferred to a submarine. On board the sub a further briefing took place. We were to land on a peninsula about forty miles east of the city of Linhai and 150 miles south of Shanghai in the province of Zhejiang. Each Chinese guide was to be with us for only one day, or until we got to the meeting place of the next guide. They had all volunteered, knowing what would happen to them at the end of their assigned service. Never before or since have I seen such dedicated people. They really believed in what they were doing.

The sub surfaced and slowly moved inshore as far as possible. We had to swim on in, so it came as close as possible. A thousand-yard swim wasn't too far for us. A rubber boat wouldn't work because no matter how well hidden it might be, it probably would be found, since we were to be gone for seven days.

The sub came in to five hundred yards offshore. We slipped over the side with our gear and swam ashore with no problems. We met our guide and started inland. Later we found out it was just as well we didn't have a rubber boat, as the Japs were all over that area before we got back. They would surely have found the boat, then waited to ambush us.

At that time I had never heard of the Sino-American Cooperative Organization (SACO), but those were the people we were working with.

Moving inland went well and was mostly at night. Water travel was by sampan but almost all travel was by land.

On the fourth night we arrived at a very small village just outside of the town of Linhai. A hut concealed a tunnel that led to a house larger than the usual size in that area. We entered it by a set of stairs. A young white man was escorted through an archway and handed over to us. Before going up to the house, we had been cautioned not to talk at all when inside. The only words spoken were by an older Chinese. "You take, no capture by Nipponese." Then he retreated through an archway.

Until then, things had gone smoothly, just like the briefings and in training. That was about to change.

Not long into the second night going back, I had the feeling things were not going to be smooth much longer. We had all concealed ourselves beside the trail. Before long we could hear Japs coming from each direction, looking for us. We let one group go past, since they were headed back the way we had just come. We started out again, keeping our point man farther ahead then before.

Soon we were being chased. It lasted the rest of the night and two more nights. One by one our people were being killed by enemy fire. We tried to stay well hidden in the daytime, but at night we moved, slowly, and still we lost more people.

By the sixth day I decided we should float downstream in a junk. With all the other junks in the water, we stood a good chance of not being noticed. It worked. By that time it was just me and the intelligence agent from SACO. We floated out beyond a small island and waited for the sub. There were Japs all over the place but they couldn't find us. We got back to the sub and we both boarded safely and I returned to my ship the same way I had come. I don't know what happened to the rescued man. I never saw the man from SACO again.

I did meet one of the SACO veterans a few years ago at Fort Pierce. There are some things not said, questions not asked or answered, and they will stay that way. Best that they be known only to me and that remarkable man I know was from the Rice Paddy Navy.

Seaman First Class Rodney Garrand
Mooers, New York

I ENTERED THE Navy in March of 1943 and took my boot training at Hampton, New York, over by Buffalo for seven weeks. After that they shipped a whole bunch of us to Little Creek, Virginia, to the Amphibious Base there. They put us to training in small landing craft. In Chesapeake Bay we learned how to beach the boats and then get them off again at high tide.

From there they sent us to Fort Pierce, Florida. We trained there with boats for a while, then they asked for volunteers for the Scouts & Raiders. I volunteered. We had a lot of hard training there: the obstacle course, lifting the logs, running in the sand up to our ankles in our combat boots with the rubber boats on our shoulders. We paddled the boats through the surf out to the ocean. We did a lot of swimming. Then they gave us demolition training over on North Island. Between us and the UDT guys, it's a wonder we didn't blow the island away. We had classes on booby traps, which were very important to us.

Once in a while we had a pass to go into town. Not all of our guys went, so when I came back I brought a bunch of hamburgers for them. They only cost thirty-five cents each. My crew at Fort Pierce included Victor Figateli, John Gagon, Comela, Billy Burd, and William Bolt. Our officer was Ensign Bobillard.

At the end of our training we had eight days of "Hell Week." We had to live off the land and eat what we could find. I was really hungry when I got back to camp, I can tell you.

In February of 1944 we shipped out of Wilmington, Delaware, and sailed to North Africa. I forget where we landed, but they put us in trucks and sent us down the coast to Ferryville. On the way down we could see the destroyed German tanks and trucks along the road. Some of them were still smoking. As I remember, Douglas Fairbanks Jr. was the commander of our base there. An antiaircraft outfit was moving in and setting up the same day we arrived.

I asked a sergeant in the outfit if they had any men in it from upstate New York. He said he did. Told me one of them, named Beebe, was walking toward us. I hollered at him and he came over. He came closer and closer and then Beebe yelled, "Rodney, is that you?" He asked me what I was doing over there in Africa. I told him we were both there fighting a war. He wasn't too far away, and while we were there we had some more visits and talked about home.

There was lots of air action at that time around our base. We weren't there long before we boarded an LST. There were six or seven ships in the harbor. There were only two teams of Scouts on the ship; the rest were on some other ships. The Jerries came out that afternoon with an air raid and all hell broke loose. I was near a guy firing at the planes. On the second pass they killed the guy. They put me in the harness where he had been and showed me how to fire the guns. That was one afternoon I'll never forget. I shot down two German planes that day.

I was upset about it. But it was wartime. I kept

thinking what they did to the people over there in Europe and after a while I got over it.

When we landed, we were in a bombed-out building with little left of it. We were there for a while, then they trucked us up to Naples near Cassino. We sometimes went into a town we called Pignoli. There was a tavern-like place where a lot of the soldiers hung out. They had dancing girls and music and drinks. About the only song the band could play was "Lay That Pistol Down."

That's where we got ready for the invasion of Anzio. It was pretty hairy, that's all I want to say about it. I lived through it. We had to do silhouetting in our training. Now we had pictures to study to help us find the beach that way. After the invasion we went back to our camp and got ready for the invasion of southern France. I worked through that one, too, and it wasn't too bad.

Then orders came that sent us back to the States and to Florida. After a few weeks we had our traveling orders. We were going to India. Later we found out we were part of the SACO. That stood for Sino-American Cooperative Organization. President Franklin D. Roosevelt and Chiang Kai-shek put the group together. Our job was to get into China and disrupt and spy on the Japanese and coast watch behind enemy lines. Most of us never got into action there. We were stuck in India partly due to interservice rivalry, and we never did get into China to do what we had been trained to do. I returned to the States and took my discharge on March 7, 1946.

Now I wish I had kept in contact with some of the guys in my outfit. I didn't.

Bronson "Tex" Howell, USN
Winter Haven, Florida

DURING THE WAR I was in a group known as Roger 1. We went through Scouts & Raiders and Underwater Demolition Training in Fort Pierce, Florida. We were especially trained as well in guerrilla warfare so we could train certain groups in China. We were sent to China for covert operations. We were part of SACO. We were first known as the U.S. Naval Group, China.

But we all were soon under the command of General Tai Li, head of the Chinese Bureau of Investigation and Statistics as the director of SACO and Vice Admiral Milton Edwards Miles as deputy director.

Our job there was to perform intelligence and guerrilla operations. They soon called us the Rice Paddy Navy or the SACO Tigers. Members of our group served hundreds of miles behind Japanese lines, establishing vital weather stations, doing coast watching to report enemy shipping, intercepting Japanese codes, and rescuing shot-down Allied airmen. There were about 2,500 of us including all branches of the U.S. services and British. All were volunteers.

There was never much information about us, since our records were all in Chungking until the end of our tour there. Even the Navy, except for a very few individuals in Washington, did not know we were in China until after the war.

After training in Fort Pierce, we took a boat from the West Coast to Calcutta, which took about forty days. One of our jobs later on was to clear the mines out of shipping channels in Japanese territory. We worked into the area, found the channels, clipped off the floating mines, moved them over to the bank, and piled them up. They needed 250 pounds of pressure on the spikes to detonate. We had three hours to get the job done. You could tell where the channels were by the depth of the water. We cut off the cables and hauled the mines out. The only equipment we had were swim fins, bolt cutters, and pants. There were fifteen of us on the job that night. The area we covered was about 360 yards long and 200 yards wide.

They gave us three hours to get the job done. When we had all the mines we could get piled up onshore, we tossed in a grenade and ran like hell. It made the biggest explosion most of us had ever seen.

When they dropped the nuclear bombs and the war was over, we moved back to Foochow. John H. Brown III (now deceased) and I were left behind when the rest of the SACO people shipped out. Our job was to turn certain assets over to the Chinese Army. Shortly after that, the Chinese Reds moved in and took over the country. We destroyed all the assets and moved on to Kiewan, where we waited for our orders to be transported to Shanghai and on home. We were told we would have to return to Foochow to be picked up by an LST. We had difficulties getting back to Foochow and it was April 1946, eight months after the war was over, before we were picked up. We at last got home.

Ensign John E. Demmer
Dearborn, Michigan

AFTER I FINISHED midshipman's school, they asked for volunteers for highly dangerous and secret work. I signed on. They sent us to Fort Pierce to Scouts & Raiders school. When we finished there, they shipped us by troop train across the country to San Pedro, California, right near Long Beach in the Los Angeles area. We were there a month or so. Many of the unmarried men rented apartments in town and rented a car and had fun driving around. We checked in every morning to see if our orders had come through, and when they hadn't, it was another day to party. Then one morning the orders were there and the party was over.

We went onboard a troop transport and forty-two days later we docked in Calcutta. It was a rough trip and almost everyone got seasick. I did as well and it was the worst feeling I've ever had in my life.

We stayed at an Army base twenty miles out of Calcutta until the Navy finished building Camp Knox right in Calcutta. It was made up of Quonset huts. We stayed there a month. In Calcutta the first man I saw had a small bucket with him. He used it for everything from washing himself to carrying his groceries and clothes and all his worldly possessions.

Some of us went to the burning ghats on the shores of the Ganges River. It was interesting to watch the ceremony where the loved one is cremated on a wooden pyre, then the ashes are put into the sacred Ganges River. One of the family walks around the pyre three times before it is set on fire.

I and a buddy, Ensign Lyle Cater, walked into the new market area of Calcutta one day. We always saw a lot of little kids, but this one little girl looked so pathetic and poorly clothed. We took her into a clothing store and bought her a new outfit of clothes and made her look real cute, then we sent her on her way. Ten days later we were in the same area and we saw the same little girl in the old raggedly clothes she had worn before, evidently looking for another sucker to buy her a new outfit.

I saw some of the most beautiful women in the world there in Calcutta. The mixed blood of English and Indian produced remarkably pretty women with darker skin and marvelous faces. For a short time we were there we enjoyed the British racetrack and the Calcutta Swim Club.

What they said about Calcutta being overcrowded was true, with people starving and dying right on the streets. That part was just terrible. In the area outside of Calcutta we saw some of the local women walking into town with what looked like dried cow dung balanced on their heads. That's exactly what it was. They collected it and sold it in town as fuel.

Then orders came down again and I was called over the hump. We flew into China to a base where a Marine major said there was no need for us there. He shipped us out to a fifth-column camp farther inside China. We went in on trucks. Ours was a 1939 Dodge, and we wound up and over the mountains. The roads were dirt and in one huge rainstorm one of our rigs went over the side and down a canyon. I spent three nights in a farmer's haystack while a small army of Chinese showed up and dug out a path with picks and shovels for the truck to drive back up to the road. Then we continued.

There were no real bridges, lots of small streams to ford, and it was slow progress working up as far as we could into the mountains. At one time we were pinned down by Communist bandits and Japanese for a few days. We worked our way out of it. During that time one of the enlisted men developed what our medic said was appendicitis. We radioed back and they sent out a surgeon. The medic had given the man sulfa pills and that evidently kept the appendix from bursting. The surgeon arrived and we put the man on an old table, and with some hot water and little else the doctor performed the operation. The man recovered.

Soon we came to the end of even that road and we had to walk through the mountains to find our new home with a guerrilla group. Along the way we went through beautiful mountains and saw a princess of some sort being carried in a fancy chair on a litter. We had a cook along with us and somebody caught a chicken and that night we had chicken and noodle soup. The kitchen man cooked the whole chicken, head, feet, and all. It tasted great.

They had local bread that we called baseballs because they were baked in about that size loaves. Most of the wheat was ground into flour on concrete blocks and some of the ground-off cement showed up in the bread, but we ate it anyway.

We got to the guerrilla camp and stayed there for a month or two. We began to make plans to ambush a Japanese patrol. We scouted it out and went out one night and lay in a ditch, waiting for the patrol to come by. We waited all night and it didn't come. We found out the Japanese would be at another spot the next night, so we went out and laid our trap. We had a man with a machine gun on a small hill above us for support. One of our Chinese guerrillas had a land mine with him. He planted it on the road with a remote detonating device.

This time the Japanese patrol came with an officer riding a horse, followed by a fieldpiece and dozens of soldiers. Our man set off the land mine right under the fieldpiece and the fight was on. It lasted for about fifteen minutes, then we took off through the mountains with the Japanese survivors chasing us. We got to a walled city and waited for them. Our guerrillas lay on top of the wall and watched for the enemy.

The rest of us retreated through the town to the cemetery and decided we'd make our stand there. I had a carbine and my .45 automatic. I sat down near a grave, and before I knew it I went to sleep. I woke up an hour later and they told me that our guerrillas had shot up the Japanese as soon as they showed. The remnants of the enemy patrol had turned around and left. The locals said we had killed fifty Japanese, but I never believed them.

We went on a couple of other operations with the guerrillas and then we got a bazooka. Our captain there asked me to go and see if I could get the Japanese commander of a small post to surrender. When we were a thousand yards away from this new small walled city, the Japanese began firing at us. Soon it began to get dark and we moved closer. We came on a grisly scene where three Chinese men had been shot in the head with dumdum bullets. It was a terrible sight.

It was a clear night with the stars out. We sent a messenger to the Japanese commander asking him to surrender to us, since we had a bazooka and could blow him out of town. We got a fancy letter back in effect saying no, he wouldn't surrender. I don't know what we would have done with the Japanese soldiers if they had come over. We called it a night and went back to our camp.

We spent some time in an Italian Catholic mission. We had good food and some local wine and goat's milk there and enjoyed our stay.

We had a Chinese man, Jackson Shih, along with us to act as our interpreter. Evidently in China every province and area has a slightly different vocabulary and accent. Our man got frustrated when he couldn't always understand what some of the locals were saying, and they couldn't understand him. But all in all he did a good job for us.

Shortly we heard about the nuclear bombs hitting Japan and word came that the war was over. A local Japanese commander arranged for a big dinner and a formal surrender where his officers gave us their swords to signify their complete surrender. I kept mine for a while, then gave it to a museum. Now I can't get it back.

We hiked out to where we could get picked up by trucks. Some of the villages we went through had Chinese celebrating by throwing firecrackers in the street. The first few times it got our attention with our nervous fingers on triggers. We eventually flew to Shanghai, where I became a manager of the officers' club.

SACO turned out to benefit both China and the U.S. The old Chinese general helped us set up weather stations all along sensitive areas, where we reported on Japanese shipping and troop movements. In exchange we sent in men to train Chinese in guerrilla warfare. The young men who came often had been survivors from terrible slaughter in Chinese villages. They wanted to fight back and serve their country. They did a good job. Usually after training the young men went back to their home villages, where they knew the terrain and how they could most hurt the Japanese invaders.

Captain Howard N. Moore USN (Ret.)
Melbourne, Florida

AFTER GRADUATION FROM Notre Dame Midshipman School and amphibious training at ATB Solomon's Island, Maryland, I joined Scouts & Raiders School at Fort Pierce, Florida. Night infiltration problems were an important part of the curriculum. On one of them my team commandeered a bus and penetrated the Port Everglades docks and oil terminals, where we "blew up" storage tanks and pipelines. The guards were humiliated.

We tried other infiltration attempts where there were Coast Guard sentries mounted on horseback. Even when a sentry didn't notice us, his horse would prick up its ears and snort and look right at us. The guard would then dismount and challenge us and capture us, and the exercise for us was over. Those horses seemed to have a sixth sense about finding us.

I was a lieutenant (jg) when I and my S & R team were assigned to the USS *Tattnall* (APD-19), which sailed for the Mediterranean in April of 1944. We helped train French commandos of the Battaillion de Choc, landing some of them on Pianosa Island during Operation Brassard on June 16, 1944.

Operation Anvil-Dragoon landing was set for August 15, 1944, and we trained the First Special Service Force troops for the mission in southern France. The targets were the islands of Port Cros and Levant, where we thought the Germans had large gun emplacements. We went in with the troops under fire. For that one they awarded me the Bronze Star, but my enlisted men deserved medals just as much as I did.

When I went back to Fort Pierce I was assigned to the amphibious Scout School, where we trained men to go into China with the U.S. Naval Group China. The class was ready to go to Fort Benning to attend jump school when the war ended.

I already had my law degree and left the Navy and spent a year in civilian practice before I returned to the

Navy, received a permanent commission, and spent the rest of my career with the Navy's JAG (Judge Advocate General) office.

Corporal Ira A. Greenberg, U. S. Army
Los Angeles, California

I ARRIVED AT the Naval Amphibious Training Base at Fort Pierce, Florida, in April 1944. I was one of 104 Army privates sent from Camp Indiantown Gap in Pennsylvania to fill out the ranks of the 11th Army Engineers Combat Battalion. We were there as guests of the Navy for the purpose of doing research, seeking solutions to combat problems engineer units had to deal with.

The one hundred men were set up to provide college studies to soldiers to prepare them to be technical specialists in the various Army branches. There must have been 100,000 or more of us tied up at universities and colleges throughout the country. After a screening at Stetson University in De Land, Florida, I was sent to Carnegie Institute of Technology in Pittsburgh, where I spent three months studying engineering subjects.

Pittsburgh was a great serviceman's town and I have fond memories of Saturday-night dances of the Waiters and Waitresses Union, where those in the service were admitted free. There developed an urgent need for Army ground forces, and almost the entire program was disbanded, as well as a good part of the Army's Aviation Cadet Program.

From the one hundred and four of us, I believe thirty were sent to each of the three line companies in the 11th Engineer Combat Battalion, with the rest going to Headquarters Company. I wound up in Company B, commanded by First Lieutenant Frederick Wunderlich.

On arriving in Florida by train, we probably were bused to Fort Pierce and then trucked across a steel suspension bridge to South Island, which was the Amphibious Training Base. It was commanded by Navy Captain Gulbranson. They told us he insisted that the island was a ship and the ground was to be referred to as the deck.

The 11th was stationed in squad tents not too far from the bridge while most of the five thousand sailors were quartered at the far end of the island. That's where the naval headquarters, the amphibious schools, the movie theater, and other structures were located.

The first day was confusing, but Lt. Wunderlich put some order into it by interviewing each of the 104 men in his tent behind the orderly-room tent. He wanted to determine the abilities of each of us.

I told him I had studied mining engineering at Michigan College of Mining and Technology. His expression turned to annoyed impatience, so I quickly added that I knew something about demolition.

His expression changed for the better and he told me I'd be working with Sergeant Mickey, who would contact me in the morning.

I had become interested in explosives in high school and tried to make my own nitroglycerine, but it didn't work. I had the wrong density of the acids I had mixed.

That night I was asleep in my pup tent—we didn't move into squad tents until later—when someone kicked my foot. A voice asked me if I was Greenberg. I said I was. He told me he was Sergeant Mickey and when the men fell out for work details after breakfast, I was supposed to stay behind near the orderly room. He said he'd come by with the crew and get me.

I did as he said and joined what then became his six-man demolition research team. We got into a two-and-a-half-ton truck and were taken across another steel suspension bridge to what was called North Island, where various buildings, research, and training projects were under way. We were separated enough so we only knew what was going on in our own area.

We had a great assignment. We were under the supervision of an Army captain who we were told came from Washington, D.C., with specific experiments for us to carry out. He was probably from Fort Belvoir, Virginia, then the Army engineering post near the capital. When the captain showed up we worked, and when he didn't we would crawl under the truck and go to sleep. Many a time we would drive back to South Island to join the rest of the company for lunch and we had clean fatigues and were puffy-eyed from sleep, while the rest of the men were filthy with sweat and cement dust. There may have been some resentment against us, which I caught up with after the demolition crew was disbanded and we were put to hard labor with everyone else.

By this time I had been assigned to a squad, and the biggest guy was Cecil "Big Ed" Edmundson. He gave me a hard time, rushing me as I struggled with a wheelbarrow full of concrete going up a narrow plank to build the three-foot-thick walls our guys and the Seabees made. Those of us in the demolition crew would blow them up later using a tank to approach and depart from the wall.

I had been doing most of the work. I had been trained as an infantry machine gunner before I went into the ASTP program and had also fired 60mm mortars. Our first research when I joined the team involved firing smoke shells from an 81mm mortar with the baseplate welded to the tank commander's seat of our Grant tank. I was the mortar operator and was the one who dropped the shells into the tube. The other team members observed from a shady spot.

Other experiments involved the tank moving up to the three-foot wall, me slipping out the side opening to plant a charge of C-2, lighting the fuse, and pulling myself back into the tank as it withdrew, or setting off the charge from inside the tank with an electric detonator. Additional experiments involved attaching a flail to the tank to destroy road mines or setting off a close charge nearby while crouching on the other side of the tank.

During these tasks the other team member watched me again from a safe place in the shade. I didn't mind, because I was the youngest and was having a hell of a good time. One experiment involved using the tank to lay bundles of slim tree trunks to make a cordouroy road. For this we all worked ourselves dizzy. We had to cut the trees armed only with machetes. It was brutal work in the hot Florida jungle.

Then Sergeant Mickey's demolition team was dissolved and we all returned to the squads we had been assigned to. But the day before we broke up, we were told the Navy had opened its Naval Combat Demolition Unit School and the Scouts & Raiders school to members of the 11th Army Engineers. If we wanted in we should put our names on the lists posted on the bulletin board.

I was one of the first to sign up for the NCDU course. Two days later when the assignments were listed, I found my name on the Scouts & Raiders sheet.

I stormed over to my First Sergeant bitching like hell. He looked at me with disgust and said, "Take it or leave it." I reluctantly took it. Forty-five years later at an 11th Engineer reunion, one of the guys told me that for that call they only took sergeants in the NCDU.

Before my Scouts & Raiders class began, I had to stay with the rest of my company. Big Ed and I developed a fierce loathing for each other. He had come from a poor family and during the Depression he had to go to work as soon as he was big enough. For Big Ed that came quickly. He missed most of his schooling and could barely read and write. I called him Lenny after the John Steinbeck character in *Of Mice and Men*, and he called me all sorts of anti-Semitic names. He wasn't anti-Semitic, just anti-Greenberg.

Later in France we got to know each other and we became buddies and teamed up together. Big Ed was one of the smartest guys in the company and invariably the big winner in poker games. I never played poker with him.

The Scouts & Raiders school began for us sometime in early summer of 1944 and after my first experience swimming from the Navy's Inflatable Boat, Small, and then climbing back onboard wearing full fatigue uniform and sneakers, I found myself enjoying it immensely. There must have been about thirty of us from the 11th Engineers and a larger group of sailors, but we didn't train together.

In the morning we caravanned from South to North Island and wound up at a beach away from the mainland where we were out of sight of everyone, and then we would go to our own beaches where we didn't see the sailors until the end of the day when we caravanned back to South Island. I know we weren't too far apart because one day there was a pile of mackerel near our beach on our arrival. They probably came after an explosion in the water. We were told to help ourselves to them but none of us did.

There were four or five boatloads of us, with each boat containing six privates who were the paddlers and one corporal who was the helmsman. That first day I learned what port and starboard were, and my position was second man on the port (left) side. We were dressed in Army herringbone twill fatigues, pants and shirts and cap, wore sneakers, and carried our M1 Garand rifles with the muzzles protected from water by Army-issued canvas muzzle protectors. After a couple of days we decided they were not good enough and used condoms from the orderly room, which were superb muzzle protectors. A week later our Lieutenant Wunderlich issued the order that nobody could get condoms unless he had a pass into town.

Our first day was spent learning about the boat, inflating it, collapsing it, and caring for it. We got familiar with it on the beach and in the ocean. This last I found especially rewarding as I always wore eyeglasses and found to my delight that ocean water ran off the glasses quickly without impairing my vision. This was not the case with fresh water.

The usual daily routine was calisthenics on first arrival, which included log PT in which boat crews would, as a team, do simple exercises with a palm tree trunk while standing or lying on their backs. As I recall it lasted about ten minutes. We also ran a half mile on the beach.

We had lectures on boat seamanship, signaling, scouting and patrol procedures, taking beach depths in fathoms, map reading and use of the compass, and other things that scouts would do in guiding assault craft to the shore. The morning's activities also included a daily half-hour lecture and demonstration of judo, the holds and throws of which we were supposed to practice on our own but rarely did.

We were also taught in formal class settings how to take out sentries, how to approach enemy positions undetected, and how to draw maps and diagrams of beaches and of anything else that might have intelligence significance. What I remember most is that we spent many long hours at night taking beach depths in our rubber boats and being bitten by sand flies during the hours we spent signaling incoming boats with our flashlights.

We were doing all of this scout work, and halfway through our course we wondered when we would get into the raiding part of the course and begin doing the commando training we looked forward to. We assumed that meant charging into an enemy position with submachine guns blazing and destroying everything there.

Our course came a short time after D-day on Normandy and we assumed there would be a need for Scouts & Raiders in the Pacific Theater. We figured we'd be assigned to the Navy for the various island invasions, and between them we'd goldbrick and enjoy ourselves. It didn't occur to us that those who survived one invasion doing the scouting work would be spending all of their time training for the next invasion.

While we privates and corporals were being trained as Scouts, on another part of North Island sergeants from the 11th Engineers were going through the Raiders part of the school, spending part of their time attacking places depicted as enemy headquarters and setting off explosives to destroy enemy equipment.

Forty-five years after our Scouts & Raiders school, I learned that our instructors had been veterans of the North African, Sicilian, and Italian invasions and we never knew it then. If we had, their training would have been much more effective and we would have given them our total attention. Maybe the Navy brass was afraid that we might leak details about those "secret" invasions.

For our final test we had to do one more night exercise. If we passed we'd get a reward. The problem was, we had to go to a part of the North Island where we had never been before, swim from our rubber boats to the beach, and then get inland quickly. Using our scouting procedures, we were to slip up on the "enemy" headquarters, where we would find a stack of oranges. We were to take one orange as proof of fulfilling our mission, then get back to the beach without getting caught. If we did that, we would graduate and get a reward.

We got our boat to the right beach and we all took off for the headquarters target. Pretty soon I was all alone, crawling quietly through the jungle. I soon found the goal, and as I paused I could hear a lot of thrashing about and yelling in the thickets to my right. I got inside the building without being seen, got my orange, rushed back into the concealment, and made my way quietly back to our beach and the boat. There were only two others at our boat. We waited for the rest. Eventually they came back after having been captured, and they had no oranges.

At the auditorium the lieutenant congratulated us and told us that the Navy had promised us a reward. All who brought back an orange were asked to step forward. We did. He said, "Now for your reward: It's the orange you brought back. You can do anything you want to with it." I looked down at my salt water-soggy orange and groaned.

In 2001 I used this incident in an early chapter of my first novel, *41 Days and the Hellsingers*, which was about the actions of a combat engineer sergeant during the North African Campaign in 1943.

The course was over. I didn't make sergeant then, and we didn't get assigned to the tender mercies of a chief petty officer. In no time we were on our way overseas. Before we left, a senior sergeant from Company B told me that he'd seen a photo of me in a tank turret about to drop an 81mm mortar round in the tube. He said it was in an Army field or technical manual. I thanked him for the news. I tried to find the manual, which came out in 1944, but never could.

Overseas, all of us graduates from the Navy's Scouts & Raiders School served as ordinary combat engineers, with the 11th Engineers being assigned to the XXIst Corps of the Seventh Army. We served in southern France and southern Germany. Then we went into the pipeline for return to the States. We were told the Army needed combat engineers for the invasion of Japan. We were slated for the March 1946 invasion of the Japanese mainland, but the second atomic bomb stopped that.

Before his death I had the honor of shaking Brigadier General Paul Tibbet's hand and say, "Thank you, General, for saving my life."

Underwater Demolition Teams

The tragedy at Tarawa, where the invasion landing craft were hung up on undetected coral heads more than a thousand yards off the beach, and men were slaughtered as they sloshed through neck-deep water a thousand yards to the shore, led directly to the forward motion of the creation of Navy units to avoid this problem in the future.

During the first week of November 1943, the Fifth Amphibious Force took the first concrete steps in the Pacific Ocean area to organize and train naval combat demolition personnel. There were two big reasons:

- Future amphibious operations in the Pacific would be directed against coral atolls. Clear passages to the beaches involved might have to be secured by demolition personnel trained in marine blasting of these coral intensive areas.
- The Japanese had never used mines or obstacles as profusely or as cleverly as the Germans, but it was not known just what kind of obstacles the enemy might employ in future landing areas, and to what extent.

A search of Navy personnel records soon discovered that there were some individuals who had experience in blasting coral. They were at the Naval Construction

Battalion, where they were clearing coral from various atolls in the Pacific at the time. Some of these men and officers were brought to Waimanalo, Oahu, Hawaii, in November of 1943 to serve as a nucleus to train other personnel in coral blasting. The beginning of this training program was given a tremendous push after the tragedy of Tarawa.

Tarawa showed that men could not be sent against an enemy beach without a complete offshore reconnaissance. It was necessary for trained men to search the water off the beaches to be assaulted for antiboat mines, tetrahedrons, and other man-made obstacles. When found, they would be blasted apart and then channels marked to the cleared beaches, and the men were to direct ship traffic into those safe lanes.

By the end of 1943 there were about thirty officers and 150 men training in underwater demolition work at Waimanalo. They were divided into two groups, which were called Underwater Demolition Teams Nos. 1 and 2. The teams were made up of the Navy coral blasters plus Army and Marine officers and men. Included were several Naval Combat Demolition Units, which had come into the program after being sent from Fort Pierce.

In December of 1943, UDT No. 2 was sent to San Diego, where it was attached to Command Task Force 53 for use in the attack on Roi and Namur in the Flintlock Operation. Commander of Team No. 2 was Lieutenant Commander J. T. Koehler, USNR.

Team No. 1 stayed in Hawaii and was attached to CTF 52 under Vice Admiral Turner to use in the planned attack on Kwajalein Island, also in the Flintlock Operation. Commander E. D. Brewster, CEC, USNR, was named CO of Team No. 1.

The combined forces teams were made up of fourteen officers and seventy men. Organizing these teams along strict military lines was difficult. Many had come from ingrained small-team operations and were loyal to their leaders. Others from the various services that had different methodologies, and molding all these different styles into one formal organization was nearly impossible.

Despite these problems, both teams made their preassault recons of the enemy beaches but found no serious obstacles to the landings. After the landings they blasted better channels to the beaches for the larger landing craft and for the LSTs. Both teams gained valuable experience under combat conditions, and this helped mold them into more integrated units.

Lessons were learned:

- The use of the four types of explosives was adequate for the four types of man-made and natural obstacles that might be encountered.
- The use of drone boats loaded with six thousand pounds of explosives to be radio controlled to sail into a beach and be detonated to help reduce or eliminate obstacles was deemed not to be practical.
- They decided that the UDT teams should have their own ship from which to conduct their operations. Getting the various groups and their supplies to the point needed in ships with other priorities proved not to be workable.

Lieutenant Commander Koehler, CO of UDT No. 2, was ordered to work out an organization plan for future teams and for a training base. It was done and, after being modified, was adopted. The basic letters covering the training and base were issued by the commander of the Fifth Amphibious Force, Pacific Fleet, on l4 March, 1944.

With two combat operations under their belts, the teams learned other valuable lessons they used to modify their organizations. They reduced officers on a team from sixteen to thirteen and increased the enlisted men from eighty to eighty-five. They also eliminated the drone personnel from the teams.

During the operation on Roi and Namur in the Flintlock Operation, UDT No. 2 used three and a half pounds of explosives per square foot to remove one-half cubic foot of coral ledge.

Lieutenant (jg) Alfred Sears, USN
Coronado, California

I JOINED THE Navy in 1928 as an enlisted man and served six years. Then I reenlisted in the Navy in 1943 and volunteered for duty with the Underwater Demolition Teams. I completed initial training at Camp Perry and Fort Pierce, Florida.

Then we were flown to England to participate in the invasion of Normandy. I was wounded on the second day of the battle on Omaha Beach. I was flown back to England. After several weeks of hospital stay there, I rejoined my outfit, which had since returned to England.

Because of my wounds I couldn't participate in future UDT operations. I was sent back to Fort Pierce and placed in the training section as an instructor in underwater demolition. In March 1945 I was promoted to lieutenant (jg). I remained at Fort Pierce until the end of the war. On June 15, 1946, the staff was dissolved and I became commanding officer of UDT Team No. 1.

After the war I stayed in the Navy in various capacities in UDT and Amphibious Training, Pacific Fleet.

Virgil Stewart, UDT No. 2

UDT TEAM No. 2 was different from any other. It was organized at Waimanalo, Oahu, in December 1943. It had a Navy CO, Lieutenant Crist, two other Navy officers, four Army officers, three Marine Corps officers, four enlisted Army men, twenty enlisted Navy men, and thirty-five enlisted Marines.

All of the Navy personnel had taken their UDT training at Fort Pierce, Florida. They acted as instructors to train the Army and Marine men in demolition. This concentrated on blasting underwater and abovewater obstacles, and the destruction of coral and coral heads.

Late in December 1943, UDT Team No. 2 boarded the USS *Schley* (APD-14), in Hawaii and sailed to San Diego. There we were scheduled to pick up four drone boats and demolition matériel. After loading the boats and explosives, they set sail with the destination of the Marshall Islands. The ship arrived at Roi and Namur in the Kwajalein Atoll on February 1, 1944.

The four drone boats went into the water each loaded with a ton and a half of explosives.

Two amphibious tractors with five men on board under Lieutenant Crist did a recon on the channels leading into the bay. The rest of the men landed on one of the smaller islands off Namur and set up camp. That night, two rubber boats with six men each went to Roi and Namur and did a recon on both beaches. No obstacles or deterrents to landing were found.

The next morning two unmanned drone boats loaded with explosives were set to be sent by remote radio control into Roi and Namur and be blown up. Rough seas came up and caused radio and equipment problems on the drone boats, and the operation was canceled.

After the troops landed on both islands, the team lived onshore for six days and blew up coral, small boats, trees—anything that would stop landing craft from sending in their troops.

Eight days after arriving at Roi and Namur, Team No. 2 boarded USS *Bolivar* (APA-34), and returned the men to Pearl Harbor and to their base at Waimanalo. Orders came down that thereafter all UDT teams would be made up solely of Navy personnel. All of our Army and Marine people were returned to their previous units. That was the end of Team No. 2. Most of the Navy men from Team No. 2 were used to form the nucleus of the newly organizing Team No. 3.

Gene E. "Nick" Nichols
Oklahoma City, Oklahoma

WE WENT TO Shima, a small island adjacent to the main island of Okinawa, where UDT No. 4 had the job of removing beach obstacles so the Army artillery could set up on Shima and shell gun emplacements and strongholds on the main island. One of the things we destroyed was a dock and related obstacles so it would be easier for wounded soldiers to be taken out to a hospital ship.

The seawall and the area near the dock had been secured. The invasion of Okinawa was early in April and the wind and water were uncomfortably cold. We tried to avoid the cold wind and random sniper and machine-gun fire by staying close to the seawall.

We received a number of wounded who were being loaded into boats to take them out to the hospital ship. We received some bad news from a stretcher bearer. He told us that Ernie Pyle had just been killed by sniper fire a short distance from where we were. Ernie Pyle was a highly acclaimed war correspondent who had only been in the Pacific for a short time. He had earned his reputation in the European Theater of operations. Ernie always was with the troops. He lived and worked and slept and ate with the servicemen and wrote wondrously about our exploits.

Ensign Lewis F. "Lew" Luehrs

WHEN SEABEE CHIEF Bill Acheson and I found out we were about to make a recon on the island of Kwajalein, we decided that if we came within range of too many coral heads, we would take off our fatigues and in our swim trunks swim in to the reef for a closer view.

The transport gave us a royal send-off, a last meal and farewell, and let us over the side for the big event. We approached the beach to within five hundred yards in the boat. When the coxswain became squeamish and the coral heads were thicker, we stripped to our swimsuits and dove over the side of the boat and proceeded toward the beach. We were in the water about forty-five minutes and were able to see gun emplacements and a large log barricade on the entire tip of the island. We found that the reef was covered with coral heads, which would prevent the landing of small boats, but we found no mines or man-made obstacles.

When we returned to the ship, we were whisked off still dripping wet to the flagship *Monrovia* for an impressive staff meeting, and to tell our story to Vice Admiral Turner, Rear Admiral Griffin, and Captain Knowles. We advised the use of amtracks instead of boats. The landing took place with the men in amtracks.

Staff Sergeant Patrick L. Finelli, USMC
Sudbury, Massachusetts

I ENLISTED IN the Marines in February 1943 and took boot camp on Parris Island, then went to Aviation Ordnance School, followed by Bomb Disposal and Explosive Demolitions School at North Island, Coronado Naval Base, in California. I was promoted to sergeant in April 1944 and assigned to MAG 45 Marine Ordnance Battalion.

In July 1944 our unit was in Santa Barbara, California, ready to ship out to see action in the South Pacific. Repeatedly we prepared for deployment with all of our gear, only to hear again that we had to wait.

They told us there was a screwup in Tinian involving the Marine Recons under Captain Jim Jones and a Naval Combat Demolitions Unit under Lieutenant Commander Draper Kauffman. The NCDUs had been sent on a mine-clearing operation but the weather and sea conditions forced abandonment of the explosives and the mission was aborted. The NCDUs didn't get to the beach, but the Marine Recons did. It also involved a dispute over "high water" responsibility. General Holland Smith felt that his Marine Recons could do the whole job of recon and clearing. The problem was, Recon was small and needed elsewhere.

General Smith sent out an order for teams to find demolition men who could be spared for underwater work in concert with his Recon men. Captain Sweet, our CO at the time, volunteered himself, me, and another Marine for this special assignment. I was a good swimmer and trained in bomb disposal and demolitions. We were dispatched to Eniwetok, where we were given physicals and swim tests. OSS (the Office of Special Services, the forerunner of the current CIA) personnel indoctrinated us with rigorous training in the use of mask and swim fins. Captain Sweet never participated, just observed and took notes. He was about thirty years old at the time, old for our kind of work.

In our training we experimented with "shot loads" to destroy Seabee-built obstacles. It was very serious, deadly, and surprisingly quiet—not much conversation at all. They told us prior demolition training was preferable, but it wasn't essential and could be taught. It would be easier to teach explosives than swimming. A higher priority was placed on swimming ability, such as strong swimming in open water. Much time was spent testing for panic levels when we were stressed despite clear visibility in sixty-foot-deep water when seen through a five-inch-diameter sea dive mask. The best advice we got was to stay calm, slow everything down, and not to get scared. We were taught to swim the sidestroke, the trudgen stroke, and the breaststroke, turning our heads to the side to minimize mask reflections. We used the crawl stroke for emergencies or extractions.

The explosives we used were a mix of what happened to be available, such as one-pound and half-pound blocks of TNT, C-3, 60 percent dynamite, tetryl, and tetrytol. We had ten-, thirty-, and one-hundred-cap blasting machines we called hell boxes. We also had Primacord, blasting caps (electric and natural), safety fuse with length formulas and calculations, delayed tetryl caps, and percussion caps.

We learned how to set charges in checkerboard and center patterns, how to waterproof connections, and, most importantly, team integrity and paired-buddy dependence. We also had some very good classroom instruction in Amphibious Landing Operations: missions and organization of combat demolition units, methods, and techniques. All in all, an intensive training program in eliminating man-made and natural underwater obstructions.

It was a marvelous addition to my Marine training. All the elements of discipline, brotherhood, and preparedness were evident and expected to be employed soon.

At the end of training, we were broken up and went different ways. My group was assigned to the USS *Clemson* (APD-31). She was a converted World War I destroyer with two stacks removed. On this mission we lost an APD when she collided with another destroyer and went down with all of the explosives from the ABLE unit. After the OSS loss, Underwater Demolition Team No. 6 took over that job and the fleet kept going. Swim teams were matched for reconnaissance on Peleliu.

Our job was to do recon on enemy-held beaches in September 1944. The Navy destroyers and battleships shelled the island while we were in the water. You could see the vortex of the shell in the air as the water rippled from the shock waves.

UDT No. 6 went in on Orange Beaches on September 12, 1944, with UDT Nos. 1, 2, and 3 and the 5th and 7th Marines. About noon, we scouted the beaches under fire and found many obstacles. Navy fighters strafed the beaches to help protect us. There was a lot of sniper fire. The tide was now low, the water shallow and showing lots of black coral.

The next day Team No. 6 prepared pathways for DUKW's and tanks over Orange Beach 2 and 3. We were swimming from seven A.M. to four P.M. There was a lot of sniper fire and the water was shallow and hot. A destroyer came in and gave us covering fire to keep the sniper's heads down.

On September 14 we continued beachhead demolitions. That morning the invasion fleet arrived. There were ships as far as I could see. From midnight to six A.M. we had no fire cover. From noon to four P.M. we had good fire cover from the Navy.

We found many two-horned antiship mines laced to horned scullies and coral cairns. They were one-hundred-pound type 98, set out about one hundred yards from the beach. Some of them were not armed: The safety pins weren't pulled. We realized that these mines were not there the day before. The Japanese had to have their own swimmers. Amazingly they had also buried some aircraft bombs in the beach with pressure fuses. We also found fuel drums laced to the fringing coral. The Japanese had had to work like hell to get that work done so quickly.

September 15, 1944. D-day. H hour was 8:30 A.M. The sea was calm, with no surf and few clouds, excellent weather but hot. The assault waves of boats had been forming up since four A.M. The noise was deafening and the smell stifling.

The first three assault waves were devastated. A great many LSTs were destroyed by enfilading Japanese fire. The beachhead was chaotic, and little penetration inland was made by the Marines. The succeeding waves of men and equipment were beginning to clog up the area. Our team was asked to help clear the beachhead. The Marine assault troops kept landing every eight minutes.

That was the end of my work with UDT No. 6. I was recalled by the Marines to work demolitions onshore. I reported to the CP at A Company, 1st Pioneers, and went up to the front with the 3rd Battalion 1st Marines in K Company.

While working with the Marines clearing and sealing caves with Bangalore torpedoes, I got caught in hand-to-hand combat with Japanese soldiers and was wounded by a bayonet. I was evacuated to Guam, then on to Hawaii.

By January 1945, I had fully recovered and returned to duty with my Marine company. I did more bomb disposal work and beach clearing until September of 1945, when I was hospitalized again due to a concussion. I was sent to the States to the Chelsea Naval Hospital in Massachusetts. I was discharged from the Marines on 26 March, 1946.

Gunner's Mate Second Class Willard W. Rudd
Cove, Oregon

I JOINED THE Navy when I was seventeen, in 1943. After boot camp and gunnery school I caught a ship to Pearl Harbor and was assigned to the USS *Sheridan*, *APA-51*. In a few days we headed for the islands of Saipan and

Tinian. We took both islands back from the Japanese. I was a radio operator and in the first wave. About the third day after the landing, our boat sank. I was with an officer, Paul Abbot. We swam to a minelayer and were taken on board. That night a Japanese bomb hit the ship. All fifty-five men on board took shrapnel wounds. The ship's skipper was killed. I picked up steel under my arm and on my side. We thought we were going to die.

We went out to the hospital ship but soon got thrown off for the really badly wounded men. The *Sheridan* left us there and the minelayer sank, so we were without a ship. We bummed around the Pacific for two weeks and hit half the islands out there. We had no food, only what we could bum. No money, no clothes. Not even a chaplain would help us. We wound up on Johnston Island. A plane took us back to Guam. From there we finally made it back to Pearl Harbor.

I'd had enough of picking up wounded Marines with no legs or arms and trying to help hold a guy's guts in as they spilled out through our fingers. Most of them still died.

I joined UDT Team No. 3 just back from Guam. We were stationed on Maui. There were about ninety men on the team. We trained hard for three months blowing up miles of coral reefs, fish, and trees. We finally headed for Iwo Jima, then got sidetracked to the Philippines. There we checked out beaches, but there was not much going on for us. We watched the great General MacArthur make his walk ashore.

We were back in the U.S.A. when the war ended. They shipped us out for Japan the same day. We went to a small town that raised cultured pearls. We confiscated all guns and swords. The houses had boxes full of cultured pearls. We took all we could find.

On the way back home on the ship we threw handfulls of pearls over the side to watch them sparkle as they sank. I got home with ten of them. A jeweler in San Diego offered me $20 each for all I could get him. Then I was sorry that we had thrown thousands of them into the ocean.

On the way home on the boat, it was Thanksgiving. The officers had roasted turkey, we had Spam. Three or four of our guys stole a turkey from the cooks. We had a great turkey feast. We threw the bones over the side but the cargo door was open below us and the bones blew back into our sleeping quarters. The officers found them. I can still hear the skipper cursing us and threatening to send us all to the brig. He never did.

Team No. 3 had it lucky: We didn't get into as much heavy action as some of the other teams. Fifty years later I attended one of the UDT reunions and I found out that the stories have all got real wild. I sure never knew we were such great heroes!

I was discharged from the Navy in 1947 after four years of duty.

From WWII UDT Historical Files: Team No. 3

UNDERWATER DEMOLITION TEAM NO. 3 was one of the first five original teams organized at Maui, Hawaii, in March of 1944. Lieutenant Crist, CEC, USNR, was operations officer of Team No. 2 and was reassigned as commanding officer of Team No. 3. Brought in from Teams Nos. 1 and 2 were twenty-two men and three officers with combat experience in the Marshall Islands. They formed a nucleus for the newly formed Team No. 3. Added to this group were men and officers who had finished their six weeks of basic demolition training at Fort Pierce, Florida. Training and operations took place at Waimanalo on Oahu and later on Maui.

Many of the enlisted men were Seabees and eleven of the officers were CEC. All were volunteers and most had spent several weeks of demolition training and physical fitness work at Camp Perry, Virginia, in addition to training at Fort Pierce.

UDT No. 3 boarded the USS *Typhon* (ARL-28), in Hawaii on 17 April, 1944, heading for the Solomon Islands. The ship arrived off Guadalcanal on May 2. From May 6 to May 16 the team lived ashore at Turner City, Florida Island. They did some maneuvers and demolition work with the Fifth Amphibious Corps during this period.

UDT No. 3 was in reserve capacity for the Saipan landings and then proceeded to Guam to begin reconnaissance of the landing beaches. The decision was made to postpone the landings on Guam in view of the First Battle of the Philippine Sea. From 16 June until 1 July the team underwent daily air attacks while on board the USS *Dickerson* (APD-21). The ship was ordered to proceed to Eniwetok.

On 10 July the team on its APD was ordered to return to Guam. They arrived on 10 July, 1944. Four days later they were ordered to start reconnaissance and demolition operations on the western coast of Guam. The *Dickerson* was accompanied by two DDs and four LCIGs.

Four UDT officers were put on board the LCIGs to coordinate fire support and remained there for the preinvasion work of Team No. 3. The same day UDT Team No. 3 made a daylight recon of two thousand yards of Asan Beach. They then did a diversionary recon of Agana Beach. A night recon to the high-water line of all landing beaches at Asan was made. At 2300 one rubber boat was hit by three bursts of machine-gun fire and contact with three men from the boat was lost. They couldn't be found. At 0015 the signal was given to withdraw.

The next morning at 0430 the DD *Donough* picked up the three missing men 2,300 yards offshore. They had been forced by our own fire and enemy fire to leave the edge of the reef and had been swimming for five hours. They suffered only slightly from exposure. The three men were Ensign M. Jacobson, Ensign W. J. Dezell, and GM 3/C J. E. Bagnall.

The team made a diversionary daylight recon on Dadi Beach. Heavy fire came from Orote Peninsula. The Battleship *Pennsylvania* silenced the enemy battery, but LCIG 469 suffered five casualties from the enemy fire.

Chief Warrant Officer R. A. Blowers was killed by enemy small-arms fire when his LCPR grounded momentarily on a coral head.

The team did night removal of obstacles on Asan Beach. LCIG 348, which had just joined the task unit, went aground and delayed operations while personnel were removed by UDT. A hundred and twenty obstacles were removed from the beach and 2,400 pounds of tetrytol was used.

On July 19 the team removed 194 obstacles in daylight work on Asan Beach. There were 4,200 pounds of tetrytol used.

On Adelup Point there were ninety obstacles, piles of coral rock with wire frames made of Cyclone-like fencing. These were three to five feet in diameter, three to four feet high, and five to eight feet apart. Some were unfinished. The enemy had been building new ones after we withdrew from a night of clearing. No mines were located.

The clearing of beaches worked this way: Each platoon of fifteen men and two or three officers left the APD in an LCPR, towing behind them two rubber boats loaded with thirty packs of tetrytol. As the LCPR approached the reef, the rubber boats were cast off with five or six men in each boat. They were paddled or dragged as close to the obstacles as possible. A Primacord trunk line was run along the length of the obstacles to be blown. One pack of tetrytol was placed alongside each obstacle and tied in with the Primacord leads on the trunk line. Two caps were used on each lead. When all obstacles had been loaded and the men had returned to the rubber boats, the firing signal was given and a four-minute fuse pulled.

On William Day, 21 July 1944, UDT personnel were on the edge of the reef to guide in the 8th wave, LCMs carrying medium tanks. They all made it to shore.

After the invasion, the team did postassault operations in clearing and removing new hazards on the beach and in the water. They completed their work there on 28 July and were released. The team gives credit to the support of the gunboats with intense and accurate fire over the UDT men's heads. They kept the enemy's heads down covering the beach with such a volume of 40- and 20mm fire that it was impossible for the enemy to give strong opposition to the UDT men.

The *Dickerson*, with UDT No. 3 on board, left Guam and sailed to Pearl Harbor. She arrived at Maui on 10 August. The men had a ten-day leave then found some changes to the team. The number of officers was dropped to thirteen and the enlisted group increased to eighty-five.

On September 15, 1944, Team No. 3 embarked on the USS *Talbot* (APD-7), and headed for Yap in the

Caroline Islands but were rerouted to Manus in the Admiralty Islands and arrived on 5 October.

They made their first trip to Leyte on 12 October, weathered a typhoon, and arrived on the beach at Leyte on 18 October and began operations immediately.

Platoons 1 and 3 made a swimming recon of a five-hundred-yard landing beach. Platoon Nos. 2 and 4 were reserve. LCPRs moved to within five hundred yards of the beaches, drawing fire from machine guns in the town of Dulag. Swimmers went right up to the beach. No mines or man-made obstacles were found. The beach was said to be ideal for amphibious assault. Swimmers moved out to sea and were recovered. The whole operation took seventy minutes. There were no casualties.

No duties were required of the team on D-1 on D-day, and the Team left Leyte on October 22 and arrived at Manus on October 27. Members transferred to the USS *President Hayes* on November 1. On November 11 the ship departed for the Hawaiian Islands.

Team No. 3 arrived at Maui on 23 November and the men were granted a leave. There followed an eight-week ongoing training program. Techniques for blasting coral and lava were added to the training.

In early April the team was ordered to the States and given leave until 1 May when the men reported to Fort Pierce. Lieutenant (jg) R. P. Marshall was named new commanding officer of UDT No. 3. Team reorganization was extensive. Ten new officers were acquired and six new enlisted men. The team trained for three weeks at Fort Pierce and was then ordered to Oceanside, California, on 19 July, 1945.

On V-J day, 14 August, 1945, UDT No. 3 embarked on the USS *Ira Jeffery* (APD-44), and headed for Manila on 16 August.

The war was over, but UDT No. 3 would see more service.

Radioman Second Class Robert M. (Woody) Wood
South Dennis, Massachusetts

I ENLISTED IN the Navy in September 1942 at Boston, Massachusetts, and took boot camp at the Great Lakes Naval Training Center. I took radio school at Pier 61 in New York City and was assigned to the amphibious force at Norfolk, Virginia.

I made radioman 3/C and was assigned to the USS *Ancon*, a former luxury cruiser converted into an AG communications ship. We were headed for North Africa port of Oran.

The ship became headquarters for the Army, Air Corps, and Navy people in the operation to invade Sicily. We went back to Oran, where I was transferred to the USS *Calvert*, an APA, and returned on her to Norfolk.

After several months there I requested sea duty in the Pacific. Our commanding officer was Douglas Fairbanks Jr., the actor. Four of us, all radiomen 3/C were given secret orders to report to Pearl Harbor for an unknown assignment. We left Norfolk at night and sailed through the Panama Canal and on to Pearl Harbor.

We disembarked early in the morning and were transported to a small naval base at Waimanalo, Oahu. That was the headquarters for the Underwater Demolition Teams Nos. 1 and 2. We were assigned to Team No. 1 and began training: swimming, boat handling, explosives, but nothing for me dealing with communications. Teams were made up of Navy Seabees, powder monkeys, Marines, and some Army men. Other members returned from the Marshall Islands about this time. The top brass decided that the UDTs would become 100 percent Navy. A new base was to be built in Maui. The naval personnel of Teams 1 and 2 now became Teams 3 and 4, with additional personnel coming out of Fort Pierce, Florida. Not only did we continue training but we also were involved in training those coming in from Fort Pierce.

A few brass eyebrows were raised when our teams requested two gross of condoms. They were not for sexual purposes but used to waterproof our firing caps, which were underwater much of the time.

We learned that we would be involved in island invasions in the South Pacific. We soon boarded the USS *Kent*, an APD. It was a converted World War I destroyer with two stacks removed. We found out later the craft was not too reliable. We arrived at Eniwetok Atoll, where the fleet would gather prior to the planned invasion.

According to ship scuttlebutt we were heading for Saipan. But this was later changed and we prepared for the taking of Guam. It would serve as an advance air base. We were told that the major landing areas were surrounded by coral heads that extend up to two hundred yards out into sea and they had to be cleared. We would have to clear channels wide enough to allow LSTs to drop their Marines directly on the beach.

Team No. 3 had one area and Team No. 4 the other. We did our first recon at night to get a feel of the situation. We then planned our first approach to drop swimmers and powder and blow the coral heads. This was now four days before the Marines were set to land. During this time we worked both days and received heavy mortar and rifle fire. We also worked at night blowing the coral heads and opening up the channels. During this time the Japs would replace the tetrahedrons and barbed wire, which we would then blow up again. My job was communications between our mother ship and the four LCI gun boats that were continually firing over our heads and keeping the Japs pinned down. We lost one man killed but no injuries. On D-day we escorted the Marines and landing craft to the already marked channels. At this point our job was temporarily done. We did help to escort wounded to a hospital ship lying off the island.

We went back to our ship and prepared for the invasion of Saipan. We would be backups to teams 5 and 6. We were issued a nip of Le John brandy, and that sure warmed us up. Prior to the landings we did screening duty for the last armada of ships involved in the landing. Once the Marines became established on the island, we headed back to Maui. We were given a week of R & R in the Islands, so a group of us went to the big island. On our return, all Team No. 3 enlisted men were awarded the Bronze Star and the officers the Silver Star. At this point I was reassigned to the Maui base as ship's company.

While at our base in Maui, there were many local Kanakas who lived nearby. These men were fishermen but during the war the Navy wouldn't let them use their boats to fish. They had to fish from the shore. We frogmen decided to help them out and train with explosives at the same time.

We would be out in one of the fishing areas on a training run in an LCP(R) and spot a school of large fish. We came over them and dropped a charge into the water with a short fuse. The ensuing explosion was enough to stun the big fish without killing them. We jumped in the water and shoved the fish in burlap bags we had brought with us. Then we brought the fish back to shore and gave them to the locals. We were their friends for life.

Edwin T. Higgins, Underwater Demolition Team

At Okinawa we moved in to our assigned beach, where the obstacles we had to blow up were only fifty to sixty yards from the muzzles of the weapons in the pillboxes and machine-gun nests: point-blank range for a blind man. All of our team made it to the obstacles without being hit and we rested for a minute, clinging to the posts, letting the Schantz packs snag to a halt in the maze of barbed wire.

Over our heads the fire support drummed a thunderous tattoo. Our ships and planes seemed determined to keep the Japs in their holes if shells and bombs could do the trick. The little LCIGs lay in close behind us, their 20- and 40mm quads and their .50-caliber machine guns pumping in perfect rhythm as they fired only a few feet over our heads at the beach. Behind them the destroyers worked back and forth across their grid patterns, slamming three- and five-inch shells in arithmetical patterns in the jungle above the shoreline. Beyond the destroyers were the cruisers and battlewagons salvoing their six-, eight-, and sixteen-inch guns in great bursts of fire that made their land targets jump and quiver, erupting in clouds of dust and debris.

The shells from the sixteen-inch guns sounded above the screaming and whining of the smaller shells, rumbling through the shattered air like runaway freight cars. High above all of this sound and fury, the F6F fighters and the TBM Avenger torpedo bombers from the carriers added their own individual tones to the murderous symphony, loosing their bombs, rockets, and machine-gun fire barely above the heads of the entrenched enemy.

Electrician's Mate Second Class Tony Provenzo
Woodinville, Washington

I JOINED THE Navy on October 14, 1943, one day after I reached my seventeenth birthday. I took my boot training in Stanford, New York, and then went to Bainbridge, Maryland, where I went to gunner's school in February of 1944. When I graduated they sent me to Pearl Harbor in April 1944. The second week in May in Hawaii, they assigned me to *LST-353*.

On May 21 there was an explosion on *353* in the harbor at Westlock there at Pearl and it involved seven ships. My ship sank after the explosion. There were several hundred men wounded and nearly two hundred killed. The event was hushed up so the Japanese wouldn't know about it. I was wounded and spent a month in the hospital at Pearl.

In June of 1944 I was released from the hospital and assigned to the USS *Sheridan* (APA-51). I wasn't pleased with my duty there. I was a young kid and I wanted to get into the war action. I was set to go to a Navy school about government. In the meantime I was a striker trying for an electrician's rate. Neither the rate nor the school happened. Two months later I noticed a call for volunteers for UDT. You had to be a good swimmer. I applied at once, the way it said, but I didn't get called. Shortly after that we left Pearl Harbor.

I took part with the *Sheridan* in the invasion of Guam in 1944 and then Leyte in the Philippines in October of that year. At Leyte I got assigned to the beach master's group and went ashore to mark it. Shortly after October of 1944 my orders came through to report for UDT training. I thought they would send me back to the States and to Florida, but instead I went to Maui to the training base there. I arrived there in November of 1944. I was among the first men from the fleet to take the UDT training. They told us we were Team Xray and that we would go into combat together. Wrong.

We went through the regular training, swimming, lots of physical work, night blasting of obstacles, reconnaissance, and much practice in taking soundings and evaluation of beach slopes. I had a swim partner and we worked with a red line and measured the depth of the water at various distances on the beach and put it down on a small plastic writing plate we carried. We looked for anything that would affect small boats landing on that beach.

We finished in January of 1945 just as several teams came in from Fort Pierce. One of them was Team No. 11. In training there they had a premature blast that killed two men and wounded several others. They needed replacements. I was one of the men who went into Team No. 11 as a filler.

We soon left for the invasion of Okinawa. We started in March 1945 doing pre-recon work and swimming with lead lines on the beach. We marked down the beach gradient, the depth of the water, type of bottom, current conditions, and any obstacles that we observed that would mess up a landing.

We took a lot of small-arms fire and mortar rounds as we were going in. Our ship was constantly firing over our heads into the beach to keep the Japanese gunners as quiet as possible. We finished up the work there the last day in March.

On April 1, 1945, the invasion of Okinawa got under way. It was Easter Sunday and also April Fool's day. That's when the Japanese kamikazes zeroed in on our beach. Quite a few of them crashed but none hit our ship. Our recon work showed new posts and barbed wire in the beach. We went in and blew them up in about six feet of water. The water was cold and we had smeared axle grease on our bodies to help hold in our heat.

We each carried two twenty-pound packages of explosives in canvas bags. We tied neoprene balloons on the packages so they would float in water. We jumped over the side of the ship and started swimming for shore. We got rid of the obstacles and the Marines landed, pushing their boats up almost to dry sand. We worked three or four more days, exploding ordnance and removing other obstacles so more ships could land.

We finished there, and in early June 1945 we and UDT No. 18 went to Borneo to check the beaches. This would be the last amphibious landing of World War II. Both our teams did recon work on the beaches. The harbor was heavily mined by the Japanese. We left our ship, the APA *Kline*, and went into the harbor on board a small minesweeper. We got in maybe five hundred yards offshore and then went on in with our rubber boat and made our recon. We did the usual work with depths at various distances, beach gradient, type of bottom, any obstacles, and currents.

We worked on Borneo for four or five days and found posts and barbed wire out seventy-five yards from the beach. Some had contact mines on them as well. We did carry a mine hook about the size of a lead pencil with a special detonator. We hooked it on the mine and activated it, and when it went off it set off the mine.

It was the last week in June when we started blasting obstacles in Borneo. We had considerable small-arms and mortar fire, but the only casualty we had in Borneo was a friendly-fire bomb from a Navy plane that killed one of the UDT men and sent six or seven others out for medical attention. I didn't get hurt in that one.

We finished that operation on July 4, 1945, and celebrated with clearing a large area of beach with large explosions.

Shortly after Borneo we were on our way back to the States. They told us the next job would be the invasion of Japan itself. They warned us that they expected a monstrous fight and that we would have extremely heavy casualty rates. They told us that anyone who wanted to ask for a transfer out of the teams was free to do so and the act would not be held against them. Some of the married guys in the teams left the unit. Most of the single guys stayed in the UDT.

In July of 1945 we were back in the States at Camp Pendleton, California, near Oceanside. We were there for what they called cold-water training. By the first of August they had arranged nine-day leaves for us with Class C priority. That meant I could bump some important person off the plane and fly commercial or military back to New York. I went home and was there when the bombs were dropped on Japan.

When my leave was over I reported back to Camp Pendleton in the morning and that same day they began loading our ships. We left the next day for a nonstop run to Japan. We landed at Nagasaki and did some recon work there, then a couple of other beaches. Late in September we headed back to the States and landed at the Amphibious Base in Coronado, California.

That completed my World War II experiences in Froggie Land. I stayed on as the teams shrank down to four with No. 1 and No. 3 based at Coronado and No. 2 and No. 4 based on the East Coast.

Lieutenant (jg) Donald Murray
Spokane, Washington

IN 1942 I was enrolled in Washington State College at Pullman, Washington. I wasn't required to take ROTC, but I heard about the Navy V-7 college study program and I liked it. Several of us went from Pullman to Seattle and passed the physical and were allowed to join the program and finish our college work. I graduated in June 1942 and received my orders as a midshipman 22 May 1943, to report to the *Prairie State*, a World War I battleship on the Hudson river in New York to attend electrical engineering school. After three months on the Hudson, I realized I didn't know much about electrical engineering. I was offered the option of transferring to deck school, be an apprentice seaman, or return home and wait for the draft. I applied to deck school and on November 15, 1943, was sent to Cornell University as an ensign to train.

Cornell was my piece of cake. I had already had basic training and as a Boy Scout I knew code, semaphore, and many other helpful things. I got the second highest grades in the regiment. I was made regimental commander for the second two months. It was fun to lead the regiment in the weekly parades and formations.

When graduation came in March 1944, I still had the second highest grades, so I had the second choice of all available billets. I chose a destroyer that was being built at Norfolk and took a seven-day leave. The last day at Cornell we were sent to a big auditorium classroom and listened to a Navy commander who gave a plea for adventuresome officers to join the Underwater Demolition Units in Fort Pierce, Florida. I didn't volunteer until my five buddies around me did and through pokes and jokes pushed my hand up. My orders were changed to report to Fort Pierce on April 1, 1944.

My UDT training was exhaustive and interesting. We swam a mile each morning and ran in the sand for miles and soon played tackle football without pads. After three months of sweat and night problems I was asked to stay and teach explosives. It was fun, and night missions were part of the job. I lost an eardrum one night when I was too close to a blast. I taught booby-trapping and shape-charge uses and also blew a hole in an antitank concrete wall four feet thick and eight feet high, wide enough to drive a tank through. This bit of explosive work blew out windows in Fort Pierce and dropped ceilings in the town three miles away.

Dottie and I were married on June 9, 1944, at the First Presbyterian Church in Fort Pierce. We found a great summer house complete with ants, spiders, and huge palmetto bugs, which were giant cockroaches. We even had our own little lizard. We could hear the voodoo drums at night from the natives' section not too far away.

On October 3, Dottie left to go back to teaching and I left for the Pacific with UDT Team No. 13: Lt. Commander Moranz, our CO, twelve officers, and eighty enlisted men from all walks of life. We arrived in San Bruno, California, after a long cattle car ride on the train across the U.S.A.

On October 9, 1944, we left on the USS *General M. M. Patrick* (AP-150). We arrived in Pearl Harbor 14 October, then went by barge to the UDT training base on Maui. We lived in Army tents and ate out of garbage cans until makeshift kitchens were finished. We had more training in the sun and on the beach areas. I was promoted to lieutenant junior grade while on that station.

On January 4, 1945, I was ordered to Pearl Harbor with a crew of four men to get supplies for our war expedition. We really loaded up. They gave us anything we wanted besides the regular-issue materiel of equipment and arms. We left on the USS *Barr*, our fighting ship. She was a destroyer escort, the *AP-54*.

Our Underwater Demolition Team No. 13 comprised our skipper, Pinkie Moran, twelve other officers, and the men of all ages and backgrounds. We had lots of rubber boats and gear of all sorts aboard the *Barr*. She was a small vessel with one five-inch gun forward, four tubs of 20mm guns, and with our .50-caliber machine guns mounted on rails all around the ship. My gun was set up on the bridge deck forward center with Robbie, my gunner's mate, at the grips.

Later, after the Iwo Jima invasion, we were in the Okinawa fracas and I spotted a Jap Betty bomber at eleven o'clock high. I shouted to Robbie, "Fire! Fire! Fire!" All I heard were a series of clicks and nothing else. My only combat order ended in a jammed gun.

The bunks on the ship were small steel rectangles of pipe that had a canvas stretched on the frame for springs. A thin mattress and a couple of blankets and a miserable pillow made up the bunk. However, I don't ever remember having trouble sleeping. We were forward in the space directly below the five-inch gun. When it went off you didn't want to be below. Light bulbs broke and everything shuddered.

I remember another eerie sensation: That was when, lying in my bunk next to the side of the ship I could hear the water rushing by outside. How thick was that hull?

The skipper was Captain Dickie, a quiet engineer type guy. The first officer was a regular Navy, sharp all-around savvy Navy. We had for a time an officer for recreation and entertainment by the name of Eddy Duchin. That's right, the famous piano player Eddy Duchin. He had brought along a collection of his records and played them regularly and kept us thinking of home. One night he had fortified his courage way too much and had a hard time staying on the piano stool. He didn't stay with us long.

We were passengers on the DE but we did some duties to help the ship's men. Generally we sat around and read or played chess, or spent time on deck as lookouts for any enemy activity.

Ten days before the landing on Iwo Jima we got orders to proceed to Iwo and erect a flashing light on some low, partly awash volcanic rock called Higashi Iwo, less than a mile from the main beaches. What a stupid order. *Boats away* is the order for us to take the pipe frame with a blinking light on it to the ragged, jagged rocks and set it up.

The Japs must have howled with glee at the fumbling efforts and amazed at an enemy ship stopping right in their front yard. You could almost throw a rock that far, and my .22 rifle would have easily made a shambles of the operation. To our amazement there was no enemy fire on us. The men returned and the light blinked and we steamed for the horizon. We were all smiles until the next morning, when we were again ordered to install another blinking light on the same beach. The Japs or the ocean had destroyed our first light. We had to do the stupid thing again.

This time the Japs were ready for us. I was on the bridge, watching the rounds hit the rocks and shrapnel splattering around us on the ship. The men scrambled around hiding in holes and finally got the blinking thing set up and going. They jumped in the LCVP and made it back to the ship without any bad hurts except some deep cuts from the volcanic rocks.

While the men were on the rocks we had a good laugh. I was watching Ensign Healy, the boat officer for the operation, running the VP craft. After dropping off the men on the rocks, he speeded away to wait for them and pick them up when done. He was looking back and saw he was being chased by twin spurts of machine-gun fire. Bob was swinging the boat in S curves to try to get away. Not funny now, but when you are tense, something like that is funny, especially when nobody was hurt and everyone escaped.

Later we learned that the venture failed to last again, but there were no more tries to get a blinker light on those rocks. During the operation we received two or three shots from shore batteries and our ship's gunnery officer quickly silenced them with several rounds from our five-inch gun.

On D-day minus two, Team No. 13 was assigned to recon the East Beaches Green 1 and Red 1. The two beaches are next to Mount Suribachi. The mountain was full of hidden and cave-mounted guns. Both beaches together measure about a thousand yards. The advanced information said the beach sand was not a hindrance to landing. Ha. Supposedly they saw flutatsune, and antitank barriers were observed, but no water obstacles. On February 14, 1945, we were to send swimmers to the East beaches in the morning and to the west beaches in the afternoon.

Then the orders were changed. UDT No. 13 would only send in one boatload of swimmers to Green Beach, next to the Mount Suribachi's most dangerous beach. Teams 12, 14, and 15 were north of us and covered the balance of the east beach. Ten swimmers went in with tremendous gunfire support. Destroyers, cruisers, and battleships poured out continuous fire at the island. The noise and dust were awesome.

I was assigned duties as information officer. My job was to debrief the men after the recon and make a report and a map of their findings. Each man was to cover a five-yard swath in and another five-yard swath out, then back out to be picked up. During this time I was sent onto one of the LCIG gunboats to observe and relay information back to the control.

At the same time two LCVPs launched from the *Barr*. One was a standby in case of need. The other one dropped swimmers parallel to the shore and came out on standby. The fire from shore was unmerciful. Bullets rained down on the swimmers. Eight-inch shells were decimating the LCIGs. Eleven of the twelve were hit. Mine was unscathed. The mortar fire was so bad and the fire so heavy that I called for smoke screens, and minutes later the shore was obliterated and things quieted down. One LCIG sank and we had many men injured. Our swimmers finished and returned. I was picked up by the second boat and, on board our ship, debriefed the swimmers and was happy to send the info that no underwater obstacles were found and landing craft could land there. The swimmers before leaving had smeared axle grease over their skin, as they wore only trunks, face mask, and fins and had a sheath knife and plastic recording slate. The water was about 60 degrees. The men were shaking from the cold when they returned, and the standard medical rum portion was distributed.

That same day Team No. 13 and the others moved to the west side of Iwo Jima and started again. UDT No. 13 was assigned the same south beach, called 31 Purple Beach, next to damn Mount Suribachi. There were no LCIGs this time but we were given aircraft support. They constantly strafed the beaches from the high-water line up and added moral support which unfortunately didn't stop the continuous rifle and mortar fire. The men stayed under the water as long as they could. One of our swimmers strayed out of our area because of the strong current and was picked up by Team No. 12. Others of the teams had bad cold-water cramps and several had to be rescued at the surf line. One UDT swimmer was killed, but there were no other casualties.

The *Barr* resumed picket duty and all appeared relaxed until news arrived that Team No. 15 on the DE *Blessman* had taken a direct bomb in the mess hall. They lost eighteen men killed and twenty-three wounded. They were our buddies and friends.

One of our duties after a recon was to assemble the information on the beaches and relay it to the Marines who were to land there on D-day. Ensign Healy was sent to the Marine transport with the information that no mines, underwater obstacles, or beach obstacles were observed on the landing beaches. The Marines always reacted in a most positive way. They offered Healy so many drinks that he was absolutely poured back aboard our ship.

On 19 February, 1945, I had the honor to lead the waves of Marines into Green Beach. I got into the LCP(R) and circled in the ocean between the beach and the swarms of boats loaded with Marines, who were in circles a quarter of a mile to sea. When D-hour arrived I stood in the boat and raised my arm, waved it in a circle, and pointed it at the beach and gave the signal *full speed*. Behind me the landing craft assembled in rows and they came on. When I got to my LCIG, I climbed on board and was thrilled to see the start of the first wave hitting the beach. I don't remember how I got back to the *Barr*.

We still had fifteen tons of tetryl and tetrytol on board the *Barr*. We loaded it on boats and took it ashore because the Marines were in dire straits, running low on powder to blast the enemy out of their bunkers and caves.

We stayed on board for another day until we were ordered to help clear the beach. The beach battalion men were unable to keep the beach clean of trucks, tanks, jeeps, barges, and other equipment. I was in charge of a crew of four: Barrett, Jordan, Evans, and Lazar. As soon as we saw the jumbled mess, I called for some LST tank supply ships to come in and send their anchor cables to the beach. We hooked them to the equipment and the ships dragged the wrecked jeeps and landing craft into the ocean and sank them. In about four hours we had the beach clean for more equipment to be sent in. The beach was not sand: It was a loose volcanic ash that settled over your boot tops with each step. All equipment bogged down until mats were sent in to provide a firm base. I was through and looked around but no one else was there. One of my men, Jordan, called out that there was a red alert and l should find some cover. A red air alert means that the enemy air is about to strike. Our small boats left us and headed back to the *Barr*. I thought my revolver might have to be tested after all. Jordan, after the all-clear, showed me the most beautiful twin-barrel small-caliber machine gun. It was an enemy gun and brand new. He asked if he could keep it. Like a good officer I said no. That was dumb. I never got smart about a lot of things.

After twelve days of beach work and night-time picket duty, we left Iwo Jima for Guam. R & R was the order. My crew knew of a UDT rest camp up in the hills of Guam and asked if I could get us up there to visit some buddies. I tried and came up with a 4 x 4 vehicle and we took off. The camp had an eight-foot-high barbed-wire-topped fence enclosure with guard towers and machine guns at all corners. I wondered about the rest part. Looked more like a prison. After finding a few friends, I found it was to keep the enemy out and the men in. Guam was not secured yet. Anyway, back to the ship, and three or four days later we headed for Ulithi, a group of atolls in the Carolinas. It was a layover and rest time. We were starting to let down some. Our skipper had a lower hold full of beer, so we went ashore and had some. After part of one, the heat, anxiety, and the beer gave me a violent headache. I couldn't see, so I got into my bunk and rested. We lost one of our men, Ray Le Blanc, there. He was a welder and offered to help the *Barr* men weld on rings lower on the sides of the ship so small rafts or boats could hold them into the ship to paint the sides. A large wave grounded him and he fell over and drowned. He was the only man we lost in World War II.

On March 20, 1945, we were on the move again, bound for the Ryukyu Islands and Okinawa. Teams 12, 13, 14, and 19 arrived. Then Nos. 4, 7, 11, 16, 17, and 21 were set to arrive later with the task force that was preparing to invade Okinawa. On March 24 the battle for Okinawa began with a bombardment by cruisers and battleships, which turned out the lights at several towns. Here we go again.

Now my fear rose. The divine wind of the kamikaze planes had been causing horrible damage. Picket duty was no longer a cruise. We had several close misses—extremely close.

We were supposed to recon Okinawa and the Kerama-Rettō Islands. Also Kiese Shima and the big island of the group, called Tokashiki. On 25 March the Team No. 13 recon of the beaches went off like clockwork. In and out with reports to the Marines, with the same results. No mines or obstacles other than coral at three or four feet below the surface. No problem for the landing craft. On 26 March we started the invasion with the UDT scouts leading the way.

Several days later we were assigned the Kiese Shima Island, two miles off the coast of Okinawa. It is a long, low island like an atoll and had small trees. We were to explore and secure it so that the Army could put heavy artillery ashore for the Okinawa bombardment.

I was in command of the LCP(R) and ten swimmers to enter a lagoon with two openings around an island in the center. We arrived under the gunfire protection of an LCIG, which was liberally spraying the area with 40mm rounds. We came around and the LCIG dropped our men and circled the island, waiting for the swimmers and zigzagging the boat so that mortar fire would be inaccurate. The most men lost in UDT operation are in the small boats with mortar fire landing right on them. Coming around the bay, I looked up and saw a giant Japanese soldier standing on the ridge above us. It took a second to see he was as amazed as we were to see each other: *The crazy enemy is down there taking a swim in our bay.* He didn't have orders to handle the situation, so he just watched. We roared around the island again and came alongside the LCIG just after one of its own 40mm rounds exploded in the gun. We found a messy gun tub.

It was time to pick up the swimmers, and at full speed we swung one after another into the boat. They waited in a straight line for our pickup. We got into the VP and went for the *Barr*. No obstructions on the beach—clear and ready for the troops.

The next operation on the small island was to clear a channel in to another beach. Large coral heads and reefs were removed with twenty-pound tetrytol satchels with Primacord leads and trunk cords. A clean approach was made and there was no enemy activity encountered. They were too busy on the big island. We had one bad day, however. Two U.S. dive bombers discovered us working on the approach to the beach and thought we were enemy. The men were dive-bombed but sustained no casualties. Radios hummed. We were suspected of being suicide swimmers, as we had suicide boats also to worry about. We used twenty-seven tons of explosives in those three days.

The invasion of Okinawa started on Easter Sunday, April 1. The *Barr* had picket duty with men scanning the skies watching for the Japanese suicide planes. Sometime before this invasion, proximity fuses were issued to most of the ships. These rounds would explode when they came close to anything—a tree, a house, or a kamikaze suicide plane. This may have been the reason we shot down so many of them.

One night in the fleet anchorage in the Kerama-Rettō, we were hit just at sunset. Several dozen "winds of heaven" kamikaze attacked our fleet, and it was a huge fight. Warships of every size—tanker, supply ships, and troop ships—were there at anchor. We saw them coming and so did the fleet gunners. The sky was full of tracers: One slug in every fifth round glowed in the back end of the bullet, so the gunners could see where their rounds were going. The sky was loaded. It was beautiful but tragic. A Japanese Betty bomber crashed with its bombs onboard on the bow of an oil tanker and the eruption was huge. War is a waste and beautiful, too, in an artistic way. We saw a number of ships hit by planes that got through the picket of ships and our own planes.

One afternoon we were alongside a tanker taking on fuel when a red air alert sounded. From straight over us a kamikaze made a dive on us and took off our antenna but landed in the water next to us. It disappeared into the ocean without a trace. Another time we had a red air alert and we saw two of our own fighter planes take off on the other side of the island. Above the next island over we saw them shot out of the sky by Japanese gunners.

UDT No. 13 was ordered off the *Barr*, as our work was done and touring aboard a picket ship was useless and dangerous. So we were sent aboard a disabled transport that had been hit by a kamikaze at the waterline. We went into the engine room and could see the plane without wings there with the dead pilot still in the mangled wreckage. A destroyer came alongside to supply power to the ship and it became a floating hotel ship for wounded and survivors.

We left after a few days on the APA *Wayne*. Aboard, we survived on two meals a day, and that was provisioned from the Aussies. It was mealy meat and bread full of weevils. We soon found that by holding a slice of bread up to the light, we could see dark spots and pick out most of the weevils. We survived by playing chess and congratulating each other for simply surviving so far.

The second night on the APA, we learned that a kamikaze had sunk our hotel ship. Lucky No. 13 had saved us again.

By the end of April we were back in our base on Maui, living in screened tents with wood floors. Our base was where Keanae Beach is now in the shadow of Red Hill and a red dusty plain. We had beautiful water and beaches, and fishing was excellent down island in the lava caves. We would fish with half a pound of tetrytol: light a short fuse and throw the bomb in the water. Soon, out would float a dozen panfish. We traded them to the native Hawaiians for steak dinners.

We got a seven-day leave, but I stayed on Maui and swam and fished.

Back on Maui, Team No. 13 men were to become instructors for UDT teams at the training and experimental UDT base. Teams 27, 28, and 29 graduated in two months. Early on, I was disgusted with the training we had for gathering information and reporting. I made a trip to the UDT headquarters. I saw Commander Kauffman, our leader, and told him what I thought of the entire info job we were doing. He agreed and made me chart and photo interpreter officer in charge of training all teams in new methods of information gathering, reporting, and mapmaking. I had a dozen photo mates and two photojournalists and we went to work. The photo journalists came to me one day and asked if we could assemble all UDT exploits and write a history with photos. Captain Couble gave us permission and asked for two copies. I didn't think to make a copy for myself. The men did a super job. I delivered the two copies to the captain and can't find any record of the work in any Navy files.

Captain Couble was a bit neurotic. His tent was stretched without a wrinkle or sag. It was surrounded by a field of gravel at least a yard wide on all sides. If anyone crossed the gravel, day or night, out rushed his lordship with a cocked .45, asking enraged questions. It was rumored that he lost his ship at Ulithi. He commanded a supply ammunition ship. A red air alert was sounded and he panicked and ran his ship aground trying to flee. When we left he was having a home built for himself closer to the water. It was nice, small, with redwood trim and screened openings and wood adjustable louvers on all the windows. Our Navy carpenters were excellent craftsmen.

Operation Olympic was the code name for the invasion of Japan. The big one was next. We heard many rumors about the cold water and the giant Japs on the northern islands. We received orders to proceed to Oceanside, California to train for the big one.

Team No. 13 was ordered to the USS *Burdo* (APD-133), bound for the States. While we were at Oceanside, the bombs dropped on Hiroshima and Nagasaki. The war was over. The team disintegrated. Officers and men went on leave or transferred or just sat in tents playing cards or, in my case, playing handball and reinventing a horse-betting formula for the Del Mar racetrack a few miles to the south.

One day at the track we watched the radio and movie star Rochester give out good-luck tips. Our commander, Vince Moranz, an attorney from Philadelpha, was forced out of the Navy by high blood pressure. We liked and respected him.

I detested inactivity, so after several weeks I asked to be transferred back into the real Navy and was ordered to report in two weeks to the San Francisco Naval District Personnel. I tried to get home on my ten days' leave by hitchhiking on military jets. It didn't work, so I called Dottie, my wife, and had her come to San Francisco.

We enjoyed San Francisco for the ten days, then I reported to the USS *Admiral Rodman* and my Navy career continued. I still had time on my required duty to serve. World War II was over. New adventures awaited me on the new ship.

Lieutenant (jg) Andy Coccari
Babylon, New York

I GRADUATED FROM Midshipman's School in October 1944 and went to UDT training at Fort Pierce, Florida. A large group of officers went through the complete UDT operation. Then I went through the second UDT training program with Team No. 24. After that, Ensign Stephen Charsky and I were sent to Mine Disposal School at Anacosta Naval Base in Washington, D.C. After that school, we went back to Fort Pierce and I went through the UDT training cycle for the third time, this one with UDT No. 30. Murray Fowler was our CO.

While I was with Team No. 30 in training, we were working on an exercise on a small island off the Florida coast. The plans were to spend a full week training there. I had the responsibility for the plan, the food, water, explosives, everything we would need. We had a big meeting with the instructors to go over the plan. I was asked the name of the venture by the CO of our UDT. I think his name was Sullivan.

I said the name assigned to the mission was "Jen-Stu-FU." He asked for an explanation of why this name was selected. I told him that the island was near Jenson and Stuart. Then he asked me what the *FU* meant. Our team's officers shouted in unison, *"Fuck you!"* Right then I was in big trouble with the CO.

The team was sent to Oceanside, California, for assignment in the Pacific Theater. Shortly after, we arrived the war ended and our team was decommissioned.

Lieutenant Wayne Palmer
Fort Worth, Texas

TEN DAYS BEFORE the invasion of Okinawa, I had a strange view of the island. I had gone ashore for recon work on the beach with my UDT team. They dropped us off about four A.M. in the dark. We swam on into the beach and did our recon work, looking for underwater obstacles, taking soundings on the depth of the water, and testing the beach bottom. After the work I somehow missed the pickup boat that came in about ten A.M. Still not sure how I missed it. It came and took away the rest of the team and they must have figured that I was listed as missing.

I was used to the water so I turned over and floated

awhile, figuring they would come looking for me. I was about a half mile offshore when I noticed what appeared to be Japanese swimmers coming toward me from the island.

They got within about fifty yards of me when a U.S. destroyer escort steamed between us, knocking me aside with its bow wave. When it had passed, the Japanese swimmers were no longer there. I don't know what happened to them.

A sailor on the DE spotted me and sent a minesweeper to rescue me from the big pond.

Ten days later I led in the first boat of the first wave of assault troops in the invasion of Okinawa. I knew where the cleared beach was. I spent the next four days ashore with the First Marine Division. All I had was the standard frogman equipment: shorts, swim fins, and a knife.

I remember Okinawa as an island with a dearth of trees and a low shoreline. It wasn't heavily defended on the beach, but the farther inland the Marines went, the tougher the fighting became.

After four days my UDT team was withdrawn from the island. They put us on a ship that was assigned radar picket duty with the other destroyers and DEs. We had three ships steaming on station when three kamikaze suicide bombers dropped out of the sky on us. The ships on each side of us were hit and set on fire, but the plane that aimed at us crashed fifty yards behind us. I remember that the plane's pilot had both hands in the air and was wearing a brown leather helmet and a brilliant white scarf. I'll always remember that scarf.

As I recall, the kamikazes sunk or damaged 368 ships before Okinawa was secured, killing more than four thousand sailors and leaving another four thousand missing.

After Okinawa I was given leave and I was home when the two bombs dropped on Japan, ending the war. After my leave, my team and I were given the mission of going ashore ahead of the surrender teams in Japan to check for submarine nets, booby traps, mines, and underwater obstacles that would upset the landing craft. We swam ashore at Hokkaidō, the northernmost Japanese island. It was absolutely eerie. People lined up along every inlet we entered, just staring at us. They didn't make a sound. There was nothing but absolute silence for the three miles or so we traveled up the inlets, looking for mines and nets. We were completely hemmed in on the land side by these silent Japanese.

Now it's hard to realize that we were there and that we did those things when we were so young.*

From World War II UDT Historical Files: Team No. 4

UDT TEAM NO. 4 formed in Maui at the Naval Combat Demolition Training base in March 1944. The team was made up of five men from Team No. 2, two officers and nine men from Team No. 1, and the rest from units trained at Fort Pierce, Florida. Lieutenant W. G. Cranberry was commanding officer. Intense retraining took place in coral blasting, swimming, hydrographic surveying and full scale maneuvers.

On April 18 they boarded the USS *Typhon* and headed for Guadalcanal. There they stayed at Florida Island for advanced training and task-force-level maneuvers while on board the USS *Talbot* (APD-7).

---

*Author's note: For his work with the Underwater Demolition Teams, Wayne Palmer received a Silver Star medal.

On the *Talbot* the team left for the Mariana Islands. They reached Saipan on June 15 with the rest of the task force. For two days the ship shelled Guam, then returned to Saipan. The team was on standby for Teams 1 and 2.

The team went back to the Marshall Islands and on 16 July arrived at Guam ready for its first combat mission. At 1520 the next day the two platoons of the team did a preassault recon of Yellow Beach Two. Their job was to determine landing conditions, locate obstacle size and numbers, and mark the landing area with buoys. A night demolition was carried out on the beach. The obstacles were coral-filled cribs made of pelu logs and barbed-wire fences. The mission was carried out and secured at 0230.

From July 18 to 20 the team did blasting work on coral heads on White Beach to form channels for the landing craft. No mines were found. Excellent support fire came on the beach area from six LCIGs, a destroyer, a cruiser, and a battleship.

It was during this work that the team erected the "Welcome Marines" sign that received so much publicity.

The next day the team members led the landing waves ashore, acting as pilots for the LCTs and the LSTs. It was during this work that Ensign T. D. Nixon was killed by Japanese sniper fire. He was the only UDT casualty of the campaign.

The same day the team blew a channel off Yellow Beach in front of Ogat Village to accommodate LSTs. Later a half-mile section of the beach near the village was cleared of all obstacles.

The team returned to Maui for further training. On September 14 the team headed for Eniwetok on the

USS *Goldsborough* (APD-132). Orders were changed and they steamed instead toward Leyte, Philippines.

Team No. 4 reached the Leyte Gulf in the morning of 18 October. The team was scheduled to check Violet Beach near Dulag. At 1500, Team No. 4, with other UDT teams, closed to six thousand yards of the beach. Three platoons went into their landing craft and headed for the beach. They met intense mortar, machine-gun, and small-arms fire.

Platoon Two got to 150 yards of the beach and launched its swimmers. As the last swimmers cleared, two hits were taken, which wounded three men. The boat, sinking, headed out to sea. Life belts on the wounded were inflated and rescue landing craft were called on the radio. Two additional hits sank the boat, and the wounded were towed to meet the rescue craft.

Platoon Four had been heading for the beach but took heavy-machine gun fire at 350 yards. When they saw Platoon Boat Two had been hit, they went to its aid. They ordered the rescue craft coming in to stand by to pick up the platoon two swimmers on the beach.

The team's APA moved in and gave fire support to the team and was hit in her number-one stack. The explosion killed two men and wounded sixteen. W. B. Kausman was killed and five other UDT men were wounded.

Platoon Two swimmers surveyed the beach, completed their recon, and withdrew on schedule to be picked up by the rescue craft.

After two days of screening duty, the team was ordered to Hollandia, New Guinea. From there they returned to Maui for advanced training.

The team's next action came on 28 March at the

Purple and Orange Beaches on the western side of Okinawa. They did a daylight recon and finished at 1530, with no opposition from shore. They found no mines but rows of posts set in four feet deep and extending the full length of the beach. The following morning Team No. 4 shooters succeeded in removing the posts.

On April 1, members of the team guided the assault waves to their assigned beaches. They did postassault demolition work under the direction of the beach master, blowing channels on Purple One and Purple Two Beaches.

On April 7 the team did preassault recons on Shima and Minna Shima. Approaches for LCMs and DUKWs were found. Green Beach on Minna Shima showed no mines or obstacles.

On April 18 the team did demo work on red T-3 and a channel was located.

On April 25, after weathering a month of kamikaze attacks, the team received orders for Guam and a shore camp.

On June 5, Team No. 4 started home via Pearl Harbor and San Francisco. On July 4, after sixteen and a half months overseas, Team No. 4 passed under the Golden Gate Bridge. The men were granted a thirty-day leave, then ordered to the Amphibious Training Base at Oceanside, California, where Team No. 4 was dissolved on 20 October, 1945.

Gunner's Mate Third Class Harold Hall
Hingham, Massachusetts

RIGHT AFTER HIGH school I tried to join the Navy, but they said my eyesight was not good enough so they put me into the Seabees and sent me to Camp Perry in Virginia for boot camp. After boot, I and ten other men were left without assignments. I was moved to the replacement area to wait. About three weeks later I was assigned to become "captain of the head" in the officer's training area. This meant I was going to be cleaning the officers' toilets. Right next to that posting was a notice that read: NEEDED: A HUNDRED VOLUNTEERS FOR DEMOLITION TRAINING. I rushed right over and asked if they had any physical limitations; they didn't, so I said, "Sign me up."

My training began right there at Camp Perry. The week was spent trying to fill a barracks with seventy men. Less than half of the men made it through the first week. Each day started with a forced march at 6:30 A.M. to the parade grounds three miles away. This forced march was pretty much a run all the way. This was followed by two hours of calisthenics nonstop. We then had a fifteen-minute rest break in which we marched around the parade grounds.

After that, we did two hours of rifle drill where the rifle was not allowed to drop below your chest at any time. If it did, you were singled out and made to duck-waddle across the field and back with the rifle held at arm's length above your head. Noontime was a welcome relief where we all went to a large outdoor pool and jumped in. Virginia is hot in the summer. We all had to stay in a stationary spot around the edge of the pool and take deep breaths and slide underwater and hold that breath as long as we could. When you came up for another breath of air, there was a Marine standing over you, ready to push your head under again. So you exhaled underwater, came up as fast as possible, and gulped in a fresh breath of air and tried to beat the foot back down into the safety of the water.

The afternoon was spent doing a diving tumble over as many men as you could. We had a few dislocated shoulders on that one. We ran round the two-mile obstacle course at least twice and did various other games, such as laying out a large circle on the ground and placing ten or twelve men inside the circle with boxing gloves on. Everyone started swinging until only one man was left standing. I lost a tooth on that one. At about 5:30 P.M. another forced march back to the barracks. Done for the day.

The next phase of our training was with the use of explosives. We learned how to blow out the side of a hill, sever a tree in half, and other things. We learned about dynamite, TNT, and fuse igniters. Also we had deep-sea diving training off a barge in the middle of the York River. We had to take various materiels down to the bottom of the river and cut things up and put things together while trying to stay upright on the bottom, holding on to an anchored rope in a very fast current. Water was between twenty-five and fifty feet deep.

The next phase of our training was in Fort Pierce, Florida. An amphibious training base was established there during World War II for the purpose of training in small-boat handling and beach landings, and for training the Scouts & Raiders, and finally for training the UDT Teams. Mornings were spent in forced marches in the deep sand along the shore and in calisthenics using palm tree logs for lifting and carrying. We had a half-mile swim out to sea and back. The afternoons were spent learning more about explosives: Primacord, igniters, fuses. Then learning to come in from the sea in a rubber boat and get off in the surf line and attach explosives together with Primacord and light the fuse igniter, then get the hell back out to sea as quick as possible.

We also had both day and night portages of the rubber boat, five men and an officer to a boat crew. We portaged across the barrier islands, paddled up and down the inland waterways, paddled up and down the coast and across the inlet waterways, and portaged across the rock jetty. We also did "sneak and peak" in the sand and dunes, coming in from the ocean at night, looking for booby traps. Lots of mosquitoes and no-see-ums. Those are small bugs that you can hardly see but they bite like hell. Lots of portaging and paddling and rolling around in the sand, surf, swamps, and shallows of the inland waterways, but no sleep.

When we went to the Pacific, we were issued swim trunks, Ka-bar knives, canvas shoes, carbines (which we never used), face masks, and inflatable life belts. Swim fins came later, between the invasions of Tinian and Leyte, if I remember right.

From Fort Pierce we went to the West Coast, then to Hawaii. We had a training base on Maui. We sailed from Maui on May 30, 1944, on the USS *Gilmer*, an APD, which is a converted World War I destroyer with two of its four stacks removed to make room for troops and equipment on board. APD stands for *attack personnel destroyer*.

The next day they told us that our destination was the island of Saipan in the Mariana Islands. Japan is twelve hundred miles to the north and the Philippines Islands lie about twelve hundred miles to the west. They told us that Saipan was one of the largest Japanese naval bases. We were ordered to do a daylight recon under the protective fire of our battleships, cruisers, and destroyers. If we found any obstacles, we would go in and blow them up after dark. The date of our work there was June 14, 1944, which was D-day minus one.

The Second Marines and the Fourth Marines would land there on June 15.

On June 2 we picked up a convoy of warships assigned to give protective fire for us. There were two airplane carriers, four battleships, three cruisers, and several destroyers.

On June 7, I made myself a hammock. It came out pretty good. I'd test it that night. The next day we pulled into the Marshall Islands to refuel. Yes, my hammock worked good.

On June 9 we sailed into Roi and Namur Islands near Kwajalein in the Marshall Islands. We got to go ashore and look at the old battleground there. We ate chow in the Seabees' mess hall, and when we went back to the ship, we found out that UDT Teams 3 and 4 were in the harbor on two other APDs.

On June 9, I found out that I and my team officer, Ensign Dolliver, would be going into the beach on a flying mattress. This is a device about eight feet long and thirty inches wide, rounded at the bow and almost pointed at the rear. An electric motor and battery were located in the center of the craft, with the motor shaft extending down into the water through a hole in the center. One man is on each side with only our arms on the mattress. This gave us a low profile in the water. They were painted dark blue.

We were to go in to three hundred yards of the beach on the mattress, then swim to the beach and make our recon of the area. We had briefings every day and we all knew exactly what our jobs were.

When we were 150 miles from Saipan, a destroyer depth-charged a Japanese submarine. One of our carrier planes shot down a Jap bomber ninety miles away that had come in under our radar.

On June 14, we went on our recon at 9:30 A.M. We were all blackened up. Our uniform was swim trunks, knife, swim shoes, life belt, and swim mask. We left the APD in our LCP(R) and approached the reef on the north flank of our Red 2 beach. At the north flank, Mr. Dolliver and I dropped off on our flying mattress and headed in on our recon. At the same time the other LCP(R)s were letting off all their recon men. Just about everyone in the team was in on the recon. Mr. Dolliver and I got in about 350 yards of the beach and noticed shells dropping in the water a little ahead of us. We thought that they were our own shells dropping short, but they turned out to be Jap mortar shells. We were both in the water low when a mortar landed eight feet in back of us. It gave me a jolt and the fear that the Japs were aiming at our flying mattress with their mortars. They were. The mattresses made beautiful targets for the Japs and they were never used again. About this time Jap machine guns and snipers started taking aim at everyone. They had waited until we were almost in and then opened up on all the teams. We were lucky and had only one man, Robert Christiansen, killed. He was shot by a Japanese sniper. The rest of us were shaken by the mortar rounds.

Then it was to work. We did the soundings, and surveyed the bottom and the currents and checked for underwater obstacles. Team No. 7 had one man killed on another beach and ten wounded. Then we swam out for pickup and back to the ship.

The Marines were pleased with our recon, and the information we brought back was important to their plan of operation for the invasion landings.

The Second and Fourth Marines went in at 8:30 on D-day, June 15, 1944. Some of our team directed the tank landings on the edge of the reef under heavy mortar fire from shore. I was in bed at the time under observation for a concussion from a mortar shell that landed close by me.

The next day we had general quarters call on our ship while on patrol. We encountered five Jap merchant vessels. We sank four of them and another destroyer got the last one. I was sleeping on deck and still considered a casualty, so I had a grandstand view. Shells were flying both ways and the boys on board had several holes to patch up from Jap rounds. One of our gun crew got shrapnel in his arm and another one had a bullet through an arm. After the ships were shot up, we picked up twenty-three Jap survivors and took them prisoners. Some of them were wounded.

The next day we put sixteen of the prisoners on board a prison ship. Three of the others died from their wounds and were buried at sea. The other four would be put on another ship for wounded prisoners.

On June 18, some of our team blew a channel through the reef so the LCVPs could get supplies to the beach. Some more of our team made a recon on another beach for landing supplies. The Marines had established a large beachhead here and were meeting stiff resistance but were pushing inland. I always thought the Marines got too much credit, but after watching what they go through, I didn't think they get half enough credit.

We had two air raids that day. The Japs were trying to bomb the beach. Only a few planes arrived and two of them were shot down.

I got out of bed that day feeling much better. Nothing was seriously wrong with me.

The Marines were moving ahead. An Army division

had landed. We still had air raids, but the Japs seemed to run out of nerve before they get there.

On June 20, the Japs blew up one of our ammunition dumps onshore and caused some excitement. Four Jap small craft came alongside one of our destroyers and wounded seven men on the bridge. The destroyer in turn sank three of the boats, but one got away.

On June 22 we went on patrol and shelled Tinian Island from ten o'clock at night until five the next morning. It kept us awake all night.

We went ashore and got four Jap antiboat mines and did some experimenting on a reef. We wanted to find out how little amount of powder it took to blow them up. We found that one block from a tetrytol pack worked.

After Garapan was secured, we would make a recon of the harbor to see that there were no mines. There were several large ships sunk in the harbor.

I went onshore for a couple of hours, looking around. It was very dusty and hot in there, and there was also an awful odor of dead bodies. There had been an air raid the night before and we shot down two Jap planes. They didn't get a chance to drop their bombs.

On June 30 we went out on patrol again and shelled Tinian all night. About 0500 we sailed into Tinian town harbor and started shelling them. The bad part was, they began shelling us back and dropped a few five-inchers close to us. We turned around and got the hell out of there.

On July 2, we were still on sub patrol. We could see the islands at all times. Tinian was about three miles from Saipan, and the Marine artillery on Saipan were constantly shelling Tinian along with the rounds from the warships.

The Marines had secured the town of Garapan, so we went in and made a recon of the harbor all along the front of the town. After the recon was finished, we had some time for souvenir hunting. I found for myself a Jap rifle and bayonet and Jap marine helmet. One Jap was found by one of our guys still alive but wounded in a pillbox. He finished the job. We were supposed to go over the ships in the harbor for booby traps, but some souvenir hunters had already been aboard and were not blown up, so we figured there are no booby traps on board.

We went in on a recon on Tinian and did a poor job. The Marines with us never got inland for their recon and our men were not sure that they were on the right beach. They said they heard Japs shouting all along the beach. The next night we went in again and this time had a good recon. Also the Marines got inland and did their recon and made no enemy contact.

The results of our recon were that we had to go back in and widen the beach from seventy-five yards to two hundred to give the Marines room enough to land.

On July 19 we went on patrol. That day we were alongside the APD *Stringham*. We were briefed by Commander Kauffman on the Tinian operation. We had a practice operation that night and another one on July 21. We went in for real on the twenty-third. The Marines landed the next day. Teams 3 and 4 would hit Guam either that day or the next. They had scullies to blow. Team No. 6 was on standby in case something happened to the other two. The invasion of Guam was expected to take place within the next three days.

Mr. Dolliver suggested using long rubber tubes to carry explosives ashore. We'd test it out. We heard that Teams 3 and 4 completed their work on Guam and were never fired on. The Marines went inland two thousand yards the first day of the invasion.

We tested the rubber tubes to carry explosives and they worked better than any other method. They were hard to see and carried a much heavier load.

On July 22, we got ready for our run on Tinian. We left at about 2200 and our blast went off about 0300. Team No. 7 had made a fake daylight recon on Tinian Town that morning to avert the Japs' attention there while we did our work at night. They had good support and no one was injured.

We had a bad night at Tinian. We had heavy rain and we missed our objective by a long way. We sat in our rubber boats a few hundred yards offshore while our scouts went in to locate the right beach. It took them four hours to find it and by then it was too late to find and blow any obstacles. The Marines landed on schedule the next morning and some LSTs were blown up by mines. Also, Tinian was heavily armed. The Japs knocked out two five-inch guns on the USS *Colorado* and made a direct hit on a destroyer, and the USS *Cleveland* suffered direct hits. We did blow up a huge ammunition dump on Tinian that morning.

Huge guns were about all the Japs had on Tinian, for the Marines didn't meet very much resistance. They moved ahead quickly.

It was tough to fail on that beach-cleaning job, but it was a good thing after all. When the Marines landed they found that the wall was all slit trenches and machine-gun nests. If we had gone in and started placing powder on that wall, we would more than likely have been cut down to a man and never have come out alive.

Two platoons from our team went to White Beach on Saipan and blew some coral heads that were in the way of the LSTs that were bringing in casualties from Tinian. The Marines were still moving ahead quickly on Saipan.

We went to Tinian and blew some more coral heads that were interfering with the landing operations of supplies. The word was that we'd be heading back to Maui in a few days. Team No. 7 was supposed to go with us, but they were ordered to Guadalcanal and join with the Third Amphibious on the next invasion. They thought it might be Peleliu.

On July 29 a platoon of our men went to Saipan to get one hundred antiboat mines that we would take back to Maui with us to use for training purposes.

The next day we went in to help run lines from a seagoing tug to the pontoon float that got broached by the heavy surf. The rope broke and the pontoon float was still broached. We had to go in the next day with another ten-inch line to the float.

At 1230 on July 31 we went on a recon of the waters in front of Tinian town. The Marines secured the area that morning. There were obstacles in the water and the beach was lined with mines. Tinian town was full of mines and booby traps.

August 1 was my birthday. To celebrate, a platoon went in to mark the channel for LSTs and look for more mines. A Navy plane crashed about two hundred yards aft of us. We rescued the gunner but the pilot and radioman went down with the plane. The pilot was hit by rifle fire from Tinian.

The next day we blew up a sunken Jap fishing boat in Tinian town harbor. We went back in and put lines around a sunken hull to try to pull it out of the way of landing operations. We couldn't move it, so we planned to back in the next morning and blow it up.

On August 3, we had a platoon in the Tinian town harbor working on blowing up and clearing out dozens of Jap fishing boats to clear the way for our own LSTs to land.

For the next three days we helped in the harbor. We salvaged some of the 3,500 pounds of anchors, blew up more coral heads, cleared screws of LSTs that had rope and clothes wound around them, and other harbor clearance work. The beach master, Commander Squeaky Anderson, was well pleased with our work.

On August 10, 1944, we left Saipan at 0600 and headed out to catch a convoy and escort it back to Saipan. We found the convoy: ten transports loaded with supplies.

After a few days on patrol around Saipan, we pulled out for the Marshall Islands. From there we would be on our way to Pearl Harbor.

We made it back to Pearl, got our citations, and then loaded on board the USS *Humphreys* (APD-12), at Pearl Harbor on September 14, 1944. We sailed out of Pearl the next day, convoying cargo vessels. Our destination was Gagil-Tomil in the Yap Islands. We were scheduled to go in for recon and removal from October 2 to 4.

We arrived at Eniwetok Atoll in the Marshall Islands on September 25. While there, we tested outboard motors on our rubber boats. We also picked up our mail.

A couple of days later we went onshore to go swimming and played baseball and had a beer party.

On September 28, our orders for Yap Island were canceled: We would escort a convoy to the Admiralty Islands.

We crossed the equator on October 2 and were transformed from pollywogs into shellbacks. What an initiation. The next day we pulled into Manus Island in the Admiralty group. A task force was forming up here.

On October 10 we were briefed. Our destination was Leyte Island in the Philippines. Seven demolition teams were to be used. We would go in on October 18, two days before D-day. When we left Manus two days later, we were with six battleships, six cruisers, nine APDs and many destroyers. In the afternoon twelve aircraft carriers joined us.

On October 18 we started in through a minefield about 0930. We passed close to an island that the Rangers had landed on the day before. They were there to silence all shore artillery. We finally got through the minefield at noon and were opposite the beach of Leyte at about 1400. We were supposed to go in at noon, but the minefield had delayed us.

We went in at 1500 with swimmers let off at four hundred yards. We drew heavy fire in the LCP(R) and we fired back with our .50- and .30-caliber machine guns. A bullet went through our motor and it stopped. We finally got it started and got out of range. Then it stopped for good. Our swimmers were picked up by the standby LCP(R) and we all returned.

One of our men, Frenchy Audibert from Maine, was shot in the head and killed while he was firing the .50-caliber machine gun on the LCP(R). We had one other casualty. Our first-aid man got mortar shrapnel under his arm and in his fanny—not too serious. Team No. 8 had eight wounded as far as we knew.

Team No. 4 had their APD hit in the smokestack and one LCP(R) sank from mortar shells. UDT men and APD men had a combined total of two dead and twenty wounded. Next to team No. 4, Team No. 3 had no casualties. One destroyer hit a mine.

The next day we had a sea burial for Frenchy Audibert.

On October 20, 1944, the Marines went in at 1000. There were very few casualties. A lone Japanese plane came over and hit the cruiser USS *Honolulu* (CL-48).

Two days later we left the Philippines on convoy duty to Hollandia, New Guinea. Three days later we changed course to head for Manus Island. Five ships left the convoy to go to Manus. At Manus we tied up alongside a tender for repairs. We went aboard the tender for chow—ice cream, Cokes, and everything. The place seemed like a city after our APD.

On October 31, I had an X-ray taken of my knee. I had injured it initially in high school playing football. I tore the cartilage and it never properly healed. But I was fit for duty. While on the teams I hurt it again loading crates of explosives. A crate banged against my knee and tore the cartilage completely loose. The Navy medics said I had to get it fixed.

I went back to Maui for the operation. I was transferred to Team No. 3 for the trip. We would sail soon on the *President Hayes* (APA-20), for Maui. Not many troops on board. Ice cream every noon for chow. Sleeping quarters nice and cool.

The APA *Mount Hood* blew up with all hands lost. Over two thousand casualties from the concussion and the blast.

We sailed on November 11 and arrived in Maui on November 23, 1944. From Maui they sent me to a hospital overlooking Pearl Harbor. They cut and fixed my knee and I was there for many weeks for full recuperation after the operation.

While I was there, a good friend from high school came to see me. He was on his way back to the States. I asked him to take some articles that I had collected home with him and drop them off at my folks' home.

Shortly I was released from the hospital and headed for the Replacement Center when my UDT No. 5 Commander, John DeBold, came to the hospital looking for me. The team had just arrived back at Pearl Harbor and was about ready to go back to Maui. I got to rejoin the team.

When we got to Maui, we were slated for a return to the States and thirty-day leaves. After our leaves were over we were to return to California for redeployment.

I beat my friend home and was waiting for him when he arrived at my folks' house. Was he surprised!

Our orders were changed and we reported to Fort Pierce at the end of our leaves. There they gave us a full Navy physical. It was much tougher than what we had for the Seabees. Now the Navy had taken over full responsibility for the UDT. About 80 percent of our teams were declared unfit for combat duty. I was among them as I was nearsighted.

The teams were broken up and re-formed with new men just completing their training at Fort Pierce. I was assigned as an instructor and worked at training new recruits for UDT there at Fort Pierce Amphibious Training Base until the end of the war.

From World War II UDT Historical Files: Team No. 5

TEAM NO. 5 WAS commissioned in April 1944 with Lieutenant Commander D. L. Kauffman as commanding officer. Lieutenant (jg) DeBold was executive officer. The team had finished advanced training at the base on Maui.

The team had four operating platoons, each with three officers and sixteen men, and one headquarters group of twenty men. The team continued to train until May using its own men as instructors.

The team had advance notice that it would participate in the operation at Saipan on 14 June. Team No. 5 would work with the Second Marine Division. The team would make detailed reconnaissances of the area from the edge of the reef to the waterline in daylight using swimmers and flying mattresses. They would deal with a barrier reef from 900 to 1,800 yards off the beaches with a lagoon inside it.

Before this, swimming had not been a main requirement of the team. Now every man would be required to swim a mile before he could go on the mission. The swimmers would bring back detailed hydrographic surveys. To accomplish this, Kauffman and his men developed the string-and-weight method of determining water depth. This system was used throughout UDT during the rest of the war.

On May 29, 1944 Team No. 5 with all of its gear and explosives, loaded aboard the USS *Gilmer*, an APD: a converted World War I four-stacker that had been stripped of two stacks to make room for the one hundred men in the team and their supplies. It was seriously cramped and overcrowded.

The team spent two days on Roi and Namur islands and left on June 9 heading for Saipan. The battleship USS *California* and the cruiser USS *Indianapolis* would give fire support as well as Navy planes from nearby carriers. The APD would not lend fire support.

Team No. 5 left the APD at 0900 on June 14, 1944, which was D-day minus one. They pushed off from the *Gilmer* ten minutes early from four thousand yards off the northern end of the beach. The Japs began firing at the ships five minutes before that, and two men on the crew of the APD were wounded. The battleship was hit in the control tower, and the damage hampered its fire support for the recon.

The landing craft zigzagged in to five hundred yards of the beach to drop off the swimmers. Swimmers were put overboard at one-hundred-yard intervals. Platoon leaders in their flying mattresses moved back and forth in front of the swimmers to make sure the men were on target. The mattresses became instant targets for the Japanese on shore. Three of the four were hit and one crewman, Robert Christiansen, S l/C, was killed.

Several of the men suffered internal injuries from the concussions of mortar rounds going off near them. Harold Hall was blown completely clear of the water by the force of a mortar round going off almost directly under him.

It was quickly determined that the team did not need to blast any ramps on the beach. The reef had such a gradual slope that an LCM could ride up on it and put off the tanks easily. They proved right, and landing craft of many kinds discharged vehicles on that reef for the next two weeks.

The team completed its recon and the officers prepared the charts and reports and sent them to the admiral. Plans were changed for landing tanks to that proposed by the recon.

The team worked for the beach master for the next thirteen days, searching for mines, making detailed hydrographic charts of both beach areas, and maintaining the team's buoys and lights in the channel.

Next in line was Tinian Island. It was only two miles across a narrow channel, and friendly artillery on Saipan could lend support.

The first recon on White Beach was a failure, with

no radar from the APD and a fog setting in and the current running opposite the way that it had been predicted. Another recon was sent in and came back with good reports and the landing was set for White Beach.

Out of two Marine Divisions that landed in the invasion, there were only five casualties. The team had done a good job of recon.

After Tinian, Team No. 5 returned to Maui, where Lieutenant Commander Kauffman turned over command of the team to Lieutenant DeBold and the team was reorganized. The team had only eleven officers and sixty-four men.

On September 14 the team sailed for work on the invasion of Yap, but the mission was canceled and the team was rerouted to Manus. After several days there the task force left Manus on October 12 and arrived at Leyte Gulf on 17 October.

Team No. 5 did recon work on Orange One and Orange Two Beaches. Fire support was good by both naval guns and aircraft.

One UDT Team No. 5 man, "Frenchy" Audibert, was killed by sniper fire. The recon showed no mines, no obstacles, good gradient, slight surf, and good exits. No demolition work was needed.

On October 23, Team No. 5 had orders to depart for Marcus. The first stop was Nouméa. The team went onshore for a two-week rest period and were awarded Silver and Bronze Stars.

Next stop was Hollandia, where the team grew restless from having to stay on board the *Humphreys* for a month.

On December 27, 1944, Team No. 5 sailed for the Lingayen Gulf, Luzon, 150 miles northwest of Manila.

Leyte was passed on January 3, 1945. The large task

force was then attacked continually by Japanese aircraft. Estimates were that the task force was diminished by 50 percent by the attacks.

This time Team No. 5 had help from Teams 9 and 15 to work the southern group of beaches. The recon swimmers reported no mines or obstacles and the beaches were well suited for the invasion. However, pontoons would be needed to unload the big LSTs and the LSMs due to a gradual gradient of the beach.

After the Marines landed on January 9 with no opposition, Team No. 5 did recon on beaches to the left and on the river.

At 1600 that afternoon, the UDT teams boarded ships and headed for Ulithi via Leyte. They soon were on board the USS *Mississippi*, heading for Pearl Harbor. Team No. 5 members had five days' leave in Pearl before reporting to Maui. On April 5 the team was off on thirty days' leave, heading for the States.

Team members reported to Fort Pierce, Florida, in early May, where they found they had only seven officers and twenty-five enlisted men left on the team: The other the men on the team had transferred out of demolition or gone on the teaching staff.

On July 11 the team was ordered to fill up to full size in preparation for cold-water training to be held in Oceanside, California.

The new Team No. 5 left Fort Pierce July 19, with a delay en route in reporting to Oceanside on 8 August. On August 15, the day Japan surrendered, the team loaded aboard the USS *Hobby* (APD-95), and headed for Japan.

Team No . 5 did various noncombat recons on Japanese islands, paving the way for troops and supply areas.

On October 13, the *Hobby* sailed for San Diego,

where the team disembarked and reported to the Naval Amphibious Base at Coronado. On October 23, 1945, UDT Team No. 5 was formally decommissioned.

Lieutenant (jg) Robert W. Parmele
Millbrae, California

I FINISHED MY Midshipman's Training on 17 March, 1944, and went to Fort Pierce, Florida, to train with the Underwater Demolition Teams. I was assigned to Team No. 10 and stayed with them through the Pacific campaigns and until the end of the war.

I took part in the Leyte Gulf landings in the Philippines, where I was awarded the Silver Star for our team's underwater-obstacle-clearing operations. My other assignments included reconnaissance and clearance of beach obstacles, reefs, and coral heads at Peleliu, Ulithi, Lingayen Gulf, and Zambales Province.

I remained with Team No. 10 my entire time with UDT and our return to the States.

When I was on an afternoon reconnaissance at Peleliu, the portal to the Philippines, I radioed from my landing craft that I saw signs of Jap activity at the point near Blue Beach. Ensign Arthur Garrett, our team's observer on the bridge of the *Rathburne* (APD-25), told the gunnery officer on the ship.

"Tell them I see Japs, that they're dragging something out of a cave up there," I told Arthur.

The gunnery officer used his field glasses and said he didn't see any Japs at that location.

"It's a howitzer, a big one," I shouted into the radio. I was near shore and I could see it. "Fire on that point," I called.

The gunnery officer said he still didn't see any Japs. About that time the first enemy shell exploded on the starboard side of the ship. A moment later another round blew up in the water on the port side. It was a professional gunnery bracket.

The ship's captain took over and gunned the *Rathburne* out of there at flank speed.

Ensign Garrett asked what to do about Ensign Parmele in the landing craft back near the beach. "Let him catch up," the captain said. Later I did catch the boat several miles at sea. Other spotters had seen the Japanese gun, and a nearby destroyer lived up to its name and blew the howitzer right off the cliff.

On September 17 our UDT Team No. 10 guided the Army Regimental Combat Team through the open channels we had cleared. The Army unit fought steadily inland. We also guided waves of tank landing craft and DUKWs ashore.

One of our men in a boat spotted an anchored mine five feet underwater three hundred yards off the beach in a landing-craft approach lane. We had no equipment to cut the heavy mooring cables, so our demolition men put up a buoy on the mine to warn friendly craft away from it. A quick search showed that we found eight such mines anchored near the hundred-fathom line. We promptly marked each mine with a buoy so no landing craft hit any of them.

After the war I returned to civilian life and went back to the University of Minnesota to complete my senior year of college.

From World War II UDT Historical Files: Team No. 6:

MEN FROM THE Seabees from Camp Perry, Virginia, made up most of what would later become UDT No. 6. Along with men from Classes 5 and 5A at Perry, these men took their training at Fort Pierce, Florida, on demolition during March and April 1944. They were in units of one officer and five men. After training there, they were sent to the demolition base on Maui, Territory of Hawaii, on April 9. There they went to an advanced course in reconnaissance and demolition practices. On May 30, Teams 6 and 7 were commissioned and left with Team No. 5 heading for the Saipan, Guam, and Tinian operation.

At Saipan on June 13 and 14, Team No. 6 was assigned standby duty, remaining in reserve in case they were needed. The team was not used. A month later, during the Guam invasion, the team received its first taste of combat. In the forenoon of July 27, 1944, Team No. 6 was ordered to blast ramps for tank landing craft over an area of seven hundred feet on the reef off Dacli Beach on the southwest coast of the island. It had to be done before 1400 the following day. The first recon indicated an irregular reef front with numerous fissures and a large number or coral heads. Lieutenant (jg) Carr was directed to take two platoons to make a test load of about three hundred feet of the reef. They began at 1400. The team placed nine tons of tetrytol and fired the shot at 1800. A check the next morning showed that the test shot had produced an excellent ramp with a clear approach. Carr took the entire team and placed charges of twenty-nine tons of powder on the obstacles. Good organization between the ship and the team under the direction of Lieutenant (jg) Methwin led to the quick transfer of the powder for the reef loading.

The shot was fired at 1245. No check was made on results, since the USS *Clemson* had to leave the area immediately.

The team was then ordered to join the task force that was assembling for attack on Peleliu in the Caroline group. At the staging area at Manus Island, the team was reorganized, additional personnel were added, and a complete outfit of battle equipment and explosives was obtained.

The team arrived off Peleliu Island on September 12, 1944. It was allotted two beaches on Peleliu. An accident taking out one team resulted in Team No. 6 being assigned an additional beach to clear and an LST area to reconnoiter. This work was finished three days before the attack. The men underwent heavy machine-gun and sniper fire but cleared the assigned areas.

Upon completion of the Peleliu mission, the team was sent to the Admiralty Islands on board the USS *Schmitt*. From there they boarded the USS *President Hayes* and were on their way to Maui. After training on Maui for several months, the team was sent to the USS *Island Mail* and sailed on January 12, 1945, for San Francisco. When they arrived in the States the men were given a thirty-day leave. On April 3, 1945, Team No. 6 members reported to Fort Pierce, Florida, and were reorganized, with most of the personnel assigned to the training staff.

First Lieutenant Frank Lahr, USMC
Stevensville, Michigan

I WAS IN school in Washington D.C., when Lt. Kauffman visited us and told us about his new organization. It sounded better than digging up bombs. Many of our group volunteered to go with him, but I went back to Field Engineering School at New River, North Carolina. Soon I got orders to report to Fort Pierce and then to Maui and became a member of Team No. 3. Originally I was liaison officer from the Third Marine Division.

Team No. 3 had a mixture of several seventeen-year olds and several thirty-plus warrant officers who had been commissioned because of their experience in blasting coral.

After Leyte, most of the older men were replaced with younger ones. One of our replacements was Clarence Mulheren. Now he's very active in our reunions.

At Guam the reef extended up to three hundred feet from shore. At low tide the reef was dry and the Japs were actually building the coral-filled cribs five feet in diameter and four feet high the week before the landing. Our UDT No. 3 team was loading them with tetrytol packs and blasting them day and night for a week preceding the landing. Team No. 5 was working on another beach at Guam. The men all received Bronze Star decorations for our work at Guam, and the officers won Silver Stars. One of our officers, Lew Luehrs, had received his first Silver Star at Eniwetok. He later was with Team No. 18, I believe, and was awarded a Bronze Star.

Dr. W. Rex Brown, Ph.D.
Maitland, Florida

IN THE SPRING of 1944 my ship was in dry dock in New York Harbor for repairs after some heavy weather damage. Following dry dock, additional training and sea trials were made. About this time a letter came to all our officers and crew. The notification said that UDT members were needed, as was later confirmed by rumors. It was thought that a large number of combat swimmer crews had been lost during the June 6 invasion of Normandy and that replacements were needed.

The contents of the speed letter interested me. I came from a landlocked state with little water experience other than raising cattle. The opportunity to experience a new type of activity and enjoy the benefits of cool-water currents, plenty of moisture, and ten days of shore leave were appealing. I sent a response letter via my commanding officer. A return reply was received within short order and authorized acceptance of me into UDT training.

I was assigned to the Fort Pierce, Florida, Underwater Demolition facility. When I reported I was assigned to a tent. I remember arriving at the town and I was impressed with the civilian area built on a bridge serving copious amounts of seafood. The instruments used to carve and consume seafood intrigued me.

Upon arrival at the active duty station, the prospective team members were met with sand fleas, mosquitoes, high humidity, and low light. The first day was devoted to teaching all volunteers to act quickly to orders.

It seemed that each day was devoted to a mile run and a mile swim with no fins or face masks to get to our duty station. At the training location instructors demonstrated how to crawl without attracting attention.

The very first order was "Hit the deck!" When first ordered, the volunteers casually moved; then suddenly a great explosion was heard within the area where we were circled, and clods of sea earth showered and struck the men. Once again volunteers were drawn to attention, and the second time "Hit the deck!" was ordered, the trainees' reaction was immediate.

After initial instructions the volunteers were taken a mile out to sea and put overboard to swim ashore. After this duty, action was taken to instruct us in the use and handling of explosives and how to attain good physical condition. You could tell us by our sunburns and cracked lips, which never seemed to heal. When I smiled, cracked lips would ooze blood from the wounds.

A highly competent instructor provided instructions. On one occasion the commander had a timed explosive in his hand and continued his explanation of how to handle it. Men in the audience had experienced explosions of similar devices and knew an explosion was imminent. This did not deter the commander even with time becoming shorter and shorter. Finally, when the men could stand the tension any longer, the commander was told the bomb was about to explode. He casually threw it aside and the timed explosion went off on schedule.

Later in the day, groups of ten men and one officer were assigned and the practice was conducted to speed up the handling of explosives.

They told us about an old house in the middle of nowhere on the base and we were ordered to find it. They told us to go in a certain direction where we would gather for lunch. One of the first obstacles was to cross a bed of quicksand and we had to figure our own way across. One man finally started to cross crawling carefully on his stomach, which worked, so we all followed. This led us to a good-sized chest-deep lake. As we moved through the water, instructors threw half-pound charges of TNT near us in order to hasten our movements.

The house was located and became more familiar as training progressed. Having arrived at the location of our next session of training, a lunch of K rations was distributed to a tired, dirty, and ragged group. As the K rations were opened a tremendous explosion took place all around us that was much larger then the first ones and caused some minor injuries to our men. This was the first time we had heard anyone call for a corpsman. Some injured trainees were taken away in trucks. We learned later that dilapidated fire hoses filled with explosives had been planted to cause us surprise. The purpose was to weed out those who thought the training was not to their liking. As training went on, more and more men were released until we were almost done and we entered into "Hell Week."

During Hell Week all kinds of fitness, physical pain, and uncomfortable situations were inflicted. I remember on one occasion, while using fins and masks, we had to go through a very rough surf. While cleaning the mask the surf suddenly washed it out of my hands. The rest of that day I spent without the mask. When I reported it to the officer in charge, he said that I would have to do a five-mile march. Later it was learned that I outranked the instructor but that didn't matter.

After our regular day of training, we were all gathered in a group and began the five-mile march by running a mile, then walking a mile, until we came to the designated location. During this run some men began to drop out due to various ailments. A return truck was sent to bring in those who could not complete the march.

Night training was involved, which included climbing over jetties with our six-man, 350-pound rubber boats while attempting to avoid cuts on our feet and hands from the huge rocks. We had to report to a certain location while moving unnoticed.

The final day of Hell Week was devoted to teams competing against one another to determine who was the best at handling explosives, making connections, and moving silently from the area. The last action was to climb over the house that we had been originally sent to find. By this time there was pain enough. However, upon returning to the duty area, a truck appeared and there were cries of joy. They hauled us back to the barracks and this was our notification of the end of our training.

I was pleased to receive the Certification of Underwater Team Swimmer and went on to take further training. I was assigned to Team No. 5.

I trained under the command of Commander John DeBold and Executive Officer Robert Marshall. I also remember Hampton Pool, a professional football player who conveyed the finer points of physical training.

I continued with Team No. 5 and took part in several Pacific Island missions until we were decommissioned at Coronado in July 1945.

From UDT World War II Historical Files: Team No. 10

IN MARCH OF 1944, Class 6A finished training at Fort Pierce, Florida, and the unit was divided into teams 8, 9, and 10. Lieutenant Commander McAdams was the commanding officer and Lieutenant H. F. Brooks the executive officer. The newly commissioned Team No. 10 left for San Francisco on 2 June where it boarded the USS *Monterey*.

The team arrived in Maui, Territory of Hawaii, on June 19. There it was joined by twenty-one men and five officers from the Office of Strategic Services, the forerunner of the CIA. This group was headed by Lieutenant A. O. Choate Jr.

All of these men had undergone special underwater swimming and explosive training and they were to be worked into the backbone of the team. When Commander McAdams left the team, Lieutenant Choate became the commanding officer and Lieutenant James Knott his executive officer.

Team No. 10 embarked on the USS *Rathburne* (APD-25), on 18 August and arrived at Guadalcanal Island off Cape Esperance, where it took part in rehearsal maneuvers for the coming operations against the Caroline Islands. Teams 8 and 10 formed the demolition units assigned to make a reconnaissance of Anguar on 14 September.

Under cover of a bombardment from ships offshore, the team left in LCP(R)s about three thousand yards seaward of Blue Beach. Swimmers went into the water three hundred yards offshore and worked their recon. Strong currents handicapped the swimmers, and scattered sniper fire menaced them. All swimmers were recovered. No demolition was needed on Blue Beach. The next day they went in on Red Beach and found no obstacles. The next day observations showed that the Japanese had installed barbed wire and jetted rails on both beaches. They were removed by team swimmers.

On 19 September orders came for Team No. 10 to join the Ulithi fire support group. After a two-day trip there, Team No. 10 was assigned to clear mines and obstacles from five beaches, each on a different island. On September 21 the team checked out two beaches and reported no obstacles. That afternoon they went to the three other beaches and found that Red Beach should have channels blown through a coral fringe to allow access to the beach at low tide. Work was completed by 1600. During the next three days Team No. 10 assisted the beach master and boat control officer with landing operations.

The team left Ulithi on 25 September on board the *Rathburne* and sailed to the Admiralties for a rest. Two weeks later the ship departed with the team for the Leyte Gulf and arrived on 18 October. Despite heavy sniper and machine-gun fire, the team did reconnaissance on the beaches and found no need for demolition. The team went ashore and watched the return of General Douglas MacArthur.

Their ship left the following morning and went to the Admiralties, where it refueled. Then it sailed for Florida Island near Guadalcanal, where it stayed for a week. Next the Team sailed to Nouméa, New Caledonia, and arrived on 8 November for a two-week rest.

The team then headed for Finschhafen, New Guinea, for a one-day stop before sailing to Hollandia, where it spent Christmas Eve. On 30 December the *Rathburne* and Team No. 10 left for Leyte Island in the Philippines. It arrived on 3 January, 1945, and went on to the entrance to Lingayen Gulf the next day.

Blue Beach was Team No. 10's assignment, but turbid water and heavy swells postponed the survey until afternoon. The recon was completed despite mortar and sniper fire.

The ship departed there on 25 January and headed

to Subic Bay just north of Manila. Red Beach was assigned for recon. A large object was noted a half-mile south of the beach. It turned out to be a grounded freighter. At 0300 four officers and eight men left the APD to conduct the recon. The sea was calm with an offshore breeze and a full moon. The job was done without incident.

The following day the beach master assigned the team to survey the beach front for suitable landing places for LSTs. A sandbar ran along most of the beach, negating landing. Some channels were found on Red Beach, but one good beaching area was discovered at Capone Cove, three miles south of the beach.

The *Rathburne* then took the team to Guam in the last week of February. On May 5, 1945, the team left for Maui and arrived on the sixteenth.

From there, Teams 9, 10, 14, and 15 were ordered to return to the States. Upon arrival all team members were granted delay–en-route leaves and ordered to report to Fort Pierce, Florida, on July 1, 1945.

After arriving in Fort Pierce, the bombs fell on Japan and the war was over. The teams underwent changes. Many officers were transferred. All men eligible for discharge were sent to separation centers. Coast Guard men were sent to separation centers. The Marines were sent to the Great Lakes. The team with new leaders remained at Fort Pierce, helping to tear down buildings until 2 February, 1946, when it was decommissioned.

Gunner's Mate Third Class Marvin Cooper
Sun City, California

I JOINED THE Navy Combat Demolition Teams at Camp Perry, Virginia, late in 1943. I was transferred to Fort Pierce, Florida, early in 1944 and trained with Class No. 5. I could not swim so I dropped out of that class after "Hell Week." I was sent to a swimming program and then joined Class No. 7 later.

Class No. 7 was the "mother of all classes." This was the time the NCDU were merged with the UDT operation. From Class No. 7, the UDT teams 11, 12, 13, and 15 were formed. Class No. 7 began its training with men from many sources, which included some residual base personnel and men left over from other classes, Seabees, men from other amphibious bases, men from the fleet, men just out of service schools, and men right out of boot camp. The officers were all from similar backgrounds. One officer for every five enlisted was the ratio to provide six-man teams for the rubber boats of the Combat Demolition Units, where we trained. The class consisted of 360 men, or sixty boat crews.

We had six weeks of day and night commando-type training for which Fort Pierce was noted. The class started with Hell Week and ended with Payoff Week. During this training period the men had learned the basics of demolition methods and all the boys were now men and called demolitionaires, or demos.

In early August the entire class was granted a ten-day leave plus travel time. Returning from leave, we had little to do except to continue our physical training. In early September, seventeen crews of five left the class and moved to the West Coast by troop train. Those seventeen NCDU crews later became Underwater Demolition Team No. 15.

During the hot and muggy month of September, the remaining crews fought the sand flies, mosquitoes, and the threat of a hurricane. The demolition area was separated from the beach by the Navy Scouts & Raiders area, and friction developed. Fights between the two groups were common events in the bars of downtown Fort Pierce. Some of the guys took weekend excursions to West Palm Beach or Miami.

September was not all liberty and play. We went down to Camp Murphy for rifle range practice and had a session of gunnery practice off the beach of South Island. A Navy plane went into the ocean off North Island. Our crews swam from rubber boats trying to locate the wreckage, but we failed and the plane was never found.

One day was spent deepening the inlet to Stuart, Florida, near Jensen Beach. The channel was deepened by well-placed explosive charges. Another day we practiced diving with deep-sea suits in the Atlantic Ocean.

On October 3 our orders came and the remaining crews of Class No. 7 boarded a troop train at Fort Pierce and began the three-thousand-mile journey to the San Francisco Bay area in California. There were about 250 men and officers on the trip.

On the morning of the seventh day of travel, we hefted our seabags and poured off the train at Camp Shoemaker, California. We were all hungry, but the base people said the mess halls were closed. We'd have to wait for the noon meal. Our officers went to bat for us and for themselves, and after pulling some rank and some arm-twisting, food was prepared for all of us.

After a short stay at Shoemaker, we moved to Treasure Island in the bay, where we got a batch of shots for the medical and disease hazards facing us in the South Pacific.

On October 14, 1944, the crews boarded the USS *General Patrick* (AP-150), and sailed under the Golden Gate Bridge and into the broad Pacific Ocean. Our ship was a nearly new Kaiser creation, a liberty ship that seemed to have a tendency to leak water in heavy seas.

On October 19 we entered Pearl Harbor in Oahu, Territory of Hawaii. We could see the superstructure of the sunken battleship USS *Arizona* sticking up out of the bay. This was the only evidence of the infamous bombing raid of December 7, 1941, that we saw in the harbor area. Our crews were moved to an LCI, which took us to the Naval Underwater Demolition Training and Experimental Base on the island of Maui, a hundred or so sea miles south and east.

Coming into Maui, we passed the town of Lahaina and then almost due east we saw the ten-thousand-foot Red Hill. The UDT base was at the foot of the mountain and about ten miles south of Kahului, Maui's main seaport.

We left the LCI and were assigned tents in the Maui dust bowl. To the north of the tent area were the smelly toilets, and south of the tents some luxurious open cold showers. To the west toward the beach were an outdoor theater, laundry facilities, administration offices, officers' quarters, and the mess hall.

At first there was no electricity in the enlisted men's tents. After we dug postholes, electrical power was brought in.

Here Teams 11, 12, and 13 were organized from the men in the Fort Pierce boat crews. Generally the enlisted men were assigned to the same team that their

Fort Pierce crew officer was assigned. Eventually the teams received men from Team Able, and an earlier team that had been in combat in the Solomons and had its ship sunk just before the invasion of Peleliu.

Lieutenant Commander Vincent Moranz became Team No. 13's commanding officer and Ensign Moore our executive officer. Lieutenant Donald Walker later replaced Moore as the XO. Lieutenant Walker came to us from Team Able, along with several enlisted men.

Our six-man crew system was replaced by a five-platoon system: four operational platoons and one headquarters platoon. The four operational ones were labeled Able, Baker, Charley, and Dog. Each platoon had an LCP(R) boat crew consisting of two platoon officers, a coxswain, two gunners, a radioman, a machinist, and ten to twelve swimmer/demolition specialists. All of the men on the boat were trained as UDT swimmer and demo men, and there were overlapping and changing assignments.

The team headquarters platoon consisted of specialists including the pharmacist's mate, yeoman, photographer, operations officer, and supply officer.

Our style of training also changed. At Maui, swimming became paramount in the training problems along with dropping and retrieving swimmers at high speed from rubber boats attached to the fast LCP(R)s. Swim fins and face masks were added to our equipment list.

Our team trained through November and December and everyone had experiences to remember. We had night reconnaissance missions, day and night demolition problems, and the high jumps from the base pier with no parachute.

The intensive physical training increased the camaraderie and organizational pride among the men. Competition with the other teams in training soon arose.

In December, Team No. 11 had an accident. On a night mission a boat crew failed to leave the target beach at the scheduled time and was there when the beach exploded. Fortunately it was only a dry run with Primacord as the explosive. Still, an officer lost a leg and several men were wounded. The team was demoralized and when the rest of us moved to the South Pacific, Team No. 11 was left at Maui to recuperate. The accident was felt by the men in the other two teams as well because the men in No. 11 were friends from our Florida training.

On January 3, 1945, Team No. 13 boarded the USS *Barr* (AP-54), at Maui. Our training was completed and we were heading west. The APD was a World War I four-stacker destroyer that had been converted into a transport for our UDT teams. Two stacks had been removed to make space for the team and its supplies.

We were loaded with tons of tetrytol, hundreds of rolls of Primacord, fuses, fuse igniters, .45-caliber handguns, Thompson submachine guns, knives, dive masks, swim fins, rubber boats, and dozens of other items we'd need in combat.

We were headed for the Caroline Islands. The *Barr* was part of a screening force of APDs for a convoy of APAs. The *Barr* was on their right flank. With the USS *Bates* (APD-47) on the left and with the battleship the USS *Nevada* as flagship, the convoy moved across the central Pacific. UDT Team No. 12 was on the *Bates*. We passed close to the Japanese-held island of Truk and we were warned to be ready for Japanese air patrols. But they never came.

We reached Ulithi in late January. This was the

staging area for the assault on Iwo Jima in the Volcano Islands about 750 miles from Tokyo. We had just settled in to wait for the big push when we heard that Teams 14 and 15 had arrived in the port. We had trained with Team No. 15. Fifteen had left Fort Pierce a month earlier, trained quickly at Maui, and helped open beaches at Lingayen Gulf in the Philippines.

In the harbor there we first heard of the "divine wind" from Japan. It's what they called their kamikaze planes. The Japanese were training pilots to fly fighters and bombers loaded with bombs and lots of gasoline for one-way suicide dives into enemy ships. They had sunk a lot of American ships during the invasion of Luzon. To help counter this threat, we brought in several more .50-caliber machine guns to mount on the fantail of our APD.

Raymond LeBlanc, one of our Team No. 13 members, volunteered to help build the gun mounts. He was a welder. While Ray was welding on one of the gun mounts, a bow wave from a passing ship washed over him and his welding gear with tons of water. Ray was knocked into the water. He was either stunned or already dead by electrocution and drifted under the ship. Teammates dove into the water to save him, but when he was pulled from the water it was on the other side of the hull of the ship. He was dead.

Ceremonies were held for Raymond LeBlanc and he was temporarily buried in a small military cemetery on Asor, one of the many islands of the Ulithi atoll group.

For a while the waters of Ulithi were a playground for swimmers of UDT No. 13. We dived from the fantail of the *Barr* in the 85-degree water. We took rubber boats to the edge of the ring of islands, searching for shells and pearls. These activities kept us in good physical shape for the work that lay ahead.

We practiced swimming reconnaissance from the open ocean into the beaches of the eastern islands of Ulithi. Then, on February 10, all four UDT teams on our respective APDs left Ulithi with the bombardment forces for the invasion of Iwo Jima.

On February 16 we arrived off the island of Iwo Jima. The weather was cool and partly cloudy. The island looked ominous. To the south rose Mount Suribachi to a thousand feet. To the north was a long ridge with a lower elevation. The island was six miles long and three miles wide. Even before the fight, the place looked devastated. It had been bombed daily for sixty consecutive days by the U.S. Army Air Corps from Saipan. Still, there were twenty thousand Japanese troops living in the caves and pillboxes that ringed the island.

My UDT Team No. 13 drew the first assignment. We were to put a navigation light on the far north end of Iwo Jima where a cluster of rocks protruded from the water a few hundred yards from the mainland. They were called Higashi Iwo. The light would warn attacking ships of the presence of the dangerous rocks. We went in on February 16 with the light and batteries. The Japanese opened up on us with machine-gun and mortar fire. Our boats responded and blasted the north end of the island. Our crew got the light established and made it safely back to the ship. It was our first wartime action.

The next day the Navy discovered that the Japanese or the waves had washed away the light and we were told to put another one up. We did, but it, too, was destroyed, and we didn't do it a third time.

Our APD, the *Barr*, had nightly assignments of cruising the picket line, which was a screen of ships forming a radar and sonar line to keep enemy submarines and aircraft from penetrating the U.S. invasion fleet area.

Two days before the invasion, February 17, 1945, was the day set for the UDT teams to open the beaches of Iwo Jima. In the morning all four teams did recons on the east beaches. Then that afternoon we went to the other side and did our reconnaissance on the west beaches.

Team No. 13 drew Green Beach No. 1, which was in the southern section of the east beaches. We swam underwater near the shadow of Mount Suribachi. It looked to be the most dangerous beach on the whole east side. We took in ten swimmers right below the awesome strength of the guns in the caves of Mount Suribachi.

We had great fire support for the teams. Battleships, cruisers, and destroyers were positioned to rain a withering fire upon the eastern slope of the small island. In close were twelve LCIG gunboats, which would pour a continuous flow of rocket fire on the enemy positions. From experience the Navy had learned that to have a successful daytime recon against heavily fortified beaches, massive fire support was necessary.

My Team No. 13 sent two LCP(R)s in with swimmers aboard one and the other as a standby crew to be used if needed. The LCP(R)s moved inside the line of the LCIG gunboats and started to take fire from shore. With throttles wide open, they turned and moved parallel to the beach, dropping off the swimmers one by one. Mortar fire and machine-gun fire rained down over and around all the recon boats until they moved out of range beyond the line of the LCIGs. So far no boats had been hit and there were no casualties.

Things were different on the LCIGs line. The Japs had poured everything they had from eight-inchers on down against the twelve LCIG gunboats. Eleven of the twelve were hit and disabled by gunfire. One sank and many crewmen were killed and wounded. Some of the casualties were UDT people who were acting as spotters on the boats. In a half hour the twelve gunboats were completely out of the fray. They were too badly shot up to continue. This was the worst disaster for the LCIGs during the Pacific War.

Team No. 13 swimmers went into their assigned beach in the frigid waters, braving the mortars, machine guns, and rifle fire. Our last swim had been in 85-degree water. Now it was down to 60 degrees. We wore trunks and swim fins and a layer of grease to help protect us from the cold. We made the recon, noting all pertinent information about the beach in less than an hour, and returned to the swimmer pickup line. The LCP(R) jerked us out of the water one at a time in a high-speed run that we had practiced so many times. Our report told that Green Beach No. 1 was clear of mines and underwater obstacles and judged suitable for landing-craft entry.

That afternoon we went to the west-side beaches. We didn't have the LCIGs, which gave us so much great in-close fire support. To make up for it, they brought in air support to work the west beaches. The planes were to lay down heavy smoke screens over the terrain just inside the surf line.

Team No. 13's beach was again the southernmost under the north slope of Mount Suribachi and called Purple Beach No. 1. Without the help of the gunboats we feared the worst. We sent in ten swimmers again. The air temperature was cold and the water colder. The LCP(R)s were under fire while dropping the swimmers, and we received heavy machine-gun and some mortar fire.

The Navy planes covered the beach from surf to dune line with a steady machine-gun and rocket fire moving up the dunes as the swimmers approached the shore. We swam just outside the surf and moved parallel to the beach for fifty yards per man. The beach was clear of obstacles, steep-sloped, and apparently suitable for all types of landing craft. We kept getting some rifle fire. We gathered and logged the information on our slates and swam seaward. The LCP(R)s came into the swimmer pickup area to make their retrieval pass.

This part of the plan broke down. Some of the swimmers had cramps from the cold water. The seas were high and some men were not in line. There was some confusion about the location of the pickup area. At least one Team No. 13 swimmer was picked up by a Team No. 12 LCP(R). A Team No. 15 LCP(R) had to race in close to the beach to retrieve two swimmers. Team No. 12 had one missing swimmer who was never found.

After the two recon operations, the swimmers had a shot of brandy and reported their findings. The *Barr* moved out to sea and resumed its assigned picket line position.

On the night of February 18, 1944, the *Barr* and the USS *Balsam* (APD-48) were on picket duty. UDT Team No. 15 was quartered in the *APD-48*. A two-engine Japanese bomber flying low under the radar beams dropped a bomb that landed directly into the mess hall of the *Balsam*. Team No. 15 had eighteen men killed and twenty-three wounded. Nearly half the team members were casualties. Many of them were our friends.

February 19, 1945, was D-day and Team No. 13 men and those of the other three teams directed the first wave of landing craft into Green Beach No. 1. The battle for Iwo Jima had begun.

After twelve days of postassault operations on Iwo Jima, Team No. 13 boarded the *Barr* and headed for Guam. We arrived on March 7. We had four days of R & R on and off the ship. Then we sailed again and went to the small island of Asor, where we had more R & R.

When we went back to our ship, the old splashes of yellow and green amphibious camouflage paint were gone. The *Barr* was painted fleet gray and had the look of a real destroyer.

On March 20 we left Ulithi with a bombardment task force bound for the Ryukyu Islands, specifically Okinawa. We were in the advance group and Teams 12, 14, and 19 were with us. Team 19 had just arrived from Maui, and Okinawa would be their battle initiation.

As we moved, other teams were assembling in the Philippines. They were Teams 3, 7, 11, 16, 17, and 21. They would come with the main task force. Our job with the advance party was to clear beaches in two groups of islands, Kerama-Rettō and Kiese Shima. The Kerama-Rettō islands were a group of many small islands almost enclosing a body of water several miles long and two miles wide. The Navy wanted it for a safe anchorage for supply ships and transports. There the ships would be safe from Jap subs, suicide boats, and kamikaze planes.

The largest of the islands was Tokashiki-jima, and Team No. 13 was picked to reconnoiter the beaches. On the morning of March 25 our platoons moved the LCP(R)s into position to drop their swimmers. The beaches were in a broad inlet with tree-covered hills on both sides. The operation went like clockwork. Enemy fire was light and some swimmers reported none at all. The swimmers worked the reefs and found no mines or obstacles but reported many coral heads. Some were less than three feet from the surface.

By going into the beach at high tide, the coral heads were avoided.

Some of the Team No. 13 men wore old-fashioned long-john underwear on the long swim and said they stayed warmer than those who used axle grease.

In three days the U.S. forces controlled the island and the planners looked at Kiese Shima, at one point only a mile of water away from Okinawa. It had a lower profile than Tokashiki-jima and in some places looked like an overgrown sandbar. The Army wanted to put batteries of 155 howitzers there to fire on some of the Okinawa invasion beaches and the city of Naha.

For three days Team No. 13 worked in the cold water almost under the noses of the Japanese. We hand placed tetrytol satchel charges around the giant coral heads and, with Primacord leads and trunk lines, cut a channel shoreward. While we worked, two Navy or Marine fighters came over and bombed and strafed our swimmers. They missed and we took no casualties.

By the afternoon of March 29, 1945, Team No. 13 had completed the channel and marked it with buoys. In three days we placed over twenty-seven tons of tetrytol, blowing out the coral.

The invasion went off on schedule on April 1, but Team No. 13 had no duties, so we stayed on the *Barr* on picket duty watching for kamikaze planes. We soon moved to a transport anchored in Kerama-Rettō. After a few days we boarded an APA, the *Wayne*, and sailed for Maui. We were glad to get back to our very own "dust bowl" and our tents.

We were given ten-day leaves and, when we assembled again, found out that Team No. 13 had been assigned as instructors in the base training program at the Underwater Demolition Training and Experimental Base at Maui. We would replace Team No. 9. We were there for two months teaching Teams 27 to 29. Shortly after that, every UDT team commissioned had orders to return to Oceanside, California, to take a course in cold-water training to prepare for Operation Olympic. That was the code name for the initial invasion of the Japanese homeland.

Team No. 13 was put back together and ordered to Oceanside.

Shortly after that, V-J Day arrived and the war was over. There were many changes in the teams after that. Some went to Japan to check beaches and ports. Eventually most came back to the States. The teams shrank to four: two on the West Coast in Coronado, California, and two on the East Coast.

A fond remembrance: Don Rose, UDT, 1950s

I RECENTLY VISITED the admiral's office at the NAVSPECWARGRUP-ONE at Coronado, California. It's located where the old UDT area was in the 1950s. What a contrast. Instead of Quonset huts on the sand, there was this large building with a security fence and senior officers all around. Looking at the Special Warfare complex, one gets the feeling that the operating fund for Special Warfare must be quite large compared to the three thousand dollars per quarter that we had in the 1950s.

Back then we lived out of everybody else's trash can. Regular visits to salvage yards as far away as Barstow, about 150 miles, were routine. The green uniforms that we wore were Marine greens with a peculiar weave called herringbone tweed. We had to black out the Marine Corps insignia on the caps and jackets. In Korea we stole vehicles to use and painted false numbers on them. We couldn't survey them, turn them in for new ones, when they became unusable, as they were stolen, so they were stripped of usable parts and buried under the sand using a bulldozer. I was surprised, with all the digging in that area, that some of the vehicles didn't resurface.

There were few drinking fountains in our UDT training area in the 1950s, which was no problem for SUBOPS. They took a five-gallon water container, filled it with ice from the galley, and picked up grape juice concentrate to give it some variety. Someone decided to jazz it up one day with a hint of wine. As time went by, there became less juice and more wine.

Personnel in those early days made a little extra money on the side by diving for lobster and abalone off San Diego's shoreline. SUBOPS went a bit further and bought an old fishing boat with a big one-cylinder diesel and parked it at the Boy Scout landing near the base. They dove on weekends or whenever time was available and called the boat the *African Queen*.

SELECTED BIBLIOGRAPHY

Barbey, Admiral Daniel E., USN. *MacArthur's Amphibious Navy*. Annapolis: Naval Institute Press, 1969.

Darby, William O., and Baumer, William H. *We Led the Way*. San Francisco: Presidio Press, 1980.

Dockery, Kevin. *Navy SEALs: A History of the Early Years*. New York: Berkley, 2001.

Dwyer, John B. *Commandos from The Sea*. Boulder, Colorado: Paladin Press, 1998.

Dwyer, John B. *Scouts and Raiders: The Navy's First Special Warfare Commandos*. Westport, Connecticut: Prager, 1993.

Dyer, George C. *Amphibians Came to Conquer*, vol. 2. Washington: Government Printing Office, 1972.

Fane, Francis D., and Moore, Don. *The Naked Warrior*. New York: Appleton-Century-Crofts, 1956.

Gormly, Robert A. *Combat Swimmer*. New York: Penguin, 1999.

Hoyt, Edwin P. *SEALs at War*. New York: Dell, 1993.

Miles, Vice-Admiral Milton E., USN. *A Different Kind of War*. New York: Doubleday, 1967.

Smith, General Holland M., USMC. *Coral and Brass*. New York: Scribner & Sons, 1949.

Young, Darryl. *SEALs, UDT, Frogmen: Men under Pressure*. New York: Ballantine, 1994.

APPENDIX 1

ORIGINAL PERSONNEL OF UDT NO. 3, APRIL 1944

Those men marked with an asterisk (*) received a Silver Star medal for the Guam operation. The rest of the men each received a Bronze Star medal.

Lt. T.C. Crist *
Lt. (j.g.) G. C. Marion *
Lt. (j.g.) W.T. Hawks *
Ens. L. P. Luehrs *
Ens. W. W. Schied *
Ens. M. Jacobson *
Ens. J. J. Breen *
Ens. W. J. Dezell *
2nd. Lt. F. F. Lahr *
Ch Carp R. A. Blowers *
Ch Carp V.O. Racine *
Ch Carp R. Barge *
Ch Carp C. L. Young *
Ch Carp W. L. Gordon *
Ch Carp E. E. Frazier *
RM3/C J. L. Allen
GM3/C J. E. Bagnell
CMM O. C. Baker
SK2/C J. B. Barfield
SK2/C F. L. Barnett

S2/C E. J. Barta
SF 1/C W. O. Behne
S1/C J. M. Bisallion
S1/C J. M. Brady
CM3/C A. L. Brokes
S1/C W. K. Brown
S1/C E. L. Carson
F1/C G. J. Canizio
MM2/C W. R. Cardoza
F1/C M. Chapman
S1/C M. B. Chase
CM1/C H. Chilton
CMM J. R. Chittum
Cox. B. M. Christinson
SF3/C W. D. Cochran
SF2/C J. Conklin
S1/C E. Davis
SF1/C J. W. Donahue
GM3/C E. W. Durden
MM3/C L. G. Foote
GM3/C D. B. Gable
S1/C J. E. Gannon
GM3/C V. D. Gilkey
MM1/C C. E. Greene
GM3/C F. C. Hart
GM3/C L. L. Harrison
EM2/C L. L. Houk
AOM1/C C. W. Hoffman
MM2/C E. Holmes
CM2/C W. W. Irish
CBM R. E. Hustead
Cox. D. C. Iverson
S1/C J. Jenkins
S1/C I. S. Johnson

Cox. L. E. Kirkbride
S1/C J. L. Lepore
MoMM3/C G. S. Lewis
CEM H. E. Little
GM3/C T. C. Maher
GM3/C H. A. Matthews
MM2/C C. M. Massey
S1/C R. L. Micheels
S1/C H. G. Mitchell
GM1/C F. C. Moore
S1/C Clarence Mulheren
S1/C R. R. Nelms
Cox E. P. Parker
CM2/C N. G. Parker
MM1/C E. Pollock
SF1/C J. F. Quiggle
GM2/C A. H. Rahn
S1/C R. E. Reid
CPhM C. V. Reigle
SK1/C J. H. Reinhardt
MMl/C R. J. Robinson
GM3/C K. J. Rylands
MoMM2/C R. M. Schantz
CCM J. Schommer
GM1/C M. Semanchic
S1/C L. A. Shaw
RM3/C E. L. Shepherd
COX H. K. Sims
CM2/C D. E. Skaggs
F1/C R. W. Smith
CM3/C M. C. Solano
CM3/C E. J. Spellman
SF2/C V. R. Stewart
F1/C A. J. Stone

RM3/C H. W. Stump
MoMM3/C W. E. Swain
Cox. W. A. Timmerman
MM2/C C. A. Tomassoni
S1/C S. R. Wagner
MM3/C R. J. Whalen
RM2/C R. M. Wood

Killed in Action

Ch Carp R. A. Blowers: Killed in action July 15, 1944, at Guam.

CM2/C W. W. Irish: Killed in a training accident in July, 1945 at Fort Pierce, Florida.

APPENDIX 2

UNDERWATER DEMOLITION TEAM No. 10 ROSTER

USS *Rathburne, APD-25*

Commanding Officer
Lt. Com. Arthur D. Choate

Officers
Ens. Frank Benton
1st Lt. C. Dockter, U.S. Army
Ens. John W. D. Dougherty
Ens. Arthur O. Garrett
Lt. Lawrence J. Gibboney
Lt. (jg) Don R. Gowers
Lt. (jg) Joseph R. Houska
Lt. Com. James Knott
Lt. Com. Paul G. Meridith
Ens. Robert W. Parmele
Lt. (jg) Harry Speaks
1st Lt. William D. Wolf, U.S. Army

Enlisted U.S. Navy Personnel
Barnhill, L. L.
Bickard, E. F.
Black, R.
Blanchard, D.

Blodgett, K.
Bostwick, D. L.
Bowlin, C. M.
Bradley, R. S.
Burkhart, J. M
Cameron, A. D.
Chambliss, K.
Christensen, W. R.
Coffield, P. Jr.
Dean, R. J.
Edwards, J. O.
Elmgren, T.A.W. Jr.
English, F. T. Jr.
Evans, F. A.
Faris, J. P.
Fialkowski, J. S.
Freeman, A. J.
Granger, C. O.
Hannigan, T. V.
Hartung, N. S.
Hawlin, R. O.
Hughes, R. G. Jr.
Jaap, C. O. III
Jewell, O.C.
Johnson, R. E.
Katsirubas, W. P.
Kelley, C. H.
Kenworthy, R. E.
Keyes, D. W.
King, D. E.
Larson, M. H.
Lathrop, R. C
Long, L. J. Jr.
Martin, W. R.

McKay, E. W.
McMahon, I.
Moore, F. L.
Moore, K. G.
Moore, W. E.
Montgomery, D. J.
Mouser, C. C.
Nichols, D.
O'Brien, W. M.
Payne, W. H.
Palaszewski, E. W.
Pechillo, J. A.
Roades, C. F.
Schultz, R. W.
Speck, G. P.
Sweeney, R. J.
Thomas, J. N.
Travis, W. S.
Vindick, R. W.
Voellinger, L. A.
Watson, A. W.
Weldon, H. T.
Willinsky, J. J.
Wislo, R. E.
Young, R. W.

U.S. Coast Guard Personnel
Beck, R.
Hobbs, R. K.
Hopper, W. D. Jr.
Mulhern, R. K.
Nikolenko, N.
Parker, R. K.

Risser, G. K.
Scoles, R. O.

U.S. Marine Corps Personnel
Bodine, L. L.
White, F. A.
Wright, W. C.

APPENDIX 3

NAVAL COMBAT DEMOLITION UNITS AT NORMANDY'S UTAH BEACH, JUNE 6, 1944

+ Awarded the Navy Cross medal.
** Awarded the Silver Star medal.
* Awarded the Bronze Star medal.
> Awarded the French Croix de Guerre ribbon.

All killed and wounded were awarded the Purple Heart medal.

All listed were awarded the Navy Unit Commendation ribbon and the French Croix de Guerre Ribbon.

Killed in Action
Demmer, P. M.
McGeary, D. C

Wounded
Angell, E. D. Jr.
Bohne, L. C.
Brennan, F. G.
Bymes, B. W.
Dellapiano, S. J. ** >
DeMase, F. W.
DiCarlo, P. J.
Dunford, J. E.
Fraley, W. D.
Hagensen, C. P.

Ladomirak, M.
Lombardo, P.
Noyes, C. R. * >
Palmisano, B.
Powell, E. L.
Wilson, C. S.

Not Wounded
Beggs, W. A.
Bierley, J. A.
Byington, C. W.
Chatas, A. T.
Church, B.
Clayton, E. P. +
Csire, L. W.
Curry, W. C.
Czawsz, F. P.
Czeszel, J. R.
Dalfino, J. R.
Dalinsky, R. D.
Dammeyer, G. W.
Deats, G. F.
DeLoreto, E.
DelToro, L.
Demerly, B. W.
Dexter, R. L.
Deutch, J. L.
DeVerna, J. J.
Dille, T. V.
Dittmer, J. A.
Dube, L. J.
Duberson, W. B. Jr.
Eberhardt, R. C.
Eckert, E.

Faltisco, E.
Flynn, J. E. * >
Gee, J. E.
Gillette, G. E.
Greaves, H. C.
Grippo, H. J.
Hartshorn, V. A.
Helfrich, R. A.
Hiesley, W. E.
Irwin, N. S.
Jeter, M. A.
Johnson, A. N.
Jones, A. L. * >
Kobelin, C.
Levine, R.
Marks, J. E.
Martini, C. F. Jr.
McNichol, W. E.
McQueen, F. N.
Menard, O. W.
Modesett, J. M. * >
Muller, W. C.
Nettleton, C. W.
Netz, L. G.
Olpp, R. E.
Padgett, J. L. * >
Penton, L.
Peterson, H. A.
Pettitt, C. T.
Phelan, J. C.
Phillips, C.
Pierce, H. L.
Polin, E. D.
Potrzebowski, F. J.

Powell, F. W.
Prall, C. B.
Prewitt, L. A. * >
Price, L. S. * >
Reinie, E.
Roloff, J. W.
Rudisill, R. B. * >
Shryock, D. W.
Simmons, G. H. * >
Sledge, R. P.
Smith, J. O.
Smith, R. C. ** >
Sprouse, J. M.
Summers, N. J.
Suvada, S., Jr.
Thomas, P. E.
Tilman, D. S.
Wakefield, O. W. * >
Walsh, M. F.
Webre, C. Jr.
Welch, R. R.
Wilmont, L. L. * >
Wirwahn, R. E. * >
Wolski, F. F.

APPENDIX 4

NAVAL COMBAT DEMOLITION UNITS AT NORMANDY'S OMAHA BEACH, JUNE 6, 1944

+ Awarded the Navy Cross medal.
** Awarded the Silver Star medal.
* Awarded the Bronze Star medal.
# Awarded the Navy & Marine Corps medal.

All killed and wounded were awarded the Purple Heart medal.

All personnel awarded the Presidential Unit Citation ribbon and the French Croix de Guerre ribbon.

Killed in Action

Alexander, H. R.
Bussell, J. E.
Cook, J. W.
DeGregorio, C.
Dillon, T. J.
Dombek, W. J.
Doran, W. R.
Drew, E. M.
Duncan, H.
Fabich, H. S.
Fleming, A. J.
Fuller, J. A.
Gouinlock, G. L.
Goulder, P. H.

Greenfield, E. J.
Harang, R. D.
Herring, A. P.
Hickey, A. B.
Holtman, O. H.
Jacobson, J. A. **
Jarosz, E. A.
McDermott, J. D.
Millis, C. C.
Mingledorf, O. C. Jr.
Olive, J. D.
Perkins, F. J.
Pienack, R. R.
Sullivan, M. F. Jr.
Vetter, A. E.
Weatherford, M. P. **
Weckman, L. I.
Woods, C. M.

Wounded in Action
Allen, C. C. L.
Barbour, L. E. Jr. +
Bard, M. W.
Barker, J. N.
Bass, R. W. +
Baumann L. H.
Blean, H. P.
Bledsoe, C. E.
Buffington, E. M. F. **
Caldwell, J. A.
Cheney, A. B.
Choffin, H. W.
Cicerone, E. W.
Conti, M. D.

Cooper, W.
Correa, H.
Cosentino, D. V.
DeVincenzia, A. A.
Dietz, C. L.
DiMartino, J. D
Dobbins, C. L.
Donahue, J. M.
Dorash, L. S.
Dracz, S.
Duffy, W. H.
Dwyer, J. J.
Fant, G. B.
Farrell, M. E.
Frashier, D. R.
Freeman, W. R. +
Glasco, R. H.
Golding, R. A. Jr.
Hurst, L. H. Jr.
Inman, S. F.
Kirkpatrick, D.
Koch, F.
Line, J. H. +
Logan, G. L.
Lokey, J. G.
Maguire, A. C. **
Markham, J. N. +
McAdams, P. M.
Mckinley, J. C.
Meyers, L. J. **
Mishler, W. C.
Mitchell, W. C.
Morgan, H. S.
Nichols, H. W. Jr.

Palacios, A. M.
Patrick, J. O.
Prefontaine, J. W.
Raymor, W. H.
Ross, J. G.
Sears, A. R. J. Jr.
Seibert, C. L.
Shelley, M. W.
Siegle, M.
Sparks, R. O.
Stocking, H. B.
Svendsen, R. L.
Thompson, W. C.
VanValkengurg, T. A.
VanWagner, G.

Not Wounded
Allen, J. C. **
Ayers, C. N.
Botens, D. G.
Brown, J. M.
Bruce, J. J.
Cameron, G. P.
Carr, D. C. #
Comfrey, J. L.
Cook, L. E.
Cook, W. E.
Coombs, R. H.
Cortez, D. E.
Covese, E. F.
Cottrell, J. S.
Crane, J. M.
Crocker, H. H.
Crossley, H. G.

Culver, W.
Daniels, L. E.
Daniels, R. F.
Darcy, F. X.
Dauphin, W. P.
DeFranco, C. R.
Dennis. J. J.
Dennison, J. W.
Diguiseppi, F. N.
Dinkelacker, W. A.
DiPietro, J. C.
Dizney, H.
Dolan, J. N. Jr. **
Domboski, L. J.
Douglas, J. F.
Douglass, H. W.
Downes, W. V.
Drake, W. F.
Drobb, J.
Dubroc, N. J.
Dumas, J. W. Sr.
Duquette, H. E. Jr.
Emi, E. A.
Fitzpatrick, E. F.
Franklin, W. W.
Fulgieri, C. C.
Galeotti, A. S.
Gallant, G. M.
Gemon, E. G.
Gibbons, J. H. **
Gooch, J. G.
Gumula, W. L.
Hall, C. T. **
Harris, G. E.

Heideman, L. L. * **
Hiester, L. A.
Hill, J. G. Jr.
Hopper, C. J.
Jenkins, W. M. +
Johnson, L. A.
Karnowski, L. S. +
Keeling, P. R.
Lapan, E. V.
Ledien, H. B.
Lehtinen, R. D.
Livesay, W. L.
Luttrell, G. P.
Marshall, G. W.
McAdoo, A. G.
McCaffrey, J. P.
McHugh, J. E.
Memelstein, A.
Mitchell, R. W.
Morning, J. M.
Munson, H. J.
Nelson, N.
Palmoski, J. A.
Peterson, W. A.
Pogozelski, S. P.
Pomponi, P. V.
Redding, J. W.
Redeye, D. J.
Reynolds, K. B.
Roah, H. W.
Scorzafava, M. J.
Sroka, M.
Stauder, K. I.
Stevens, L. F. * **

Talton, J. C.
Tezman, L.
VanDusen, R. J. Jr.
Vaughn, W. M. #
Vinion, B. R.
Waddell, R.
Walczak, L. J.
Walters, A. J.
Wells, L., Jr.
Weston, E. E.
White, W. F.
Wren, W. R.

APPENDIX 5

NAVAL COMBAT DEMOLITON UNIT ROSTERS

NCDU No. 11
Robert Bass
Matthew Conti
C. DeFranco
Carl Dobbins
Michael Farrell
William Freeman
Lawrence Heideman
Ozie Mingledorf Jr.
Jesse Olive

NCDU No. 22
Loran Barbour Jr.
Richard Coombs
Walter Cooper
Henry Correa
G. M. Gallant
Chester Hall
John Line
Lester Stevens
Milton Weatherford

NCDU No. 23
D. E. Cortez
Ernest Converse

D. V. Cosentino
Harold Duncan
Andrew Fleming
Preston Goulder
Arthur Herring
John McDermott
Alvin Vetter

NCDU No. 24
D. G. Botens
G. P. Cameron
Julien Cottrell
John Crane
W. Culver
Joseph DiMartino
E. A. Emi
William Livesay
A. G. McAdoo

NCDU No. 25
Angelos Chatas
Edward Clayton
William Curry
Frank Czawsz
John Czeszel
Edmund Eckert
Carroll Prall
Leland Prewitt
Charles Weber Jr.

NCDU No. 26
Billy Church
James Dalfino
Max Jeter

Alvie Jones
James Marks
Oliver Menard
Leonard Price
Jack Smith
Leonard Milmont

NCDU No. 27
Henry Alexander
Charles Bledsoe
W. P. Dauphin
James Dwyer
John Fuller
Richard Harang
O. Heltmon
Orvid Holtman
Phillip McAdam
McCaffre

NCDU No. 28
Gordon Deats
Ernest DeLoreto
Herbert Greaves
Horton Grippo
Louis Netz
Fredric Powell
R.C. Smith
Steve Suvada Jr.

NCDU No. 29
Larry Bohne
Bernarde Bymes
Louis Deltoro
Bryan Demerty

Robert Eberhardt
Lewis Hursh Jr.
Charles Martini Jr.
Jackson Modesett
Paul Thomas

NCDU No. 30
James Bierely
Charles Byington
Roy Deter
Joseph Deutch
George Gillette
Carl Hagernson
Clarence Nettleton
Floyd Potrzebowski

NCDU No. 41
Milton Bard
Angelo DeVincenzi
Charles Dietz Jr.
Joseph Donohue
Robert Golding Jr.
John Nichols Jr.
Frank Perkins
John Prefontaine
Melvin Shelley

NCDU No. 42
Louis Cook
Anselmo Galeotti
John Lokey
Kenneth Reynolds
Herbert Roach

Marino Scorzafava
Leon Teizman
William Thompson
Calvin Woods

NCDU No. 43
J. C. DiPreto
Walter Dombek
William Drake
Wallace Franklin
John Jacobson
William Jenkins
Norval Nelson
Melvin Sroka
Keith Stader
Edward Weston

NCDU No. 44
Leon Dombroski
William Duffy
Raymond Lehtinen
Paul Mishler
John Palmoski
Stanley Pogozelliski
William Raymor
John Talton
Lawrence Weckman

NCDU No. 45
Edward Cicerone
Lawrence Dorash
John Douglas
G. B. Fant

Clarence Hopper
Lawrence Kamowski
Lester Meyers
Conrad Millis
Robert Svendsen

NCDU No. 46
John Bussell
Harold Crocker
William Downes
Elmer Drew
Henry Fabich
Carmine Fulgieri
Jerry Markham
James McHugh
Raymond Pienack

NCDU No. 127
John Dittmer
William Duberson Jr.
Edward Faltisco
J. L. Padgett
Myron Walsh
Raymond Wirwahn

NCDU No. 128
Lester Baumann
John Comfrey
H. Dizney
John Dolan Jr.
James Dumas Sr.
Herbert Duqutte Jr.
Donald Frashier
Abben Maguire

NCDU No. 129
Jack Caldwell
Jak Choffin
John Drobb
James Gooch
Paul Keeling
Wade Peterson
Gordon Van Wagner
Lewis Hureh Jr.

NCDU No. 130
John Bruce
Alan Cheney
John Dennison
W. A. Dinkelacker
Nelson Dubroc
James Redding
Dean Redeye
Billie Vinion
Robert Waddell
Andrew Walters

NCDU No. 131
W. E. Cook
Carmine DeGregorio
Ernest Gemon
Walter Gumula
S. F. Inman
Friedrich Koch
Harold Morgan
Alfredo Palacios
Jasper Ross

NCDU No. 132
John Flynn
John Gee
Ray Levine
Floyd McQueen
C. R. Noyes
Richard Olpp
Orville Wakefield

NCDU No. 133
Lloyd Daniels
Richard Daniels
F. N. Diguiseppi
George Logan
Robert Mitchell
Joel Morning
P. V. Pomponi
Louis Walczak
Levi Wells Jr.
William Wren

NCDU No. 134
Virgil Hartshom
Carl Kob
William McNichol
Leroy Penton
Clint Pett
James Phelan
Cushing Phillips
Eli Polin
Richard Welch

NCDU No. 135
Francis Brennan

Raymond Dalinsky
George Dammeyer
Robert Rudisill
Gilbert Simmons
Richard Sledge
J. M Sprouse
Norman Summers

NCDU No. 136
Walter Beggs
Louis Csire
William Hiesley
Harold Pierce
Edward Reinie
J. W. Roloff
Dennis Shyock
Daniel Tillman
Francis Wolski

NCDU No. 137
Harold Blean
James Brown
Edmund Buffington
H. G. Crossley
Lee Hiester
Louis Johnson
Gilbert Luttrell
James Patrick
William White

NCDU No. 138
John Allen
Francis Darcy
Joseph Dennis

Stanley Dracz
Edward Greenfield
Arthur Hickey
Dean Kirkpatrick
Harold Ledien
Herman Munson

NCDU No. 139
John DeVema
Thomas Dille
Robert Helfrich
Nate Irwin
Alfred Johnson
Phillip Lombardo
Warren Muller

NCDU No. 140
Clarence Ayers
Donald Carr
John Cook
E. F. Fitzpatrick
James Hill Jr.
George Marshall
James McKinley
Ralph VanDusen Jr.
Wendell Vaughn

NCDU No. 141
Clifford Allen
James Barker
Thomas Dillon
William Doran
Ray Glasco
George Gouinlock

Edward Jarosz
Clarence Seibert
Maurice Sullivan Jr.

NCDU No. 142
Harry Douglass
Guy Harris
Ethan Lapan
Aaron Memestein
William Mitchell
Alfred Sears Jr.
Robert Sparks
Howard Stocking
Thomas VanValkensburg

Men on Unknown Teams
Francis DeMase
Lewis Dube
Joseph Gibbons
Herbert Peterson

APPENDIX 6

OPERATION RECORDS OF SPECIAL SERVICES UNIT NO. 1, THE AMPHIBIOUS SCOUTS, 7th AMPHIBIOUS FORCE

September 11–13, 1943: Men of Special Services Unit No. 1 were transported by two PT boats of Commander John Bulkley's squadron and performed reconnaissance of enemy-occupied Finschaffen and acquired valuable intelligence despite aerial bombing. In the party were Capt. "Blue" Harris AIF, Lt. Allen Lane AIF 9th Div., Lt. Victor Nelson AIF, 9th Div., a sergeant with AIF, Lt. (jg) Henry Staudt USNR, and Agana natives Masa and Yuli.

September 24–Oct. 5, 1943: Reconnaissance performed in vicinity of Cape Bushing, New Britain, by men of Special Services Unit No. 1 within an enemy-patrolled area. Included in party were Lt. (jg) Rudolph A. Horak USNR, 1st Lt. Dailey P. Gambol, Australian, Lt. Andrew Kirkwall-Smith AIF, 1st Lt. John Bradbeer USMCR, and Agana natives Sabra and Tablo.

October 5–26, 1943: Performed reconnaissance in enemy territory, west of Gasmata, New Britain, under adverse conditions, radio trouble extending their mission. Were finally brought out by PT boat. Included in party were men of Special Service Unit

No. 1: Lt. (jg) Donald G. Root USNR, Lt. Beckwirth, Australian, Lt. L. C. Noakes AIF, and natives.

November 14, 1943: Prereconnaissance of Cape Gloucester by members of Special Service Unit No. 1, Lt. (jg) A.E. Gipe USNR, 1st Lt. R. B. Firm USMCR, Sgt. Elmer Potts USMCR, and Cpl. Americus Woyciesjes USMCR. Left after twenty minutes.

November 20–2l, 1943: Reconnaissance of Cape Gloucester by men listed in Operation No. 4. Despite the area being strongly held and well patrolled, they completed a recon of the beach, acquiring information of great intelligence value.

November–December 1943: Arawe. Special Service Unit No. 1 members Lt. (jg) Frank Meredith USNR, Lt. (jg) John Goodridge USNR, GM 2/C Richard Bardy USNR, BM 2/C Bob Hayden USNR. Reported to Alamo Scout teams for recon mission. Mission canceled.

November 24, 1943: Special Service Unit No. 1 ordered to Milne Bay. For the first time they are identified as the 7th Amphibious Scouts.

December 13–15, 1943: 1st Lt. John C. Bradbeer USMC and Lt. G.H. Maarsland RAAF and two natives completed a recon mission at Gasmata.

December 18, 1943: Capt. John Murphy AIF captured on recon mission at Gasmata.

December 25, 1943–January 12, 1944: Lt. (jg) Frank Meredith USNR, Phm 1/C Edwards, and RM 2/C R. Toman, served with beach party in initial assault on Breen Beach, Cape Gloucester. Remained there for eighteen days.

January 3, 1944: Saidor—Lt. (jg) A. E. Gipe acted as assistant beach master with beach party No. 2 and with 6th Army 32nd Division in initial assault.

March 3, April 8, 1944: Men of the 7th Amphibious Scouts were engaged in making tidal studies in the Admiralties in the following groups:

At Saidor—Lt. (jg) David De Windt, BM 2/C J. H. Bardy, and RM/2 C R. Toman.

At Long Island—Ens. W. A. Ramage, MoMM 1/C Rosaire Trudeau, BM 2/C P. L. Dougherty, and RM 2/C T. J. Reynolds.

At Purdy Island—Lt. (jg) Donald G. Root, Cox. C. W. Byrd, MM1/C M. J. Kolb, and RM 2/C Taylor.

April 12, 1944: Lt. (jg) A. E. Gipe sent to Los Negros as an observer during landing there.

March–April, 1944: Lt. (jg) Henry E. Staudt, Col. Melvin Brown USMC, BM 1/C J. Sufferan, BM 1/C James, and BM 2/C George Sackman aboard USS *S-47* prepared recon of Aitape; while en route were ordered to abort.

April 10, 1944: Lt. (jg) Henry E. Staudt ordered to temporary duty to LST 221 and participated in initial assault on Aitape.

April 10, 1944: Lt. (jg) Rudolph A. Horak sent with assault party as photographer for Naval Intelligence on first wave at White Beach at Hollandia.

April 11, 1944: All scouts aboard APAs and LSTs as observers for landings at Aitape and Hollandia.

April 11, 1944: Col. Melvin G. Brown USMC, OIC Amphibious Scouts Unit No. 1, 7th Amphibious Force, participated in landing at Aitape, acted as captain of the port. He transferred troops and supplies from there for Wakde-Tooem operation.

April 10–22, 1944: Lt. (jg) A. E. Gipe and BM 2/C John E. Grady were assigned to Tanahmerah Bay, west of

Hollandia, and participated in initial landings as beach party No. 3. Encountered difficulty unloading due to lack of successful beach reconnaissance. This was the area in which Capt. "Blue" Harris AIF and his party were annihilated.

May 1, 1944: Lt. (jg) H. E. Staudt assigned as cargo officer on LST 462.

May 20, 1944: Lt. (jg) A. E. Gipe, BM 2/C J. E. Grady, as preparation for Biak landing, were sent aboard as observers.

May 20, 1944: Lt. (jg) H. E. Staudt was cargo officer on LST 462 in initial assault at Wakde.

May 12-26, 1944: Lt. (jg) D. G. Root, Cox. Calvin Byrd, with Alamo Scouts attempted recon at Biak; however, due to incapacitation of the PT transporting the party, the mission was canceled after three attempts.

May 26, 1944: Lt. (jg) Gipe and BM 2/C J. E. Grady served with beach party No. 6 in initial assault at Biak, remaining ashore over two weeks.

May 26, 1944: Lt. (jg) H. E. Staudt served as cargo officer during initial landing aboard LST 462.

June 7, 1944: Lt. (jg) H. E. Staudt served as cargo officer during landing and unloading at Noemfoor.

June 7-July 14, 1944: Lt. (jg) D. G. Root and Cox. Calvin Byrd aboard the submarine USS *S-47* training for Sansapor mission. This included four days' reconnaissance in enemy territory.

July 14-18, 1944: Lt. (jg) A. E. Gipe and BM 2/C J. E. Grady with Alamo Scouts, performed reconnaissance for four days in enemy territory at Sansapor.

Col. Melvin G. Brown USMC, OIC amphibious Scouts Unit No. 1, 7th Amphibious Force, prepared the reconnaissance of Sansapor.

According to Adm. D. E. Barbey USN, "Sansapor was the most thoroughly reconnoitered landing in the Southwest Pacific."

July 18, 1944: Lt. (jg) H. E. Staudt landed on Sansapor D-day as the cargo officer on LST 462.

August 30–Sept 8, 1944: Lt. (jg) A. E. Gipe assigned duty with beach party no. 5 to train for Morotai invasion.

September 15, 1944: Lt. (jg) A. E. Gipe, Lt. (jg) D. G. Root, Lt. (jg) Robert Eiring, BM 2/C J. E. Grady, and Cox. Calvin Byrd participated in initial landing at Morotai with beach party no. 5. Met coral reef difficulties which NCDU officer resolved.

September 15, 1944: Lt. (jg) H. E. Staudt participated in initial landing at Morotai as cargo officer of LST 462 on D-day.

September 15, 1944: Lt. (jg) David De Windt participated in landing at Morotai coming in with the PTs.

September 20–21, 1944: Reconnaissance in enemy territory in Salebabu Island in the Talaud group for 24 hours by Alamo Scouts party including Lt. (jg) D. De Windt.

October 16–31, 1944: After battling storms to land, two parties of Amphibious Scouts installed and manned as directed navigation lights on Homonhon and Dinagat Islands, remaining for fifteen days.

Homonhon Island: Lt. (jg) A. E. Gipe, BM 2/C J.E. Grady, and GM 3/C J. J. Hedderman.

Dinagat Island: Lt. (jg) D. G. Root, Cox. Calvin Byrd, and BM 2/C P. L. Dougherty

October 20, 1944: Leyte, Tacloban, Samar. All other Amphibious Scouts served as beach master personnel.

October 20, 1944: Lt. (jg) D. H. De Windt landed with a beach party at Leyte.

October 20, 1944: Lt. (jg) Rudolph A. Horak participated in landing on White Beach as first lt. on LST 455.

October 20, 1944: Lt. (jg) Henry E. Staudt as cargo officer on LST 465 participated in D-day landing on Red Beach.

November 15, l944: Ens. J. T. Davis, BM 2/C Wm. J. Ryan, Cox. Billy Cardwell, Cox. Connors, and SM 3/C B. Connolly participated in initial landing in Mapia Islands and made beach reconnaissance to bring in future landing craft. Remained there for five days.

November 19, 1944: Ens. W. C. Sheppard, Cox. Leonard Hood, Cox. J. A. Di Pietro, and S 1/C Calvin C. Lovern participated in the initial landing on the Asia Islands and made beach reconnaissance to bring in future landing craft. Remained there for five days.

January 6, 1945: Lt. (jg) D. H. De Windt and Ens. W. C. Sheppard went to Lingayen Gulf with Underwater Demolition Team No. 6.

January 9, 1945: All amphibious Scouts participated in the initial assault on Luzon, Lingayen Gulf, worked with the naval beach parties five days. Teams led by Lt. (jg) D. E. De Windt, Lt. (jg) S. S. Chapin Jr., Lt. (jg) Davis, and Ens. W. C. Sheppard.

January 15–31, 1945: Lt. (jg) D. H. De Windt and Ens. W. C. Sheppard did a beach reconnaissance of Santiago Island, Lingayen Gulf, with an Army scouting party. On January 21, they participated in the assault landing of that island.

February 16–20, 1945: Lt. (jg) S. S. Chapin Jr. reported to 8th Army for a scouting mission in the Zamboanga area of Mindanao. Stayed ashore for four days.

March 9–13, 1945: Lt. (jg) S. S. Chapin Jr. with BM 2/C J. Cappa, MoMM 2/C K. W. Kachline, and Lt. (jg) J. T. Davis, with BM 2/C W. J. Ryan and S 1/C Cardwell, participated in D-1 day operations plus the assault landing at Zamboanga, Mindanao. Lt. (jg) J. T. Davis was seriously wounded and hospitalized on March 9, 1945.

March 10–12, 1945: Ens. W. C. Sheppard with Cox. L. Hood and GM 3/C J. J. Hedderman did a recon of the southeast coast of Panay, near Floillo.

March 17–Apr. 2, 1945: Ens. W. C. Sheppard joined the Alamo Scouts for a reconnaissance of the Legaspi Area on southern Luzon. Stayed ashore sixteen days.

March 22–23, 1945: Lt. (jg) S. S. Chapin Jr. with BM 2/C R. J. Cappa and MoMM 2/C K. W. Kachline did a reconnaissance of Western Negros Island near Pulupandan town vicinity.

April 9, 1945: Ens. W. C. Sheppard did a hydrographic recon of Fort Drum in Manila Bay.

April 10–May 9, 1945: Lt. (jg) S. S. Chapin Jr. with BM 2/C R. J. Cappa and MoMM 2/C K. W. Kachline were assigned temporary duty with COMPHIBGRP 6 and participated in the assault landing of Tarakan Island, northeast Borneo, on May 1, 1945.

April 12, 1945: Ens. W. C. Sheppard with BM 2/C W. J. Ryan and GM 2/C J. J. Hedderman did a recon of Paligpigan Bay and Carabao Island in Manila Bay.

April 17–May 7, 1945: Ens. W. C. Sheppard, with BM 2/C W. J. Ryan, Cox. L. Hood, and GM 3/C J. J. Hedderman, were assigned to COMPHIBGRP 8 for temporary duty. Participated in assault on Davoo. Made hydrographic survey of beaches at

Digos Point and Santa Cruz and Talama in Davoo Gulf.

May 26–July 21, 1945: Lt. (jg) S. S. Chapin Jr., with BM 2/C R. J. Cappa and MoMM 2/C K. W. Kachline, reported to COMPHIBGRP 6 for temporary duty. On June 7, 1945 they arrived at Brunei Bay area with fire support group. On June 8–9 they did a recon of Green Beach, Brunei Bluffs, and White Beach, Muara Island. Landing was June 10, 1945.

APPENDIX 7

U.S. Navy Ship Designations

ACG: Amphibious force command ship.
AF: Provision store ship.
AG: Miscellaneous auxiliary.
AGP: Motor torpedo boat tender.
AP: Transport.
APA: Attack transport.
APB: Self-propelled barracks ship.
APD: High speed transport.
ARL: Landing craft repair ship.
AS: Submarine tender.
ATB: Amphibious training base.
BB: Battleship.
CA: Heavy cruiser.
CVE: Small aircraft carrier.
DD: Destroyer.
DUKW: Or "Duck," amphibious truck.
IX: Unclassified miscellaneous ship.
LCG: Landing craft gun.
LCI: Landing craft infantry.
LCIG: Landing craft infantry with guns.
LCM: Landing craft mechanized.
LCP(R): Landing craft personnel ramped.
LCVP: Landing craft vehicle, personnel.
LST: Landing ship tank.
PA: Short form of APA.
PT: Motor torpedo boat.

INDEX

Abbot, Paul, 244
Acheson, Bill, 238–39
Admiralty Islands, invasion of, 10, 12
Alamo Scouts:
 at Biak, 11
 formation of, 26–28
 at Panay, 205
 at Sansapor, 13–14
 training, 26
 at Vogelkop, 26–28
Allen, John, 107, 108
Allen, Oliver, 154
Allen, Ross, 154, 156
Allen, Steve, 156
Allied Intelligence Bureau, 4–5
Amphibious Scouts:
 formation of, 4–6
 medical officer, 22–25
 operation records, 354–61
 roles of, 25
 training of, 6, 7
 volunteers for, 19–20
Amphibious Training Base, 135, 136
Anders, Lloyd, 6
Anderson, "Squeaky," 289
Anderson, W. E., 189

Andreasen, Grant, 121
Anzio, Italy, 185, 214
APD (attack personnel destroyer), 281
Army, U.S.:
 Airborne Division, 73, 112, 189–90, 206
 Alamo Scouts, 11, 13–14, 26–28, 205
 Cavalry units, 10, 153
 Combat Demolition Unit, 54
 Combat Engineers, 72, 113–14, 223–26, 229
 Engineer Demolition Teams, 52, 54, 64, 68, 119
 Gap Assault Teams, 119
 Joint Training Force, 120–21
 march across France, 73–74
 Seventh Army, 231
 Sixth Army, 18–19, 20, 21, 26, 205–6
 Sixth Rangers, 16–17
 V-Corps Provisional Engineer Group, 114–15
 Western Task Force, 74

INDEX

Army, U.S. (*cont.*)
 XXI Corps, 231
Arnn, Roy, 118
Arthur, Charles, 156
atomic bombs, 70, 125, 155, 188, 203, 221, 271, 308
Audibert, Frenchy, 290, 291, 295

Bagnall, J. E., 247
Barber, Gilliam, 143
Barbey, Daniel E., 10, 24
Bardy, Richard, 6
Barnette, Robert, 143
Bat Island, 10–11
Becker, George, 191
Bell, Ensign, 126, 150
Berry, Earl T., 175
Biak Island, 11–12
Blean, Harold P., 79–82, 115
Blowers, R. A., 247
Bobillard, Ensign, 212
Bolt, William, 212
Bookout (wounded), 119
Borgen Bay, 21
Borneo:
 NCDU in, 112–13
 UDT in, 208–9, 256–57
Bosco, Robert, 155–56
Bradbeer, John, 20
Bradley, Omar, 67
Brandau, Jack, 6
Brewster, E. D., 233
Bricky, Chief, 85
Bristol, Ray B., 178–88, 183*n*, 187*n*
Brooks, H. F., 305
Brown, James M., 56–58, 80

Brown, John H. III, 216
Brown, W. Rex, 301–5
Brunei Bay, 145, 202, 208
Brunei Bluffs, 200–201
Bryon, Jack, 121
Buchanan, "Shorty," 150
Bucklew, Phil H., 121, 126, 178, 180, 182–87
Buffington, Edmund M. F., 80
Burd, Billy, 212
Burma Road, 157
Bussell, John E., 62, 65, 66
Byrd, Calvin W., 6, 7–18, 27–28

Cairns, Australia, training in, 20
Calcutta, 217–18
Caldwell, J. A., 119
Camp Pendleton, cold-water training in, 257
Camp Perry, Virginia:
 mosquito control in, 85–86
 NCDU in, 70
 training in, 71, 279–80
Cappa, Robert J., 196, 198, 200
Carberry, Lieutenant, 105
Cardwell, B., 196
Caroline Islands, 306–7, 313
Carr, Lieutenant, 299
Carrick, Clare Chips, 143
Carter, Donald J., 144
Castilow, George A., 144
Chanley, Jack, 205
Chapin, Sidney S., 144, 192–201

INDEX 365

Charsky, Stephen, 272
Chiang Kai-shek, 214
China:
  guerrilla activities in, 218–21
  intelligence operations in, 209–12, 214, 215–16
  recon of South China beaches, 147
  SACO in, 188–90, 210–12, 214, 215–16, 221
  travel in, 218–19
  Unit Buck in, 187–88
China-Burma-India theater, 153–54, 155
Choate, Arthur O. Jr., 306
Christiansen, Robert, 283, 294
Churchill, Winston, 77, 172
Chyz, Ernie, 151
coast watchers, 4, 9
Coccari, Andy, 272–73
Comela (S&R training), 212
Connolly, Andrew B., 144
Cooper, Marvin, 309–21
Cooper, Walter "Scotty," 69
Coppa, Robert J., 144
Couble, Captain, 271
Coultas, William F., 7–8, 9, 19, 22
Coulter, Edward J., 144
Craig, Wilber, 156
Cranberry, W. G., 275
Crist, T. C., 137, 236, 245
Crocker, Harold Henry, 64

Davao, scouting operations at, 128
Davis, J. T., 196
DeBold, John, 292, 295, 305
DeMerritt, Grantville, 153
DeMerritt, Warren, 152–54
Demmer, John E., 216–21
Dennis, Joseph, 107
De Windt, David, 7
DeWitt, William P., 176–78
Dezell, W. J., 247
Dickie, Captain, 261
Diedrichsen, Lloyd, 154–57
Dinagat Island, 15–18
Dittmer, John A., 92–103
Dolliver, Ensign, 282–83, 286
Donaldson, L. V., 64
Donnal, Lieutenant, 176
Donnelly, Jerome, 121, 185
Dougherty, Paul L., 6, 16
Dove, John, 11, 129–30
Dracz, Stanley, 107
Drew, Elmer Malcolm, 64
Dube, Lewis, 93
Duberson, W. B. Jr., 93
Duchin, Eddy, 261
DUKWs, 146
Dunford, John, 93, 97–98, 102

Edmundson, Cecil "Big Ed," 225, 227
Eichelberg, Lt. Gen., 194
Eisenhower, Dwight D., 177
Ellsworth, Lieutenant, 205
Engineer Aviation Battalion, 836th, 27
Eniwetok, training at, 240–41
Ernest, W. W., 189

Fabich, Henry Samuel, 62
Fairbanks, Douglas Jr., 213, 250
Falsetto, Ed, 93
Fazekas, Edward J., 137–40
Ferdinands, 5
Fergusson Island, 8–9, 18, 20
Ferry, John S., 147–50
Figateli, Victor, 212
Finelli, Patrick L., 239–43
Firm, R. B., 18–19
Flynn, John, 113
Flynn, W. F., 71
Forrestal, James V., 15
Fort Pierce, Florida:
   choices in, 137–38
   decommissioning of, 308
   "Hell Week" in, 35, 61, 90–91, 104, 127, 148, 213, 304–5
   Navy SEAL/UDT Museum, 140
   NCDU in, 34–35
   training in, 34–35, 39, 40–41, 60–61, 71, 79, 82, 90–91, 104, 122, 124, 126–27, 128–29, 132–35, 138–40, 147–49, 150, 158–68, 171, 191, 192, 202–3, 206–7, 212–13, 222, 259, 280–81, 299, 302–5
Fouch, David, 143
Fowler, Murray, 272
France:
   Battaillion de Choc, 222
   invasion of, 144
   march across, 73–74
   southern, invasion of, 77–78, 147, 214
   southern, securing islands offshore, 172–74
   training in, 222
   see also Normandy invasion
Francis, Darcy, 107
Freeman, William R., 30–32
Fulgieri, Carmine Carl, 62

Gadd, William, 143
Gagon, John, 212
Gambill, Daily, 20, 21
Garland, Bill, 117
Garrand, Rodney, 212–14
Garrett, Arthur O., 297, 298
Gee, John, 108–13
Gelwick, Deal, 156
Gerow, Leonard T., 114
Gipe, Alva Earl, 6, 10, 11, 16, 19–20, 129–31
Givens, Terry "Tex," 37–39
glider-borne troops, 73, 112
Goephert, Jack, 156
Goldberg, Marshall "Biggy," 140
Goodridge, John C., 6
Grady, John, 10, 11, 16
Green, Robert, 156
Greenberg, Ira A., 223–31
Greenfield, Edward J., 107, 108
Green Island, 43–44
Griffin, Robert S., 239
Griggs, BM 1/C, 7
Groeschell, Paul, 156

Guam:
  clearing of beaches, 248, 301
  invasion of, 255, 286–87, 299
  R&R at, 266
  recon at, 246–48, 251–52, 276–77
Gulbranson, Captain, 224

Hall, Harold, 278–92, 294
Hall, Robert C., 175
Hallowell, Lieutenant, 203
Halperin, Robert, 121
Hamilton, Lieutenant, 6
Hammer, Clyde C., 189–90
Hardenbrook, Rev. Don, 188–89
Harris, "Blue," 9, 11, 22
Healy, Bob, 262, 264–65
Hedderman, J. J., 204–5
Heffelfinger, Cliff, 140, 154
Herrick, Robert, 121, 150
Hickey, Arthur, 107
Higgins, Edwin T., 253–54
Homonhon Island, 15–16
Hood, Leonard, 204
Horak, Rudolph A., 6, 19–22
Howe, Jack, 156
Howe, Kenneth E., 121, 185
Howell, Bronson "Tex," 215–16
Hund, Lieutenant, 93

Île-de-France, 143–44
Île d'Hyères, 172
Impampulga Island, 144–45, 198

India:
  ammunition dumps cleaned up in, 149–50
  Calcutta, 217–18
Ivy, Minden, 117
Iwo Jima:
  assault on, 106, 314, 315–19
  beach recon, 262–66, 316–17
  flag-raising on, 49, 106
  light installation on, 261–62, 315
  Mount Suribachi, 49, 106, 262–64, 316, 317

Jacobson, M., 247
Japan:
  atomic bombs dropped on, 70, 125, 155, 188, 203, 221, 271, 308
  kamikaze pilots, 256, 267, 274, 314
  occupation forces in, 128
  planned invasion of, 70, 140, 190, 203, 257, 271, 321
  surrender of, 113, 203, 221, 296
Jerick, CPO, 46
Johnson, Charles H. Jr., 122–23
Johnson, John, 121
Jones, Jim, 239

Kachline, Kenneth W., 143–45, 196, 198, 200, 201–2
Kanaka fishermen, 252–53

Kassell, Kenneth G., 64
Kauffman, Draper L., 34, 40, 239, 270, 286, 292, 293, 295
Kausman, W. B., 277
kayaks, folding boats, 180
Kaye, Matthew W., 150–52
Kaylor (training), 150
Kendall, O. Melvin, 136–37
Kennedy, John F., 3
Kerama-Rettô Islands, 267, 269, 319
Kiese Shima Island, 267–68, 319
King, Adm. Ernest J., 33–34
King, Lieutenant, 45, 106
King, CBM Ray B., 145–47
Kinner, David, 171–74
Kirkpatrick, Dean, 107
Knott, James, 306
Knowles, Captain, 239
Koehler, J. T., 233, 234
Kolb, Milton J., 6
Krueger, Walter, 26
Kwajalein Island, 238–39

Lacovers, Don, 194
Lahr, Frank F., 300–301
Lanier, S. E., 207
Last, Alvin, 119
LCI (landing craft, infantry), 165, 184
LCM (landing craft, mechanized), 116, 121, 179
LCP (landing craft, personnel), 121
LCPL (landing craft, personnel, large), 121

LCPR (landing craft, personnel, ramped), 121, 249
LCT (landing craft, tank), 116
LCVP (landing craft vehicle, personnel), 73, 75, 263
LeBlanc, Raymond, 266, 314
Ledien, Harold Benjamin, 106–8
Ledo-Burma Road, 153
Lennox, Fritz, 156
Lent, L. B., 207
Leonard (recon specialist), 184–85
Leu, Don, 155, 156
Levine, Ray, 113
Leyte Gulf:
　landing at, 22, 297
　preparation for attack, 16–18, 255
　recon operations, 249, 277, 290, 295–96, 307
L'Heureux (recon specialist), 184–85
Long (wounded), 119
Long, Lt. Col., 198, 199
Lowell, Walter, 155, 156
Lowrey, Clarence W., 194
LST (landing ship, tank), 175
Luehrs, Lewis F. "Lew," 238–39, 301
Luger, Bill, 6
Luttrell, Gilbert, 80
Luzon:
　assault landing on, 144
　Japanese invasion of, 314

INDEX

Lylne, Allen, 23
Lyon, Richard, 126–28

MacArthur, Douglas, 113, 129, 244, 307
MacDonald, Ernie, 191
Macy, John, 202–3
Maddox, BM1/C, 158
Mandalena, Australia, training in, 42
Mann, Paul, 175
Marines, U.S.:
  First Marine Division, 5, 21, 243
  Fourth Marine Division, 282, 283
  at Iwo Jima, 264
  MAG 45 Ordnance Battalion, 239–43
  at Peleliu, 241–43
  Raiders, 141
  Seabees' support for, 29
  Second Marine Division, 282, 283, 293
  training, 60–61, 104–5
  "Welcome Marines" sign, 276
Marion, George C., 87
Markham, Jerry N., 58–70
Marshall, R. P., 249, 305
Marshall Islands, 236–37, 282
Martin (recon specialist), 184–85
Martin Mars (airboat), 144, 193–94
Martz, Vernon, 175
Maruea, James S., 175

Marusa, Mike, 175
Mason, BM2/C, 158
Mathews, "Beach Jumper," 6
Maui, training on, 69, 249, 255, 292, 306, 311, 312–13, 321
McAdams, Lt. Commander, 305, 306
McGraw, John Paul "Pappy," 136
McGuire, James T., 190–92
McHugh, James Edward, 62
McQueen, Floyd, 113
Meredith, Franklin, 6
Merrill, Ed, 131
Methwin, Lieutenant, 299
Metz, Robert, 143
Mickey, Sergeant, 224, 226
Miles, Milton Edwards "Merry," 188, 215
Miller, William, 191
Mindanao Sea, 47–48
Molero, Paul "Sabu," 157
Montaign (gun accident), 151
Moore, Howard N., 221–23, 312
Moran, Pinkie, 260
Moranz, Vince, 259, 272, 312
Morotai, invasion of, 15
Morrisey, William G. III, 150
Morro Bay, 161–62
Mosher, Alvin F., 64
Mount Suribachi:
  flag-raising on, 49, 106
  recon of area beaches, 262–64, 316, 317

INDEX

Mulheren, Clarence "Mullie," 83–92, 301
Munson, Herman, 107
Munson Lung, 43
Murphy, Ed, 46
Murphy, John, 21
Murray, Donald, 258–72

Naples, Italy, NCDU in, 112
Navy, U.S.:
  amphibious landing experiments by, 1–2, 5, 38–39, 120, 223
  beaches cleared by, 248
  Bomb and Disposal squads, 29
  college study program, 258
  Combat Demolition Units, see NCDU
  Construction Battalion, 232–33
  crossing the equator, 289–90
  determining water depth, 293
  Fifth Amphibious Force, 232, 235, 246
  flying mattresses, 282–83
  Joint Training Force, 120–21
  Naval Intelligence School, 124, 127, 135, 149, 202, 207
  Physical Training Program, 121
  Scouts & Raiders, see Scouts & Raiders
  Seabees, 29, 58–59, 79, 85, 299
  SEALs, 1–3, 126, 207
  ship designations, 362
  Special Service Units, 2, 4–7, 178
  Third Fleet, 43
  UDTs, see Underwater Demolition Teams
NCDU (Navy Combat Demolition Units), 4, 25, 33–119
  Civil Engineer Corps in, 70
  democratic organization in, 61–62
  disbanding of, 69, 82, 92
  formation of, 33–35
  mission of, 35
  on Mother's Day, 94–95
  name of, 37
  and Normandy, see Normandy invasion
  training, 34, 62–63, 79, 91, 93, 104, 106–7, 109, 127, 133, 148
  and UDTs, 133, 309
  volunteers for, 40, 60, 79, 106–7, 109
Newcastle, Australia, training in, 5
New Guinea:
  Alamo Scouts in, 26–28
  Sixth Army in, 26
Nichols, Gene E. "Nick," 237–38
Nixon, T. D., 276
Noel, Will, 176

Normandy invasion, 12,
56–58
  casualties in, 111
  destroyers' cover fire for,
    67–69
  Omaha Beach, 36, 54–56,
    63–69, 75–77, 80–82,
    107–8, 111, 113,
    114–19, 185–87, 336–42
  panzer divisions in, 75
  preparation for, 36, 50–53,
    54–56, 72–77, 95–103,
    107–8, 113–14, 235
  Utah Beach, 36, 50–53,
    109–12, 332–35
Norris, Max, 119
North Africa:
  invasion of, 146, 178–79
  postinvasion cleanup in,
    151–52, 213–14
  preparations for invasion
    of, 29–30, 124
Noyes, Carl R., 50–56, 113
Noyes, Humphrey, 156

Oahu, UDTs on, 233, 236,
  237, 250
O'Brien, Arthur, 156
Ohman, Charles E., 64
Okinawa:
  invasion of, 142, 209, 238,
    253–54, 255–56, 260,
    268–69, 274, 320
  model of Brown Beach,
    207
  preparation for invasion
    of, 49–50, 124–25,
    208–9, 267, 273, 278

Okinawa Safety Operations
  Plan, 125
Olpp, Richard E., 113
Omaha Beach, *see* Normandy invasion
Operation Anvil/Dragoon,
  172, 222
Operation Brassard, 222
Operation Flintlock, 233, 235
Operation Husky, 180–82
Operation Neptune, 54–56
Operation Olympic, 203,
  271, 321
OSS (Office of Strategic
  Services), formation of,
  78–79

Padgett, J. G., 93, 100
Palmer, Lloyd J., 131–36
Palmer, Wayne, 273–75
Panay, operations in, 203–5
Parmele, Robert W., 297–98
Patrick, James O., 80
Pearl Harbor, 169–70, 311
Peddicord, Lloyd E., 2, 121
Peleliu:
  invasion of, 105, 242–43
  recon on, 241–42, 297–98,
    300
Peterson, Herbert, 50–56
Petoniak, Theodore, 64
Petoskey, Ernest J., 206–9
Petoskey, John, 136
Pettis, Wayne, 6
Phinney, Ernest, 209–12
Pianosa Island, 222
Pienack, Raymond Rudolph,
  62

Pirro, Carmen F., 185
Pizzo, Del, 46
Ponds (training), 150
Pool, Hampton, 305
Powell, Elmer, 93, 94, 101
Provenzo, Tony, 254–58
Pulupandan, beach recon at, 197–200
Pyle, Ernie, 238

Queen Mary, 109

radar, early use of, 44
Redmond, Gordon Alva, 190–91
Repertus, General, 21
Reutzel, Emil Jr., 123–25
Ridgeway, Matthew B., 73
Roosevelt, Elliott, 207
Roosevelt, Franklin D., 214
Root, Donald E., 6, 11–12, 15, 16, 19–20, 27–28
Ross, Robert E., 82–83
Ross, Wesley, 114–19
Rudd, Willard W., 243–45
Ruhl, Fred, 143
Ryan, W. J., 196

Sabra (native), 20, 21
SACO (Sino-American Cooperative Organization), 188–90, 210–12, 214, 215–16, 221
Saipan:
 clearing beaches of, 287–88
 invasion of, 283–84, 293–94
 preparation for invasion of, 252, 281–84
Salerno, Italy, 37–38, 182–84
Sansapor mission, 12–15, 129–31
Scouts & Raiders, 120–231
 disbanding of, 128, 129, 135
 formation of, 2, 147
 as occupation forces, 128
 teams of, 149
 toughness of, 140, 146, 153
 training, 124, 126–27, 128–29, 138–40, 141, 143, 152–53, 154–56, 171, 176, 191, 192, 202, 206–7, 212–13, 216, 227, 228–29, 230
 transfers to UDTs, 135–36
 Unit Buck, 187–88
 volunteers for, 131, 138, 143, 146–47, 150, 152, 158, 176, 202, 212, 216, 226–27
Seabees, USN:
 roles of, 29
 training, 59, 85
 and UDTs, 299
 volunteers for, 58–59, 79
SEALs, 1–3, 126, 207
SEAL/UDT Museum, Fort Pierce, 140
Sears, Alfred, 235–36

Sebou River, 29–32
Sheppard, William C., 203–6
Shih, Jackson, 220
Shima Island, 237–38
Sicily:
  operations at, 175, 177, 180–82
  preparations for invasion of, 250
Smith, Harry, 143
Smith, Holland, 239–40
Smith, Jack, 157–71
Smith, Kirkwall, 20
Snyder, Randy, 143
Special Service Unit No. 1:
  formation of, 2, 4–7, 178
  medical officer, 22–25
  roles of, 2, 25
  training, 8–9
  volunteers for, 8, 19
Spencer, Bill, 141–43
Sprouse, James M., 70–79
Stameris, Bill, 156
Standard Landing Craft Units, 5
Starkey, Lieutenant, 200
Staudt, Pat and Hank, 4–7, 9
Stewart, Virgil R., 236–37
Stilwell, Joseph W. "Vinegar Joe," 153
Struble, Arthur D., 205
Subic Bay, 308
Sullivan, Warren, 128–29
Sweet, Captain, 240

Tablo (native), 20
Tai Li, General, 188, 215
Tarawa Island, 1, 8, 40, 232, 233
Taylor, RM 2/C, 6
Taylor, Ustus, 83
Thomas, Robert, 6
Thompson, Dick, 156
Thompson, George S., 27–28
Throckmorton, Allen, 205
Tibbet, Paul, 231
Tichener, Morris B., 7
Tinian Island, 285–89, 294–95
Tipson, Big John, 121
Tokashiki-jima Island, 267, 319–20
Toman, R., 6
Tripson, Big John, 150, 192–93
Trudeau, Rosaire, 6
Tunney, Gene, 121, 146, 206
Turner, R. K., 233, 239

Underwater Demolition Teams (UDTs), 2–3, 232–322
  Able, 45–47, 105, 312
  beaches cleared by, 248
  NCDU personnel transferred to, 133, 309
  No. 1, 233–34, 236, 250–51, 258
  No. 2, 233–35, 236–37, 250–51, 258

374 INDEX

Underwater Demolition Teams (cont.)
  No. 3, 237, 244–50, 251–52, 258, 301, 324–27
  No. 4, 237–38, 251, 258, 275–78
  No. 5, 292–97, 301
  No. 6, 241–43, 299–300
  No. 7, 309–11
  No. 9, 296
  No. 10, 297–98, 305–8, 328–31
  No. 11, 208, 255–56, 309, 311, 313
  No. 12, 309, 311
  No. 13, 259–71, 309, 311, 312–21
  No. 14, 49–50
  No. 15, 264, 296, 309, 310, 314, 318
  No. 18, 256
  No. 19, 319
  No. 25, 69, 83
  Scouts & Raiders personnel transferred to, 135–36
  Seabees in, 299
  training, 88–91, 124, 129, 137, 147, 203, 250–51, 270–71, 309
  volunteers for, 87–88, 136–37, 235, 259, 300–301
USS *Arizona*, 170, 311
USS *Balsam* APD-48, 318
USS *Barr* AP-54, 260, 263–69, 313–20
USS *Blue Ridge*, 10, 12, 15–18
USS *Brigit* AKA-24, 135
USS *Charles Lawrence* APD-37, 141–43
USS *Clemson* APD-31, 241–43
USS *Dickerson*, 246–49
USS *General Patrick* AP-150, 311
USS *Gilmer*, 293–95
USS *Honolulu* CL-48, 291
USS *Missouri*, 113
USS *Mount Hood*, 291
USS *Nevada*, 74, 313
USS *Noa* APD-24, 45–46, 105
USS *Ommaney Bay* CVE-79, 47
USS *S-47*, 12–14, 27
USS *Tattrell*, 172–74
Utah Beach, *see* Normandy invasion

Van Alen, Commander, 193
Vanfebilt, William, 64
Vest, Melvin, 115
Vogelkop Peninsula, 26–28

Wakefield, Orville, 113
Walk, Myron, 93
Walker, Donald M., 103–6, 312
Walsh, Myron, 98–99, 101
Walters, Bob, 205
Watson, Glen, 205
Weintraub, Joshua, 6
Wheeler, William F., 194

White, William, 80
Wihrwohn, Raymond, 93
Wildgen, Bernard C., 7, 22–25
Wilson, Harold, 39–50
Wise, Fred, 33
Wise, John, 131
Wood, Joe, 121
Wood, Robert M. "Woody," 250–53
Wunderlich, Frederick, 224, 228

Zamboanga, preassault recon of, 145, 194–97, 202
Zimmerman, Sergeant, 151

Experience the fight up close and personal with the best in Military Nonfiction from Pocket Star Books

THIRTY SECONDS OVER TOKYO
Captain Ted W. Lawson
Edited by Robert Considine

After a daring bombing raid on targets in Japan, several B-25 twin-engine bombers had to make emergency landings in Japanese-controlled China. This is the miraculous story of their escape to safety.

WINGS OF FURY
From Vietnam to the Gulf War—The Astonishing True Stories of American Elite Fighter pilots
Robert K. Wilcox

From the training grounds of Miramar to combat in Vietnam and Desert Storm, these are the stories of those who defend the skies—and the dramatic evolution of modern air warfare.

CROSSHAIRS ON THE KILL ZONE
American Combat Snipers, Vietnam through Operation Iraqi Freedom
Craig Roberts and Charles W. Sasser

The enemy is never safe from the sniper's crosshairs on the kill zone.

THE PROUD BASTARDS
One Marine's Journey from Parris Island through the Hell of Vietnam
E. Michael Helms

The true story of a young marine's life in Vietnam, this memoir describes the day-to-day life of a combat infantryman in unforgettable detail.